D0427480

◆ The Bad Attitude Survival Guide

Also by Harry E. Chambers

No Fear Management

◆ The Bad Attitude Survival Guide

Essential Tools for Managers

HARRY E. CHAMBERS

▲ **Addison-Wesley**   Reading, Massachusetts

Many of the designations used by manufacturers and sellers to distinguish their products are claimed as trademarks. Where those designations appear in this book and Addison-Wesley was aware of a trademark claim, the designations have been printed in initial capital letters.

Library of Congress Cataloging-in Publication Data
Chambers, Harry (Harry E.)
    The bad attitude survival guide : essential tools for managers / Harry Chambers.
        p. cm.
    Includes bibliographical references and index.
    ISBN 0-201-31146-1
    1. Supervision of employees. 2. Employees—Attitudes.
3. Negativism.   I. Title.
HF5549.12.C43   1998
658.3'045—dc21   97-40871
                                                                   CIP

Addison-Wesley is an imprint of Addison Wesley Longman, Inc.

Cover design by Suzanne Heiser
Text design by Jean Hammond
Set in 10-point Minion by Vicki L. Hochstedler

123456789–DOH–020100999897
First printing, December 1997

Addison-Wesley books are available at special discounts for bulk purchases in the U.S. by corporations, institutions, and other organizations. For more information, please contact the Corporate, Government, and Special Sales Department at Addison Wesley Longman, Inc., One Jacob Way, Reading, MA 01867, or call 1-800-238-9682.

Find us on the World Wide Web at
http://www.aw.com/gb/

To Chris
It just keeps getting better!

To Patrick, Shari, and Mike
We are so very proud — be proud of yourselves!

To Papa
and the loving memory of Grandma June

To Richard and Elizabeth Kern
Thanks for your daughter

◗ Contents

◆ Acknowledgments

This book is the result of years and years of workplace experience with input from many talented and generous people along the way. Sincere thanks are owed to a number of people for their encouragement, support, and contribution to this book. My family, specifically Chris and Patrick, offered total support and willingly sacrificed to allow me to complete this book. I am grateful to Nick Philipson, Executive Editor at Addison Wesley Longman, for his encouragement and willingness to risk. Many thanks to Production Manager Pat Jalbert, for her efforts at keeping us on track, and to Julie Stillman, a very gifted editor. Her guidance and insights were invaluable. The entire staff of Addison-Wesley was extremely supportive in this effort. My assistant, Mickey Beatty, was her usual competent self and once again proved her ability to make a silk-purse manuscript out of many sow's-ear rough drafts! Thanks to Rick Kern for his research help. Thanks to some special teachers: Joretta Kelley, Roger Morin, Dr. Morris Speir, and countless others, who made contributions far more than they'll ever know. And to those who offered opportunity: especially Carol Miller, Christie Ward, Diane Montgomery, Dennis McClelland, and Drew Gierman. If they hadn't opened doors, many things may not have happened.

Three Critical Challenges in the Workplace: *Bad Attitudes, Poor Performance, and Organizational Change*

"Life is difficult" is the opening line of M. Scott Peck's book, *The Road Less Traveled*. If you think life is so difficult, try management. Not only are you accountable for yourself, you also bear responsibility for the performance and behavior of others. A tall task! The challenges facing today's managers and leaders are unparalleled in the history of industrialized America. Never before have we faced the multitude of new situations and changes we face today.

Consider the challenges you deal with in leading people through

- The break in the bond of workplace loyalty
- The disruptions of short-term contractual relationships and increased outsourcing
- The turmoil of downsizing, rightsizing, upsizing, resizing (or whatever the euphemism of the day may be)
- The hair-trigger litigious nature of the workplace
- The avalanche of laws protecting employees while restricting and mandating much of management's behavioral options
- The shift of priority in the role job/career plays in people's lives today
- The change in the expectations people have of their job, organization, and manager, and the never-changing importance of the role people play in the workplace

No matter what we do, we do it with people. People create the technology. People implement the technology. People make it all happen. People ultimately use whatever it is we create. No matter how small your organization or how technical its process, it takes people to be successful. What makes your organization different from that of a direct competitor or that of a similar entity is probably not your technology—it's your people. Globalization expands the pool of people. We have more people to interact with and more differences in people to be considered. The people dynamic is the common denominator, and it will never go away.

Managing the technological side of your organization may be relatively easy; managing the people is not. People present the ever-challenging dynamic of blending emotions, perceptions, motivations, ethics, morals, likes, and dislikes into an imperfect performance machine you must lead toward greater results. Given the inordinate amount of time people spend on their jobs today, the workplace has become the stage for acting out much of life's drama.

> In a counseling session with a poorly performing employee, Susan, a recently appointed new manager, looked her problem employee in the eye and said, "and another thing I would like to discuss with you is you have a bad attitude." The employee smiled and replied, "Well, you ought to love my attitude because you gave it to me!" Surprised, Susan inquired, "You acknowledge that you have a bad attitude?" The employee responded, "Yes!" (She was very proud of her attitude.) Susan then said, "And it's my fault that you have this attitude?" With obvious satisfaction, the employee smiled and said, "You and all the other managers like you around here. You're all giving me and everyone else a bad attitude."
>
> Perplexed, Susan then posed the following questions: "Why do you willingly give away control of your thought process and behaviors to me or anyone else? Why are you making me such a powerful person in your life and allowing me to exert such a negative influence over you?"
>
> Susan continued, "I would never want anyone else to have that kind of control over me. I would never want anyone else to control how I think and act. If I choose to think or behave a certain way it is because I made that choice, not because someone else made me. When will you begin to take responsibility for your own thoughts and your own behaviors?"

In reality, blaming Susan for her bad attitude was an easy, comfortable way for the employee to distance herself from taking responsibility for her own negative actions and beliefs. As we have become more of a "blaming society," we hold ourselves less and less responsible for our own behaviors and decisions. The emerging negative philosophy of "Because you did that, I'll do this and blame you for it" results in people acting out all kinds of minidramas and holding us responsible! In our role as managers, we have become a convenient focal point for blame. Managers have moved from guideposts to whipping posts and frequently bear the brunt of

- Employees' personal feelings of insecurity and inadequacy
- Outside problems that filter into the workplace
- Employees' lack of personal preparation and failure to position themselves for tomorrow's workplace opportunities
- Stalled careers

Today's management challenge is to meet these realities head-on and increase overall productivity simultaneously. To further complicate things, this must all be accomplished in an environment where we are all being asked to do more and more with less and less.

There is no single cause, nor simple strategy for overcoming bad attitudes. The issue is a complex one. Interestingly, blaming employees' poor performance or disruptive behavior on their bad attitudes has become a frequently used crutch for managers. Just as employees put the blame on their managers, many managers respond in kind with their own version of the blame game. Positive outcomes are impossible to create if both parties blame the other while holding themselves harmless of any responsibility. If employees aren't performing to company standards or to their own capabilities, we assume they are choosing to do so. If employees disagree with us or don't support new organizational directions and initiatives, we blame their bad attitudes and negativity. It just isn't that simple. Bad attitudes may be the disease; however, more often they are merely the symptom and there are other issues involved. Bad attitudes are not created by spontaneous combustion. There is a consistent connection between bad attitudes and other workplace realities. In this book, I will address bad attitudes comprehensively as part of an overall management challenge package.

Show me any organization today, and I'll guarantee that managers at every level are dealing with the three-cornered challenge of bad attitudes, poor performance, and organizational change. From the new frontline supervisor to the seasoned executive, from human resource professionals to training managers, all are dealing with these three critical, inescapable issues on a daily basis. To a significant degree, the success of the organization as well as individual management careers may well be determined by their proficiency in dealing with these interconnected challenges.

Many books have identified these as separate and distinct issues; however, they are interwoven from their conception—you won't experience

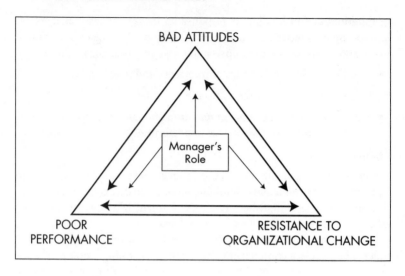

one without the others. Attempting to correct them individually is the equivalent of treating only one lung when both are infected!

This is a "how to" book. Talking about "what" to do is relatively easy; knowing "how to do it" is the real challenge. You will not only learn what to do, you will acquire specific implementation skills to increase productivity (both yours and your employees') through successful management of these three critical challenges.

■ Bad Attitudes

We are experiencing an epidemic of bad attitudes in the American workplace today. Our workplace has rapidly become narrowly me-focused and less we-focused. In an environment of uncertainty and unpredictability we tend to react negatively to any situation not perceived to be in our own personal, parochial best interest. Bad attitudes flourish when employees perceive their best interests are at cross-purposes or antagonistic to yours or the organization's.

Bad attitudes have become mainstream. Irreverence, criticism, and disrespect are at the forefront of our humor, entertainment, media, political discourse, and everyday conversations. We see this in our increased bickering, in the narrow focused partisanship dominating our politics, and in the frequency and intensity of personal attacks upon one another.

These personal attacks and "character assassinations" occur so often, they are no longer shocking or noteworthy. We have become desensitized to such attacks. We do not just disagree with someone's ideas and actions; we attack their intelligence, ethics, and morals! We label them or assign demeaning names to what we perceive they are. We search people's pasts for vulnerabilities. People who disagree with *us* are demonized. We have no opponents; we have only enemies. Our lives are evolving toward disconnected individualization and away from connectedness and intertwined commonality.

In the last thirty to forty years, we have experienced an erosion of respect for people, positions, and institutions. For a multitude of debatable reasons, the respect automatically given to those in positions of authority in the past has diminished or disappeared. Consider the decline in respect for politicians, teachers, law enforcement officials, and even parents. The previously deified medical doctor is automatically subjected to the "second opinion!" Our first impulse is no longer to trust and respect, it is now to question and doubt, fed by our escalating cynicism. Leadership in the workplace today no longer enjoys automatic high trust, respect, or regard. Perhaps considered automatic in the past, today these things must be carefully earned, nurtured, and maintained.

The us-versus-them mentality has become the dominant theme of the day. There is always someone or something to be against. Antagonism is fashionable. Our lives are played out at such a rapid pace, we have a need to quickly categorize someone as a good guy (one of us) or a bad guy (one of them). There is no middle ground. We tend to make very quick, subjective, emotional decisions in judging people or issues. We tend to think in absolutes.

- "*Every* decision they make is wrong."
- "They are *always* out to get me (us)."
- "*Everything* the boss does is wrong."
- "*Everything* the company does is wrong."
- "*Everything* the other department does is wrong."
- "The company will do *everything* they can to get me."

Second guessing has become an "industry" in America today. Whether in the form of workplace gossip, print media, radio, or television, we ravenously attack the actions and decisions of others. Just listen to the feeding frenzy of negative attacks on talk radio in any city, at any time of the day. People who aren't out there making things happen, sit there and criticize and ridicule those who are! With the advantage of hindsight, elapsed time, and observable results, we have become experts at being post-event critical. People who do not want to risk actually doing it can always sit back and talk about how much better they would have done if they had tried! These after-the-fact geniuses are glorified as media stars or beacons of guiding light. Such hindsight-based criticism has become the pulpit and platform for those who are not secure enough to put themselves on the line and take risk. The stature of malcontents has been elevated and a legitimacy extended to their perceptions as never before in our history.

In this book you will learn

- Where bad attitudes come from
- Why bad attitudes grow and develop
- Specific actions to turn around bad attitudes
- The role unresolved conflict plays in perpetuating bad attitudes
- Why bad attitudes can be a successful employee strategy (if we allow it)
- Strategies to reduce the influence of bad attitude employees on those around them

You will also learn the most important facts concerning bad attitudes:

◆ You cannot change someone else's attitude.

An attitude is nothing more than a personal thought process. It is how people choose to think, and you cannot change how someone else thinks. You do not have the power, control, or influence to change someone else's thought process, nor do you have the right! Few, if any, things in America are valued more highly than the right to think any way we want. Men and women have died in wars, sacrificed their lives so that we can think any way we choose. Trying to change bad attitudes is a fruitless pursuit.

◆ Bad attitudes must be described as behavior.

Focus on behavior—it is something you *can* change. Behavior can have consequences. You can create a positive consequence for positive behavior and a negative consequence for negative behavior; however, you cannot possibly apply a consequence to how someone thinks.

Attitudes can be used as weapons. In fact, they are used as effective tools by many employees to control or disrupt their manager. Why? Because we respond subjectively and emotionally to people's attitudes. There is no rational thought process or objectivity in our response to attitudes. Employees use your subjective response to their attitudes to their advantage and your disadvantage.

We have all heard those sagacious words: "Never discuss religion or politics." Why do we not discuss them? Simply because they are personal thought processes, and when people don't agree with or criticize someone else's political or religious thought process, emotional overreactions are the result. Think of how you respond when someone tells you that your religion or politics is "wrong" and theirs is "right" and you need to abandon yours and follow theirs. Take a history book and chronicle how many wars have been fought and lives lost over those types of issues.

In the earlier example where Susan confronted her employee about her attitude, she made a very critical error. Confronting people about their attitude should be avoided at all costs. Saying to someone, "You have a bad attitude" translates to "You have a thought process that I don't approve of." The truth is they couldn't care less whether you approve of their thought process, and once they know it antagonizes you, they will use it against you very effectively. Telling someone he or she has a bad attitude is tantamount to giving the following instruction: "On the computer keyboard of life, let me show you the H.T.G.T.M.R.B. key." (How to get to me real bad!) Once they learn that key on your keyboard, they will use it consistently to disrupt, disturb, or control you.

Here, you will learn to focus on employees' behaviors, which you *can* influence, and to abandon the unproductive focus on their disruptive sideshow of attitudes.

◗ Change behavior and attitudes *may* follow.

When you successfully address negative behaviors, the attitudes of employees may also change. The key is learning to eliminate the payoff they perceive they achieve by demonstrating these behaviors. Their payoff may be watching you squirm in frustration over having to deal with them. You will learn very specific "how to" techniques to eliminate these payoffs for their bad attitude behaviors.

In the real world not all of these issues and behaviors can be overcome. The roots of the bad attitudes employees have may be very deep and internal and not within the influence of you or the organization. You cannot address employees' internal issues, only they can. They maintain total control of how they choose to think and interpret the events they experience. Bad attitude employees may be committed to the cultivation and proliferation of their negative behaviors and thought processes. You can create an environment that reduces the incidents of bad attitudes. The costs of bad attitudes are high. Frequently they are hidden, or experienced covertly, and reveal themselves in

- Acts of sabotage
- Higher levels of conflict
- Reduced levels of workplace cooperation
- The infectious spreading of antimanagement or anticompany sentiments
- Reductions in the quality of products or services provided

■ Poor Performance

In this era of doing "more with less" and addressing savagely competitive economic situations (unlike any we have ever faced in our economic history), poor performance is an issue influencing the very survival of many organizations. Typically we have

- Fewer people available to do the job
- Fewer dollars available to fund our activities
- Fewer resources available to accomplish the tasks

While we are calling upon our employees to rise to the occasion and become more efficient, productive, and successful, many are choosing performance patterns of mediocrity or worse. In reality, manipulation of personal performance levels is one of the few weapons employees have within their control to fight back against policies, decisions, and management styles with which they disagree. Poorly performing employees frequently enjoy legal protections that were nonexistent or unavailable in the past. Protection of poor performance can actually be institutionalized through collective bargaining agreements, selective service provisions, tenure policies, and "special status" through legal entitlements. It is much more difficult to remove a poorly performing employee today than ever before in our economic history. The old hair-trigger reaction of firing people at the slightest infraction is impossible today (in many cases rightfully and humanely so). In the past it was easy. If someone was not performing or you did not "like" him, you could easily just dismiss him. Maritime captains forced their problem employees to walk the plank or abandoned them on remote islands. We have come a long way since then!

In today's litigious environment, many managers and organizations are hesitant to take any action with a poorly performing employee for fear of legal repercussions. With the unpredictable and sometimes inconsistent reaction of our courts and governing agencies, this fear may be well founded. Just as employees must have legal protection from capricious and unfair actions by their employer, organizations must have the right to correct or dismiss those who are not performing to reasonable standards and expectations. There is a balance to be achieved in protecting the interests of all involved; this balance has yet to be reached.

The costs associated with poor performance are enormous:

- The loss of productivity. (A cost that can never be recovered.)

- The value of the manager's time. (Inordinate amounts of time are invested in the poor performer. If performance improves, it is time well spent. If performance doesn't improve, it is a valuable resource thrown down a black hole.)

- The greater reduction of overall productivity levels as poor performance spreads to others in the group, department, or team.

- The costs of replacement.

Replacement Costs

Author Carol A. Hacker in her book, *The High Cost of Low Morale*, states: "The estimated costs to replace an employee range from 30% of an employee's annual salary for entry level and unskilled workers to five times the annual salary for executives."

Replacement costs may include:

1. Separation expenses: severance pay, unemployment compensation, continuous extension of medical benefits (COBRA).

2. Covert damage/loss: acts of sabotage prior to separation, client/customer lists that disappear, damaged customer relationships, loss of other employees who may be enticed to leave.

3. Recruiting/hiring costs: ads, investment of management and human resource departments' time, travel/lodging expense, competency testing, medical exams, etc.

4. New hire orientation costs: training, uniforms, equipment, etc.

5. Initial period of low productivity from the replacement employee.

6. Compensation for the new hire during the lesser productive probation or evaluation period.

Replacement Costs   *Total*

1. Separation costs of the previous employee	Separation pay?	Unemployment insurance?	Extended medical benefits?			
	_____ + _____ + _____					= _____

2. Recruiting/ new hire costs	Advertising costs?	Travel expenses?	Costs of medical or skills testing?	Hours of staff spent in recruitment	Estimated staff hourly compensation	
	_____ + _____ + _____ + _____ × _____					= _____

3. New hire/ orientation costs	Training materials	Uniforms, equip, etc.	Hrs. spent in orientation/ training	New hire's hourly compensation		
	_____ + _____ + _____ × _____					= _____
	Hrs. of staff providing orientation & training	Estimated staff hourly compensation	New hire's benefits (33% of comp.)			
	_____ × _____ + _____					= _____

4. Related Costs	Costs of loss or reduced profit?	Estimated loss of customer goodwill?	Additional estimated covert damage/loss costs?			
	_____ + _____ + _____					= _____

Total estimated cost of replacement
of poor performing employee   _____

It is estimated to take eighteen months to recoup training, recruiting, and loss of productivity costs before an employee actually becomes profitable to the organization. Many employees never even reach the break-even point.

Obviously, developing and implementing successful turnaround strategies has a significant impact on expenses and contributes to profitability. It is in the best interests of the manager, the employee, and the organization to avoid the costs and increase the productivity.

Management's Inadequate Response to Poor Performance

An often overlooked and highly significant contributing factor to poor performance is the lack of managerial training in America today. Managers are not equipped with the skills or tools they need to successfully address poor performance.

◆ Managers are not trained to be managers.

Our traditional model has been to promote the best performer. We tend to make managers of people who are good "technically" at what they do, with no regard for assessing their management or leadership potential. Hence, the top teacher becomes the principal; the top salesperson becomes the sales manager; the top machine operator becomes the foreman; and the top administrative assistant becomes the office manager.

Management training in America has become permanently stalled at the level of on-the-job training (O.J.T.). We promote people and then throw them headlong into the job with little or no preparation. We judge them harshly if they fail, but we do not prepare them to be successful. This is the equivalent of throwing someone into a swimming pool to see if he can swim. If he sinks we pull him out and repeat the process until we find a "bobber." When we find the bobber who can at least stay on top of the water, we leave him in the pool, hoping he will teach himself how to maneuver successfully around the pool. Longevity and internal political connections, along with technical proficiency, determine initial moves into management. However, continued success and future promotions are determined by managers' ability to get others to perform well. Success is getting the job done with and through other people. This calls upon an entirely different skill set, and these skills frequently remain undeveloped.

Typically, we promote someone by saying, "You're doing a great job; now you get to be the boss." They respond, "Cool. I'm really happy about this. Now, tell me what I should do." Our response is, "Just go get people to do what you did. You're good; you should get them to do it just like you." Typically they say, "That's great. How do I do that?" The response is, "I just know you'll be able to do it, I have every confidence in you. I'm behind you 100%. Go get em, tiger!"—Surprise, Surprise! We have an explosion of bad attitudes and poor performance.

The assumption that just because someone can do something well, he can also teach it and manage it well, is a dangerous one that costs us millions of dollars every year in inefficient management practices and the inevitable poor employee performance. It results in a cadre of managers/leaders who are not prepared to deal with the challenges of today's workplace.

Routinely, managers at all levels are not taught the skills of interdiction, counseling, and correction to effectively deal with poorly performing employees. This results in managers frequently practicing avoidance behaviors. The problems are not addressed proactively and interactively, but are avoided in the hopes they will correct themselves. (If I ignore it maybe it will go away.) When we do not know how to correct poor performance, we put up with it. The problems compound, and we become managerially defensive and begin to make excuses for employees' unacceptable performance (usually blaming their attitude). This continued level of poor performance becomes the new acceptable standard by default. Every manager and organization will receive the performance they are willing to tolerate. Usually our willingness to tolerate is based not in high levels of patience, but in our lack of confidence or inadequate skills. Along with the lack of training, managers have limited opportunity to actually practice whatever skills they may have self-acquired. If we accept the premise that 80% of your problems come from 20% of your employees, you are not called upon to utilize these correction skills with the bulk of your people. It is tough to be good at something you are not trained to do and have little opportunity to practice! Managers are not necessarily born, they must be trained and developed. This book will increase your inventory of management and leadership skills.

You will learn

- The six primary root causes of poor performance

- The importance of training, recognition, and feedback

- When to use disciplinary procedures effectively

- How punishment is inappropriately used in attempts to correct poor performance

If you are committed to taking an active role in increasing the productivity of your department, team, group, or individual employees, this book will help you to learn and implement effective strategies to do so. While not all poor performance can be corrected, you will realistically be prepared to assess your options, opportunities, and limitations.

■ Organizational Change

Much has been written about organizational change. Most current material addresses the importance of change, the inevitability of change, and why we must learn to live with change. In this book we broaden the focus. We address change as contributing to and intertwined with bad attitudes and poor performance. We will look specifically at the role of the manager in guiding and implementing successful change and will consider the negative consequences of poorly managed change initiatives.

> ♦ **The change strategies implemented by management ultimately determine the success or failure of the intended change.**

To exist in today's economic environment is to experience change. If you are successful, then you are dealing successfully with change. We often hear people say, "Things are changing so rapidly around here, I just can't keep up with it." Frequently change is seen as negative. In reality, change is necessary to survive. People and organizations that are not changing have positioned themselves in a "funeral procession." They are on their way to the cemetery! The trip may be long or short, but the arrival at the burial ground is inevitable. The ultimate result of resistance to change today can only be obsolescence. To refuse to change is to become inconsequential and irrelevant.

Today's change comes in many forms:

- Changing markets
- Explosive growth
- Developing technology
- Restructuring of process
- New leadership, ownership, etc.
- Downsizing, rightsizing, upsizing, etc.

While the outcomes of these changes create rejuvenated and more competitive organizations, the journey through implementation is a major contributor to bad attitudes and poor performance.

▶ We all want the positive results of change—we just don't want to make the trip to get there!

Perhaps if allowed to remain in their own current comfort zone, many employees would not display their bad attitudes or act out their disruptive behaviors. However, when their changing environment demands compliance with a deluge of constant redefinitions of policies, procedures, priorities, and processes, the bad attitudes emerge with acute intensity. If we weren't changing so profoundly, perhaps we wouldn't be experiencing the explosion of the bad attitude epidemic.

Here you will learn

- Why employees resist change
- How resistance can be neutralized or overcome
- The manager's role in increasing workplace flexibility
- The pitfalls to avoid in introducing, implementing, and managing change

The only constant, predictable, guaranteed reality in any organization today is "change happens." Change is not an enemy to be defeated; change is not a cancer to be cured; change is not an erosion to be avoided at all costs. Change is the appropriate response to the differences of today and tomorrow. As our workplace challenge redefines itself everyday, so must our behaviors and responses.

▶ **Yesterday's behaviors will not support tomorrow's growth.**

■ Looking Ahead in Our Journey

In the next two chapters, we are going to examine the root causes of bad attitudes. We cannot begin to positively impact any problem until we accurately diagnose the actual cause. Symptoms are only a smoke screen, and our tendency to react to these symptoms in knee-jerk fashion has only driven the problems deeper. We are going to penetrate to the basic core of these attitudes and clearly identify the tributaries that feed the raging rivers of bad attitudes and negativity.

In Chapter 4, we will take an in-depth look at the authoritarian management styles that have rapidly become obsolete and unproductive. We will identify the participative leadership alternatives that are critical to creating top performance in today's organizations. Things have changed! We will help you to assess your management style and identify the behaviors that you may be utilizing either to help or to hinder the turnaround of bad attitudes and poor performance. We will also address the role the overall organizational culture plays in creating environments that actually nurture these problems.

In Chapters 5 and 6, we identify the pervasive, negative impact of unresolved conflict and why our tendency to avoid or deny its existence is causing significant organizational and individual problems. We will expose the typical negative responses to conflict; the actual impediments to positive conflict resolution; the varying, escalating degrees of conflict; and most important, we will introduce successful resolution strategies. We will also discuss effective techniques for mediating or arbitrating the conflict between others.

You will meet Marty, Tanya, and Billy in Chapters 7 and 8, as we spotlight thirteen very specific negative behaviors demonstrated by employees with bad attitudes. Along with in-depth definitions and descriptions of these behaviors, we will offer very clear, concise strategies for gaining behavioral turnaround. Not every one of these can be fixed every time, but we will structure the steps necessary to achieve whatever level of correction is possible.

Have your bad attitude employees ever refused to comply with your requests or become defiant in the presence of others? In Chapters 9 and

10, we will address insubordination and the five additional most prevalent and pervasive negative behaviors related to poor performance. We also look at the critical issues of poor performance: definitions, root causes, tools for diagnosis, and strategies for achieving positive outcomes.

The disciplinary process can be a necessary and valuable tool for turning around problem employees. Its value is not to punish or just terminate people legally. Chapter 11 looks at the effective use of the disciplinary process to teach and reverse performance declines with problem employees. Used properly, counseling sessions and the disciplinary process are effective tools; used improperly, they are squandered opportunities.

Motivating employees and the shifts in job satisfaction and incentives in today's workplace are the subjects of Chapter 12. We discuss the very real limitations on the ability of today's leaders to exert motivational influence and the ineffectiveness and futility of attempting to motivate predominantly by verbal or emotional appeals.

Bad attitude employees and change are the focus of Chapter 13 as we look at the growing influence of change on the attitudes of today's workers. We reduce change to its most empirical and simple foundation and present critical do's and don'ts, along with strategies to implement successful, ongoing, never-ending change. Managing change is a challenge you cannot avoid and a skill that will have significant impact on your future success.

■ Why Does All of This Matter?

> ♦ **Just doing your best isn't good enough anymore. Today we have to get it right.**

This book fills many of the gaps in the training and development of today's workplace leaders by filling in the blanks and answering many of the questions that remain unasked and unanswered. The goal is to help you help your employees to be more productive and more positive and, perhaps, to increase their quality of life. The negativity and diminished performance of some take a toll on many, and not only in the workplace. The tentacles spread among family, friends, and other activities and arenas of life. Everyone's job can be more satisfying and more enjoyable if we can turn around the problem employees we all have to deal with. "Work is overrated" is a current buzz phrase being widely proclaimed. While work may be overrated, it still remains a necessary part of life, and it doesn't have to be a hassle or an experience that devalues and emotionally consumes the people involved. Few things in life are more rewarding than a job well done or a period of extended high productivity. Few things contribute more to a person's self-confidence or self-worth than knowing he or she is an effective performer, a key contributor, and a major cog in the organizational wheel. This book will help you and the people you are responsible for experience the exhilarating payoff of overcoming the negative, debilitating influence of bad attitudes and poor performance. It will help you and those around you to "get it right!"

Few management achievements are more rewarding than actually turning around a problem employee. The ability to create such performance turnarounds is one of the most valued and sought after traits in successful managers. Your ability to defuse the negative influence of bad attitudes and correct performance problems and increase productivity will only enhance your career and your value to the organization. Instead of viewing bad attitude, poorly performing employees as problems, they may, in fact, be your ticket to leadership stardom. None of your employees offers you a more visible opportunity to make your mark and demonstrate your exceptional leadership qualities than the employees you may perceive to be your biggest problems. (How's that for a paradigm shift!) Let's go forward and embrace that challenge.

To put this into the proper perspective, you as supervisor, manager, department head, or top executive do not bear total responsibility for your employees' bad attitudes, poor performance, and resistance to change. The ultimate responsibility for all of these problems appropriately lies solely with them. However, if you are willing to be an active partner in the learning process, this book will help you to influence others and help them to take increased responsibility for themselves. You can raise their awareness of what their poor performance, bad attitudes, and resistance to change is doing to them, their careers, and perhaps their families.

This book is not written to satisfy the intellectual community; it is written as a guide to help the men and women actually leading the American workplace. It is a tool for the growth and development of the people who are actually making it happen as well as those who someday aspire to be leaders in the workplace.

▶ **Management may be difficult, but it doesn't have to be painful.**

Let's meet the challenge and have some fun.

2 Bad Attitudes: *Root Causes*

How are bad attitudes created? Unfortunately, there is no easy answer to such a complex question. There are a multitude of factors that exist individually or blend together into a kaleidoscope of forces resulting in bad attitudes. I have identified six primary root causes and several secondary contributors. As you face bad attitudes in your workplace, the cause is undoubtedly somewhere in this mix. This chapter will cover the first three primary causes. Chapter 3 will discuss the remaining primary causes as well as the secondary contributors.

The primary root causes of bad attitudes are

- Low self-esteem
- Fear
- Boredom
- Unresolved conflict
- Inability to accept change
- Resentment

Secondary contributors to bad attitudes include

- Stress/burnout
- Physical conditions
- Lack of understanding of organizational goals, mission, vision
- Past experiences
- Lack of feedback
- Lack of recognition

■ Low Self-Esteem

Acknowledging that people who have low self-esteem probably display bad attitudes is not an earth-shattering revelation. However, confronting the magnitude and pervasiveness of low self-esteem in America today may well be a shock. Jack Canfield, co-author of the best-selling series of books beginning with *Chicken Soup for the Soul*, estimates only one out of three

Americans possesses or demonstrates appropriate levels of high self-esteem. Two-thirds of Americans deal with issues of low self-esteem—some to greater levels of intensity than others.

▶ **Low self-esteem is an epidemic in America today.**

Symptoms in the Workplace

Low self-esteem is often contributory to subpar performance. It should be one of the first places we look when analyzing an employee's poor performance, but unfortunately it is usually the last place we look—if we go there at all. Employees who do *not believe* they can do a job well are right—they can't. When employees do *not believe* they can become a top performer (or at least in the top 10%) within the organization, they are right—they won't. Frequently, low self-esteem employees will stake out the lowest level of performance and take pride in how little they accomplish. They become motivated to see how little they can do without being fired. This is not unlike a student who doesn't believe he will ever achieve straight A's or become class valedictorian so he becomes the class clown.

People with low self-esteem will talk about others behind their backs. They are critical of management, peers, friends, family members, and other departments, but rarely in their presence. They level criticisms at those who are not there to defend themselves. This is an attempt to enhance their own self-esteem at the expense of others. In this criticism is a clearly implied message of "I am brighter, smarter, superior, and above all the things the other people do." This implied superiority is not the result of achievement or increased personal value, it is merely an attempt to lower the value of the people around them. Low self-esteem people devalue others just to keep themselves competitive!

Here's an interesting exercise. Concentrate on conversations, either those you are involved in or those going on around you (you have permission to eavesdrop). Ask yourself this compelling question: What is the true topic of conversation? It can be a sobering experience to realize that perhaps as much as 50 to 60% of the conversations we are involved in or those we overhear are *critical of people who are not there to defend themselves.* These conversations are attempts at raising someone's own self-perception at someone else's expense.

Are such discussions and criticisms always examples of low self-esteem? No. The key is whether the discussion is a prelude to positively confronting the issues or behaviors with the absent other, or whether it is merely intended to devalue, demean, or fuel the venting fires of negative frustration. Are we going to be proactive and attempt to do something about the problem or be reactive, weak, and victimized, and just complain and whine?

Blowing out someone else's candle does not make yours burn brighter. However, a whole lot of people try to disprove this truism every day. To blow out someone's candle, they will

- Consistently reject others' ideas
- Treat others with disrespect and lack of dignity
- Demean and ridicule others at every opportunity
- Blame others for their own mistakes and choices in life
- Refuse to teach, train, or assist others in growth and development
- Frequently attribute others' mistakes to stupidity, lack of intelligence, or dishonesty

Causes of Low Self-Esteem

The causes of low self-esteem are numerous and far beyond the scope of this book to analyze effectively. We will mention several here, but all causes of low self-esteem are related to issues of acceptance or affirmation by the individual involved. We are all in control of our self-esteem.

> ◗ **No one can give someone else low self-esteem—it can only be self-accepted.**

Negative comparison between ourselves and others is a substantial cause of low self-esteem. These scenarios often begin early in life when parents measure children by the achievements of an older, or perhaps gifted, sibling. These children grow up believing they are not as good as other prominent people in their lives, and this easily transfers to negative comparisons in the workplace.

Children may be influenced by ongoing messages of "You're not good enough, don't even try," or when their attempts to win approval from parents always seem to fall short. Teachers may label students with descriptions frequently carried into adulthood (slow, math-deficient, poor reader, etc.). Other causes include:

- Identifying with failures, not successes. How many people do you know who could easily describe ten of their weaknesses or failures and would struggle to identify five strengths or successes? So many of us are quick to identify what we aren't rather than what we are!

- Embracing self-blame for failures. "Life is a series of opportunities to fail our way to success." Low self-esteem flourishes when failure is interpreted to be an affirmation of inadequacy instead of an opportunity to learn and increase our next performance. ("I made a mistake—this proves I'm a bad person.")

- Perceptions of loss of control related to victimization. When people believe they have no control over life's events and outcomes, low self-perception blossoms, fostering feelings of inability, inconsequence, and "getting what I deserve."

- Demeaning or negative self-dialogue. Some psychologists estimate that we think 50,000 thoughts a day, giving us untold opportunities to affirm ourselves with positive thoughts or deluge ourselves with self-criticism and doubt. We talk to ourselves twenty-four hours a day—consciously in thought and reasoning, unconsciously in dreaming—and those whose dialogue with themselves is critical, demeaning, or destructive, ingrain low self-esteem.(Note: Some believe that talking to yourself is insanity. It is *not*. Arguing with yourself and losing—that may qualify!)

- Feelings of being different, or not fitting in, contribute to low self-esteem. Everyone wants to be accepted and part of the in crowd. The pain of those who are not can do significant self-perception damage.

Self-esteem issues are reinforced in the workplace in many ways, including criticizing mistakes versus correcting them, perfectionist bosses who are never satisfied, assigning responsibility without delegating authority, withholding recognition, devaluing employees, and maintaining a wide gulf between employees and management in positive perks and payoffs. We will address these issues throughout this book.

Turnaround Tools

Dealing with low self-esteem in the workplace is a significant challenge because the root causes are often very deep, personal, and longstanding. The options available to management for correction are limited. You are not a therapist. No one can impart high self-esteem to someone else; it is truly a self-generated, self-controlled perception.

Why should you even concern yourself with the issues of an employee's self-esteem? Quite simply—it is about productivity and the overall work environment. You are judged by the performance of your people. If you can help them to develop a more positive self-image, you will benefit through their enhanced performance. You cannot dismiss someone for poor self-esteem, but you may have to live with its results. Your only realistic option is to help employees make positive corrections. Certainly you can dismiss them if their performance becomes unacceptable; however, these employees frequently hover just above the line of dismissable performance. It is in everyone's best interest to do everything possible to promote positive self-esteem.

As a manager, you can promote self-esteem in the following ways:

- Appropriate use of recognition
- Encourage employees through self-assessment and creative goal-setting
- Depersonalize errors (focus on *what* happened, not *who* did it)
- Let employees out of jail
- Assign (delegate) work into employees' strengths
- Training
- Suggest personal counseling

The appropriate use of recognition   Recognition can be used to raise people's value. Few employees are truly recognized appropriately for their work. Low self-esteem employees, whose performance is probably mediocre at best, may not receive *any* positive recognition at all. Silence has become positive recognition. "If I'm leaving you alone, you are doing a good job." Silence isn't enough.

▶ **Recognition may be the single most powerful tool available to turn around low self-esteem employees.**

Traditionally, the standard recognition model has been: the employee performs, recognition is offered, the employee continues to perform. For the person struggling with low self-esteem, the model must be adjusted to: recognition is offered for something the employee does well, the employee performs, recognition is offered again, the employee continues to perform, recognition continues to be offered. In reality, recognition may have to come *before* performance and be continued in a consistent cycle.

▶ **With bad attitude employees, recognition must be front-end loaded.**

For many managers this may be a tough pill to swallow. It does *not* seem fair, nor is it easy to recognize low self-esteem employees. They do not earn recognition as top performers. You probably don't even like them! While you may not relish giving them positive recognition or reinforcement, low self-esteem employees probably need it more than most and will probably respond very positively to receiving it. No matter how frustrating these employees are, *they do something well!* Identify what it is and give them positive recognition. This means we may have to recognize people for the intangibles, such as honesty, politeness, integrity, consistency, promptness, or perseverance.

Obviously, using recognition as a tool to turn around bad attitude employees has an inherent problem. You run the risk of severely alienating other positive, highly productive employees by offering praise and recognition to those who may not be performing at their level. There are three key issues to consider:

- Giving recognition privately
- The abundance of recognition
- Specific versus general praising

The prevailing wisdom has always been to give praise or recognition publicly and criticism in private. This is giving way to the new wisdom which says, "Give praise/recognition in private, and use public praising sparingly." Obviously, if you are extending public praise to your problem employee in the presence of others, the high producers would demonstrate an acutely negative response. Using recognition as a tool does much less damage when used in private. Also, when we praise publicly, we may be putting the recognized employee in an uncomfortable and embarrassing situation.

Consider the case of "Super Manager" (a very personal experience):

Many years ago, as a young new manager, I perceived myself to be "super manager." Having read all of the management books and knowing all of the buzzwords, I was a self-proclaimed "great" manager. The only thing missing was a red S on my chest and a blue cape on my shoulders.

Steve, an employee in our production department, had reacted very quickly and decisively to avert a potentially serious problem. Few people were even aware of his action because he took it so quickly and efficiently. Within moments, the problem had surfaced, been corrected, production was cranked back up, and everything continued business as usual. Had he not reacted so quickly and decisively, everyone would have known about the problem, and the negative effects would have been felt over an extended period of time.

As his manager, I wanted to give Steve some well-deserved recognition, and, according to all of the management books, I was supposed to do that publicly. I happened to see Steve huddled with some members of the department in the lunchroom. I approached and said, "Steve, you did an excellent job yesterday in reacting to that potential problem. You took decisive action that avoided potential injury and certainly saved us a lot of time and money. We would have had a major problem if you had not reacted as quickly and effectively as you did." I then turned to his peers and said, "You guys would have really been impressed. Steve did an excellent job yesterday. We should all be very thankful for his quick response." In returning to my office I thought to myself, "Super Manager strikes again! I did my usual excellent job of following all of the rules of the perfect manager."

A few hours later, Steve came to my office and asked to talk with me. As I invited him in, I thought to myself, "He is probably here to compliment me on my excellent managerial abilities. He is so impressed, he wants to come in privately to pay homage." As I pumped up my feathers and preened in preparation for his acknowledgment of my superior managerial ability, he looked at me and said, "Don't ever do that to me again." He went on to say, "I appreciate your kind words, but you said them in front of that group of vultures in the lunchroom. For the past few hours, they have been walking around blowing me kisses, rubbing their noses, and making smooching sounds every time I approach. I don't need that kind of pressure. If you have something to say, please do it privately. I appreciated your acknowledgment, but it isn't worth having to deal with all the teasing and hooting that I have been getting."

Crushed by his response, Super Manager learned a valuable lesson; praising can be a powerful tool, but much like fire, if not handled properly, it can do significant damage and be counterproductive.

Let's address the abundance of recognition. If all of your employees are receiving appropriate recognition, no one will react negatively when you give positive recognition to the low self-esteem problem employee. But negative reaction can be intense when there is limited availability of the desired resource. What's the message? Be sure that everyone under your influence receives appropriate recognition. When they do, they have little interest or concern about the recognition you extend to others (including your bad attitude employee).

The framing of the recognition is also very important. General praising is better than a sharp stick in the eye, but it really does not contain the positive impact of specific recognition. Praise should be given by recognizing specific behaviors or assignments that have been performed well.

Specific praising is very effective because it indicates a personal interest in the employee and awareness of his or her challenge and performance. General praising does not have the same impact.

◆ Recognition—the more specific, the more effective.

A typical example of ineffective general praising is the high-level manager visiting from the home office who positions himself at the time clock to shake hands with employees as they report to work. He tells each employee to keep up the good work and that the company appreciates his or her efforts. Most employees react negatively to this encounter. They are probably saying to themselves, "You don't even know who I am or what I do around here. You don't have a clue as to the quality of my work or the intensity of my efforts. I resent the fact that you think I can be conned by your blanket insincerity."

◆ Recognition—the more general, the more insincere.

Encourage employees through self-assessment and creative goal setting
Encourage employees to

- Determine their personal strengths
- Identify what they like about themselves
- Analyze their weaknesses
- Identify areas for improvement
- Analyze the barriers that are holding them back

You can help your employees create improvement strategies by addressing these questions: What are they good at and how can they get even better? How can they do even more of what they do well? What are their weaknesses, and what can they do to overcome them? How can barriers be neutralized or removed?

You can assist your employees in setting specific goals for improvement. Design strategies to help them achieve their improvement goals, support them in the achievement of those goals, celebrate goal achievement, and then create the next phase of incremental goals for improvement.

Help your employees to surround themselves with positive people, to identify and avoid negative circumstances, and to concentrate on developing a positive outlook and overcoming negative interpretations of their lives and the events they experience.

All of these efforts will effectively rebuild or enhance self-esteem. However, they are *not* easy, they are *not* a quick fix, and for many, they may be an ongoing challenge of daily life.

◆ **Enhancing self-esteem through positive achievement pays long-term dividends.**

Depersonalize errors (focus on what happened, not on who did it)
Errors are a fact of life in the workplace. While you do everything possible to reduce their frequency, errors happen in the real world. People make mistakes. Bad attitude employees will often distance themselves from responsibility for errors. They will deny mistakes, explain away their actions, or blame others while refusing to take any personal responsibility. Bad attitude employees avoid blame because they see blame as very damning. It is one of the primary tactics they use to effectively devalue others. They focus on *who* did it, not on what happened, which allows them to distance themselves from any responsibility. If they allow themselves to be blamed, it would provide a basis for others to devalue them. They avoid being slashed by their own sword.

The key is to focus on *what* happened and not on *who* did it—depersonalization! When errors are depersonalized or "deblamed" by managers, the results are successful correction and an overall reduction in the perceived assault on self-esteem.

Blaming people with low self-esteem is a destructive strategy with huge downside risks. It yields little or no payoff. What does materialize is wrath, resistance, and a cornucopia of passive-aggressive behaviors. In reality, the egos of low self-esteem, bad attitude employees will *not allow* them to accept blame; however, their egos do encourage them to be a part of the solution. ("Ego" is not a bad word. Everyone has one, and we must find nourishment for our egos, or we all tend to plunge into the abyss of bad attitudes.) Help bad attitude employees to find success by correcting errors and fixing future behavior while avoiding past blame.

◆ **Blaming gets you a continuous replay of the past, not successful changes in the future.**

Let employees out of jail   Allow employees to overcome any *corrected* past problems. Many managers cultivate and maintain a laundry list of employees' past sins. This inventory of infractions is never allowed to expire or go out of print. There is no statute of limitations! The list is continuously updated, and with the slightest misstep by an employee, all his past violations and infractions are recalled, chapter and verse. In this scenario, people are never forgiven, and the past is never put to rest.

In our legal system, if a person commits a crime, is prosecuted, and is found guilty, he or she completes the sentence and is free to go. Do the crime! Do the time! You're done! A person cannot be retried for the same offense, and the punishment cannot re-occur. This is often not the case in the workplace. When employees commit a "crime," not only are they punished, but they are kept under suspicion and surveillance forever. Many managers do not let people out of jail for even the slightest infractions.

This type of managerial action results in the escalation of employees' stress and frustration, as they realize they will continue to be held responsible and punished for past problems. Since the past cannot be changed, why continue to revisit it? Your focus should be looking forward, fixing future behavior—not getting bogged down in what has already happened.

> ● **The past cannot be changed. Acknowledge it, but don't dwell there. Move on.**

Assign (delegate) work into employees' strengths   Every employee has strengths and weaknesses. Those with low self-esteem frequently identify primarily with their faults. They are much better at describing what they *can't* do than what they *can* do. As you evaluate the strengths and weaknesses of employees, it is important to assign them tasks complementary to their strengths. Assigning tasks to the weakness of a low self-esteem employee merely perpetuates frustration and failure. Low self-esteem is exacerbated. You are better off not assigning the work at all rather than inviting the low self-esteem employee to a banquet of failure.

Unfortunately, decisions of work assignment and delegation are too often based on who is available, closest, or least likely to complain. One employee told me that when she sees her boss coming, she runs away as fast as she can. "It's like the wild kingdom around here. The slow ones in our herd don't get eaten—they get delegated to. You get out of here as fast as you can."

> ● **Build confidence by assigning tasks to an employee's area of strength.**

Delegating into employees' strengths helps them to accumulate successes, building momentum and confidence to meet new challenges.

The legitimate point can be made that assigning tasks only to employees' strengths does not provide them opportunities for growth, development, or skill enhancement (they are never given anything new). Obviously, you do want to give employees new challenges and unfamiliar tasks to create opportunities for new success and to broaden their skills. The key to assigning employees new tasks is to couple the new delegation with complete and effective training. Learning new tasks and skills enhances self-esteem; assigning new tasks without training depletes it.

> ● **If you cannot provide the appropriate training, do not delegate the unfamiliar task.**

Training   Training is an extremely valuable tool in positively impacting employees' self-esteem. Giving people the opportunity to learn and expand their inventory of skills increases their sense of self-worth and self-confidence and makes them more valuable to the organization. Timely, effective training is one of the most positive motivators in the workplace today. Unfortunately, low self-esteem employees are the least likely to be involved in new skill training and development. Most of the training they receive tends to be a "remedial review" of past learning. Regularly scheduled, basic, fundamental review is an important component of training, but ongoing exposure to new skills and new tasks is also necessary. In the real world, low self-esteem employees are rarely selected for new projects. When they receive additional tasks, they are picking up the routine and boring tasks of others, as the more productive employees are freed up to do bigger and better things. The low self-esteem, bad attitude employee probably has the least opportunity for growth and development.

In Chapter 4, we will address specific training issues in greater depth. Suffice it to say at this point that any legitimate and reasonable opportunity to expose low self-esteem employees to additional effective training will enhance their self-worth.

> ◆ **Training well done enhances self-esteem; training poorly done tears it down.**

Suggest personal counseling   The issues influencing low self-esteem are often very deep and long-term and may be embedded in an employee's personal life. They may, in fact, be very serious emotional or mental disorders. You are not trained or qualified to advise them, nor is it appropriate for you to do so. While you cannot mandate it or become an active participant, you can offer suggestions to seek outside help. You can assist an employee in identifying counseling options.

Support and counseling could be available through

- Employee assistance programs (E.A.P.s)
- A personal physician
- The organization's medical providers
- A religious affiliation
- Competent mental-health-care providers
- Various support groups and 12-step programs

You may introduce these options by sincerely saying to an employee, "There may be some things going on where you could use some help or guidance. Here are some suggestions you may want to consider." You cannot dial the phone and make the appointment, but you can provide the number and a quarter to make the call. It is important for these suggestions to be sincere and compassionate. If you are not sincere in your interest to actually help the employee, don't pretend. Your lack of sincerity will speak volumes. Insincere intervention may be more harmful than no intervention at all. When in doubt, do not become involved. Employees may choose to take your advice or reject it. The control is entirely theirs. If they take offense (which is highly unlikely), so be it. Keep in mind you were motivated to offer options in their best interest.

We now move on to the next root cause of bad attitudes.

■ Fear

Bad attitude employees are frequently fearful people. They fear an inevitable, impending doom. The fear may be nonspecific, perhaps a generalized dread of bad things that are bound to happen. "Something bad is going to happen. It's going to happen soon, and it's going to happen to me!"

Symptoms

People with bad attitudes seem to gravitate toward opportunities to be fearful. They embrace the minutia and can parlay a small, petty incident into a predictor of future disaster. The fear of the bad attitude employee can be described by the longstanding acronym: False Evidence Appearing Real.

Consider "Negative Norman," the quintessential fear-based bad attitude employee. Norman goes to the supply cabinet to get a legal pad. There are no legal pads to be found. What are his options?

1. He could choose to be helpful in solving the problem—going to the supply storage area and transferring some legal pads. However, it is very doubtful he will pursue this action. Bad attitude employees like Norman are problem identifiers, not problem solvers. It is much easier to respond angrily or catastrophize about terrible outcomes than it is to fix the problem.

2. He could find someone to blame for the lack of legal pads. This reinforces his belief that whoever is in charge of resupplying the cabinet or ordering supplies is an idiot. "They are not even capable of keeping enough legal pads for me to do my job. How can I be expected to be successful when they can't even give me the tools I need to work?" It gives him someone to blame—it distances him from any responsibility.

3. He can take the path of negatively analyzing why there are no legal pads and create a fear-based, threatening scenario.

"There are no legal pads in the cabinet."

"I'll bet our legal pad supplier has refused to ship us."

"I'll bet we have not paid our bill."

"I'll bet we are having financial problems."

"I'll bet this is just the beginning of supply shortages."

"Soon all our vendors will probably turn against us."

"I'll bet we are in serious financial trouble."

"I'll bet my next paycheck is going to bounce."

"I'll bet we will be in Chapter 11 very quickly."

"I'll bet I am going to be out of a job very soon."

"I may lose my house and my boat, and I won't be able to educate my children because the leaders of this company are so stupid and have mismanaged us so badly we are going to be forced out of business."

Obviously, Norman chooses the third scenario. He seeks out other negative confidants and shares his contrived fears, expanding on them as he goes. With each telling, the story gains validity, legitimacy, and momentum. Damaging rumors and innuendo result. Soon the tentacles of these rumors spread throughout the company, and they begin to take on the aura of fact. Management hears the rumors and decides to react by calling a meeting to deny any financial problems. How do Norman and his compatriots react to this denial? They proclaim, "This proves it! That's what management *always* says just before they file for bankruptcy. They call a meeting to deny everything and then . . . Wham! They pull the plug."

People with fear-based bad attitudes take a sliver of fact or observation and expand it into horrible, inevitable, impending doom. Norman chose to see the lack of legal pads as proof of impending bankruptcy. He refused to consider any other possible (and less catastrophic) reasons why the pads weren't there.

Mark Twain is reported to have said, "I've experienced many horrible, awful, terrible things in my lifetime—a couple of which actually happened!" The things that tend to knock us for a loop are the unanticipated events of life. Franklin Delano Roosevelt, realizing the debilitating and insidious effect of fear said, "We have nothing to fear but fear itself."

Causes

Where does this fear come from? The causes may be intertwined with low self-esteem. Fear-based bad attitudes frequently reflect people's inability to see themselves as successful, either now or in the past. They do not take credit for the good things or the successes they have experienced. They feel they lack any ability to influence or control future outcomes. Their days are spent floundering perilously close to the jagged rocks of the shoreline, and they have little belief in their ability to take any positive action to avoid the pending devastation awaiting them on the shore. They are at the mercy of the wind gods, and they are powerless to influence their fate.

People with fear-based bad attitudes often attribute any success they do have to outside forces other than to their own skill, competence, or ability. They often credit successes to luck or "karma" (being at the right place at the right time). They do not give themselves credit for their accomplishments. They believe success and positive outcomes (past and present) are dependent upon those external forces (such as luck) over which they have no control.

The fear of bad attitude employees is frequently based on the capriciousness of luck. They fear their luck is inevitably going to run out. "I was lucky. I am lucky. It is extremely doubtful I will continue to be lucky." No one's luck can last forever. That is the *inevitable, impending doom.* The fear is rooted in the belief of

◆ "Today is the day my luck runs out."

Does luck really play a part in life? Of course it does. The late legendary University of Alabama football coach, Bear Bryant, has been quoted as defining luck this way: "Luck is when preparation meets opportunity." The opportunities of life are something you cannot control. However, preparation is something you can. People with bad attitudes frequently do *not* prepare themselves. Why? Because they believe the opportunities will not happen for them. When opportunity does knock, they haven't made the necessary preparations, so they are not in a position to take advantage of it. This becomes more proof of their victimization and further affirmation that nothing good ever happens to them. "I told you so. I never get the lucky bounce."

People whose confidence and belief in themselves encourages them to prepare for future opportunities are prepared to seize them when they do appear. Bear Bryant also said: "The harder I work, the luckier I get." In other words; the harder you work, the more you prepare yourself, and the more of life's positive opportunities seem to come your way.

◆ Preparation is the key to being lucky.

The people who win the lottery have at least bought a ticket! If you want the opportunity to win, prepare yourself by investing in a ticket. If you do not buy the ticket, do not lament the lost opportunity. Do not read the winning numbers in the paper; do not watch the live lottery drawing on television. You will probably have a bad attitude if your lucky numbers are pulled and you have not prepared properly.

Bad attitude employees often predetermine their lack of opportunity and excuse themselves from preparation. ("It will never happen to me!") It is easy—and it gives them something to blame.

Turnaround Tools

There are a number of managerial tools you can use when dealing with fearful employees.

Instill internal credit for good events, and depersonalize blame for mistakes or failure   Help people focus on their ability and see the future as something they can influence with their competence. Reduce the fear of the unknown by instilling confidence in their control. When people believe their past and present successes resulted from their capabilities and competencies, reflecting their influence and control, the future is much brighter. "I was capable and competent; I am capable and competent; I *will be* capable and competent." The future is much less fearful. They believe in their ability to create positive outcomes, and it is something they can control.

Training   (Help people to prepare for the opportunities of tomorrow.) Train employees in the skills and competencies necessary to face the challenges of tomorrow. The future is much less scary when you are prepared for it!

Establish clear goals and accountability   Contrary to popular belief, goals, responsibility, and accountability are not fear inducing, they are fear reducing. They establish the rules of the road, raise employees' awareness of their boundaries, and let them know what is expected of them.

> If we place a dog in a yard equipped with an invisible fence, the animal quickly learns that certain movements will result in its receiving a mild shock. If the dog is unclear of the boundaries or they frequently appear to change, he becomes fearful of movement and tends toward inactivity. Human beings react in very similar fashion. Unclear goals and boundaries usually cause fear and low initiative.

Defuse the fear   Help employees articulate the fear or inevitable impending doom, and address the issues honestly, including: What can be done to make sure this won't happen? How will we know if it is happening (identify early warning signs)? How will we react or correct it if it does?

■ Boredom

Boredom can be a major contributor to employees' bad attitudes. However, it is not the traditional boredom defined by inactivity. Rarely in today's workplace do you have employees bored out of their skull, standing around with nothing to do. (Those employees were probably downsized long ago.) Today's workplace boredom is driven primarily by repetition.

Symptoms

The symptoms of boredom include

- Escalation of absenteeism and tardiness
- Increased quality problems, including epidemics of minor mistakes indicative of lack of focus or concentration
- Lack of perceived job worth, indications of what I/we do isn't really important
- Higher prevalence of negative behaviors such as surliness, whining, and complaining

Causes

No matter how technical or challenging the task may be, doing the same thing, the same way, over and over, day in and day out, makes it boring. Repetition, monotony, and the absence of different challenges contribute to today's boredom-based bad attitudes.

This repetition is frequently a catch-22. We are good at what we do, so we get to do more of it. When you don't allow employees to branch out or routinely expose them to changes in their routine, you invite escalations of boredom. Our complex brain rebels against the monotony of repetition.

It is not uncommon for employees with bad attitudes to be assigned a disproportionate share of boring tasks. The "bad attituders" tend to be the dumping ground for other employees' boring tasks as you try to give the favored/productive employees some help in freeing up their time for new challenges. It is not uncommon for bad attitude employees to pick up everyone else's crumbs! Boredom escalates their negative attitudes, further embedding the employees' perception of being picked on, disregarded, persecuted, or devalued, and reinforces their lack of influence and control.

▶ **Boredom based on idleness is a thing of the past. Boredom based on repetition is an attitude destroyer of today and tomorrow.**

Turnaround Tools

Boredom is an issue to be constantly reviewed by leaders at all levels of all organizations. "How can we break up the boredom around here?" should be an ongoing question. Is there anything you can do to help relieve the repetition-based boredom of your people? Many boring tasks cannot and should not be avoided. Just because something is boring does not mean it may not be critical to your mission, and the responsibility for effective completion cannot be waived just because it is not fun. However, there are some adjustments that can be made.

You can reduce boredom by

- Task rotation
- Job rotation
- Analyzing and eliminating unnecessary, repetitive tasks
- Cross-training

Task rotation   Identifying some of the highly repetitive and monotonous tasks that may lend themselves to sharing or rotation is an excellent, quick way to reduce boredom. Even tasks that invite boredom are *not* monotonous initially.

If the department or team is truly rotating some of the boring tasks, it may be appropriate for the manager/leader (you!) to take a turn in the rotation. While this is certainly not necessary, it does provide concrete evidence of your willingness to participate. You are probably familiar with the dogsledding metaphor, "In sledding, unless you're the lead dog, the view always remains pretty much the same." Key question: How can you "improve the view" of everyone in the pack?

Peers can also begin to address their own issues of boredom. Workmates or teammates may each be doing repetitive tasks whose high levels of boredom are driving them to distraction. Is it possible they could rotate their tasks on a "sometime" basis? One person's poison may be another person's challenge. Learning something new can be fresh, different, and exciting. Giving employees the empowerment to address their own issues of boredom can help relieve bad attitudes. It gives them some measure of influence and control.

Job rotation   While not always possible, allowing employees to rotate their normal jobs is extremely helpful in reducing boredom. When some jobs are more desirable than others, it is also an effective way to share the pain. Successful job rotation programs also help the organization insure itself against the problems of absenteeism, turnover, and vacation scheduling.

Analyzing and eliminating unnecessary, repetitive tasks What are we requiring our people to do that just doesn't matter? Many irrelevant, repetitious, or boring tasks frequently are traditional to the organization (we have *always* done it), inherited from others (permanent delegations never rescinded when the need had passed), or qualifiers for the catchall job description category of "other duties as assigned." Can they be eliminated?

Interestingly, opportunities to eliminate repetition are often found in internal reporting systems. In many organizations, people are required to spend enormous amounts of time compiling reports that nobody reads. In many circumstances, reporting has degenerated to "prove to me you have been busy." Instead of assessing actual results and productivity, we ask employees to invest their time justifying their existence by explaining actions and accomplishments already taken and achieved.

Cross-training Cross-training is an inherent part of job rotation. Obviously, employees must be trained if they are to assume new duties, even on a rotated or occasional basis. However, many jobs cannot be totally crosstrained or rotated. Job requirements such as educational background and licensing or certifications may restrict movements and rotations. Even in these circumstances, cross-awareness training is extremely effective in reducing repetition and monotony. Employees may not be trained to the extent of actually being able to perform the duties of another job description or classification; however, they can be trained to the level of being aware of the intricacies and demands of the job and the prioritization of the tasks involved.

Cross-awareness training allows employees to "walk a mile in another's moccasins." (This also helps to reduce miscommunication and internal competition.) Awareness increases cooperation.

▶ **Productivity, quality, and safety are all positively influenced by reducing repetition-induced boredom.**

In Chapter 3 we'll continue to discuss primary root causes of bad attitudes as well as examine secondary contributors.

3 Bad Attitudes:
More Root Causes and Secondary Contributors

In this chapter we will consider the three additional root causes of bad attitudes: unresolved conflict, the inability to accept change, and resentment. Unresolved conflict and the issues of change are so critical to our understanding of bad attitudes that each is further addressed in separate chapters later in the book.

We will also address a host of secondary contributors to bad attitudes: stress, physical conditions, past experiences, lack of understanding, lack of feedback, and lack of recognition.

■ Unresolved Conflict

The impact and magnitude of unresolved conflict is frequently underestimated and misunderstood. Our discomfort and lack of understanding of how to positively resolve conflict produces conflict paralysis. We do nothing in the face of conflict and hope that it goes away. We blame others for the conflict's nonresolution, and we pursue behaviors of active avoidance. We avoid the conflict, the people, and the responsibility—the long-term results of this avoidance are devastating.

◆ Unresolved Conflict = Bad Attitudes and Poor Performance

Symptoms

Conflict is inevitable and it can become dysfunctional. When avoided or addressed ineffectively, it escalates and, in the extreme, results in acts of violence and retribution. Unresolved conflict turns inward and spawns passive-aggressive behaviors that are intended to get even, or fight back covertly under the cover of darkness. Unresolved conflict will inevitably show itself in the erosion of quality of work. Unresolved conflict causes workplace factions (cliques) and a prevailing us-against-them mentality. It can also take its toll on employees physically and emotionally, through increased levels of stress and deteriorating issues of health. Sabotage, espionage, theft, destruction, tardiness, and absenteeism are some examples of the destructive results of unresolved conflict.

Many issues negatively impact bad attitude employees in their attempts to deal with conflict, including their

- Lack of conflict resolution skills
- Feelings of "exclusion" and "victimization," which are fed by conflict situations
- Perceptions of low trust in management and peers
- Tendency to personalize conflict
- Lack of solution orientation (quite different from mere identification)
- Historical perspective to conflict
- Narrow field of vision (high regard for self, low regard for others)
- Reaction to conflict that is emotion-based not content- or objective-based
- Ultimate perception that prolonging the conflict may be in their own best interest

Causes

Perhaps the primary cause of conflict is not getting what we want since we tend to react badly when our expectations are not met. Other significant causes are

- Personality differences
- Disagreements (facts, data, observations, strategies)
- Goals (what we are going to do)
- Workload (perceptions of unfairness or overload)
- Cultural differences
- Values (boundaries/limitations and perceptions of acceptable/unacceptable behaviors and conditions)

The Realities of Conflict

Conflict, whether real or imagined, is as consistent and predictable a challenge in today's workplace as in personal relationships. Conflict is not always bad. Conflict can make a very positive contribution to the organization. Creativity, innovation, and change can all have their stirrings of birth in conflict. Conflict can also serve as an early warning sign of potentially serious problems. It also invites us to look inward for solutions as well as to force collaborations with others to create resolutions. Conflict can be a very unifying force. Strong relationships are forged in conflict. Successful relationships, whether they are workplace, personal, or global, frequently share a common foundation, having recognized conflict, committed to its resolution, and partnered interactively to achieve successful outcomes beneficial to all concerned. Conflict, faced head-on and resolved, bonds parties tightly together. Bad attitude employees whose conflict remains unresolved, do not experience the benefits of the bond. They remain on the outside looking in.

These issues and others, including in-depth assessments of conflict levels and positive strategies for solutions, will be discussed in Chapters 6 and 7.

■ Inability to Accept Change

Bad attitude employees frequently react negatively to change—change equals threat. Resisting change is a very predictable and normal (perhaps instinctive) human behavior. In actuality, the most intense, initial negative reaction to change may come from your most positive, top-producing employees. Why? Because they have the most to lose! They are doing very well under the current process. For them, "it ain't broke so don't fix it." Change impacts their performance, comfort, and security. However, when change is inevitable and unavoidable, positive employees who take appropriate internal credit for their achievements can and do embrace change successfully. Bad attitude employees who lack the ability or willingness to see themselves as successful resist change. Change is a threat, it calls upon their reservoir of luck, and that supply may be dwindling or gone. Many employees will move from passive to active resistance as they perceive the threat of change to escalate. While they perceive themselves to be victimized, unrecognized, and unappreciated under the current process, at least they are surviving. What they are now experiencing, no matter how bad it is, is better than the fear of what the future may hold. Change may pose a threat to their survivability. For many, the only thing worse than their current situation is the "unknown threat of change."

For many bad attituders, change itself *is* the inevitable impending doom. If they are not confident of their ability to be successful, any threat to the status quo is fearful indeed. The dilemma for bad attitude employees is that change is everywhere. Change is the one constant ingredient that permeates every successful organization. No matter where they go or which way they turn, bad attitude employees are confronted with change. If things are left as they are, their attitudes may become dormant. However, the threat of change causes their attitudes to flare and remain in a high state of constant agitation.

Symptoms

Change stimulates fear and increases perceptions of loss, and these feelings may become overwhelming and unmanageable for the bad attitude employee. These fear and loss issues include

- Fear of failure (or perhaps success)
- Threat to the "comfort" of stability
- Loss of face
- Loss of perceived prevailing advantage
- Loss of influence
- Decreased visibility
- Escalation of unfairness

Because of the tendency of bad attitude employees to personalize their issues, they perceive change as a personal criticism of their current and past performance and contributions. Having to change means "I haven't been doing it right." They internalize this "blame" and react by distancing themselves from responsibility. They do not see change as dictated by the differences of today and tomorrow; it remains an attack on their past.

A statement attributed to Winston Churchill concerning his thoughts on change:

> ◆ **"There is nothing wrong with change if it is in the right direction. To improve is to change. To be perfect is to have changed often."**

What does this say about the bad attitude employee whose energy is focused on resisting change? What does this say about organizations and people who are still doing things "the way we have always done them around here"? These issues and many others will be addressed in Chapter 13, "Bad Attitude Employees and Change."

■ Resentment

When people experience resentment, the explosion of bad attitudes is a natural progression. Resentment is a very strong emotion that can be highly damaging as it may cause people to respond with negative actions.

Our consideration of resentment will be twofold:

First we will look at the causes and turnaround tools to deal with the very real and painful issues of legitimate resentment in the workplace today. While many of these issues are uncontrollable (at least at your level of the organization), they are nonetheless very real and a cause of significant concern for your employees.

We will also look at the myriad causes driving the shallow, self-centered, illegitimate resentment frequently embraced by those who are seeking reasons to lower their performance, blame others for their circumstances, and conveniently perceive themselves as victims. We will introduce tools for turning around a significant amount of this illegitimate resentment.

Symptoms

The symptoms of resentment range from uncooperative behavior (refusal to work overtime; do unpleasant, unappealing tasks; or participate in organizational functions) to covert and overt attempts to disrupt management and the workplace. These include

- Sabotage (acts of omission escalating to commission)
- Escalating conflict (violence is not unheard of)
- Formation of cliques with ostracizing or punishment of those not aligned (or deemed too cozy with management)
- Withholding of support for management issues
- Efforts to unionize
- Unacceptable and expensive high rates of turnover

Causes

Three significant contributing factors to these feelings of resentment are

- Issues of unfairness (legitimate or illegitimate)
- Realistic changes in today's workplace
- Issues of loss or disenfranchisement

Legitimate issues of unfairness

1. Compensation

   When employees are denied raises while high-level executives draw massive bonuses or the disparity in pay between employee and management is huge, resentment will flourish. According to *Business Week* magazine, in one year alone, 1996, total compensation of CEOs rose

54%, which was preceded by a 30% increase in 1995. The average factory worker's compensation increase for 1996 was 3% and a white collar worker's was 3.2%. Top executive pay is 200 times that of factory workers.* Do you think there might be some resentment related to this compensation issue?

2. Downsizing

The callous elimination of jobs with no regard for employees or their family's well-being escalates resentment to bitterness. In fact, many executives and shareholders profit during these cuts as the stock market reacts positively to the strategy. It is an interesting phenomenon: management makes mistakes and puts the company at risk, workers are downsized while managers maintain their jobs, and managers are rewarded for their decisive actions with stock profit windfalls.

3. Discrimination, Abuse, and Harassment

These very real issues take numerous forms: gender, age, sexual issues, sexual orientation, race, nationality, disability, religious beliefs, appearance, and so on. When people suffer any form of discrimination, resentment is a natural conclusion.

4. Gray Areas

In reality, many incidents of unfairness are not clearly defined, nor can they be proven by evidence or documentation. While not being clearly proven, they are very real nonetheless.

- "Was the other person really more qualified for the promotion, or does the boss just not like *me*?"
- "Are other people really better performers? Do they get the good assignments because of their relationship with the boss?"
- "The people on the other shift don't work as hard as we do, and they always leave their messes for us to clean up."
- "I work harder than anyone else in the department, but we all make the same amount of money."

All of these statements are based on opinion or interpretation, and the biggest challenge with the gray areas is that we all see things in our own best interest. It is very difficult to be objective when things are not going our way. Determining whether unfairness is real or imagined is

---

* *Business Week*, "Executive Pay, Special Report," April 21, 1997, page 59.

extremely difficult because perceiving we are being treated unfairly is another avenue for distancing ourselves from responsibility. Perceiving a lack of promotion to be the boss's bias is easier than looking in the mirror and saying, "Maybe it's me." Perceiving unfairness can be a great way to avoid pain and reality. When we perceive we are being treated unfairly, we don't have to ask ourselves to change our behavior or make any adjustments. Their unfairness is something we can do nothing about, and we frequently choose to respond with passive-aggressive behaviors through the reducing of performance or contribution. It gives us a convenient opportunity to excuse our negative behaviors.

Turnaround Tools for Legitimate Issues of Unfairness

Our goal in the workplace is to eliminate all forms of discrimination and to hire, fire, compensate, and promote employees solely upon the basis of their productivity and overall value to the organization. We are not yet there, and anyone who thinks we are is in severe self-serving denial. Any allegations of discrimination and harassment must be taken very seriously. Employees must be instructed how to document their allegations and how to pursue the formal process for correction and elimination. Your role as a leader is to ensure that your employees receive effective training and have the necessary awareness and knowledge to properly pursue their allegations and to avoid committing these acts against others. All employees must receive training to raise their awareness of existing laws, the definitions of unacceptable behaviors, and their personal, as well as organizational, liabilities. Zero tolerance is mandatory and moral.

Unfortunately, for some, allegations of discrimination and harassment are comfortable places to hide, convenient opportunities to attain an unfair advantage or to pursue ill-gotten monetary gain. Fraudulent allegations and pursuits must also be dealt with decisively and to the full extent of the law.

Employees confronting real workplace unfairness have three options.

Acceptance   Confront the reality of the circumstance, acknowledge there is nothing to be done, and choose one of two paths.

- Continue their current level of performance and maintain a positive outlook in the hopes that the circumstance will change. (Help them to focus on the good, not just the bad!)

- Covertly fight back through performance reductions, subtle sabotage, and resistance to change initiatives. (Let your employees know this is *not* acceptable and will put you in a position antagonistic to theirs, which you do not want but will deal with effectively, if necessary.)

Attempt to change the situation   Employees can choose to address inter-actively their perceptions of unfairness through positive communication based on objective content, not subjective emotional discussions based on self-serving perceptions and observations. Procedures must be established to encourage employees to present their perceptions in an adult, busi-nesslike manner, and management must demonstrate a high willingness to consider the employee's point of view. Real or imagined, these incidents of unfairness are legitimate in the employee's eyes, and that perception must be addressed. Pursuing legal action is an ultimate option.

Leave the organization   If, in fact, the unfairness is intolerable, employees must take steps to relocate and seek employment opportunities where they perceive they will be treated equitably. The decision to separate should not be made arbitrarily or impulsively and should be done in a thoughtful manner. The employee should make this decision based on self-interest, not to somehow punish the boss or the organization. Management can, in fact, be helpful in assisting an employee to transfer or seek employment opportunities with another organization if, in fact, the perceptions of unfairness cannot be satisfactorily addressed by all concerned.

■ ■ ■

Now we consider the issues of self-serving, illegitimate perceptions of unfairness.

Illegitimate issues of unfairness   These develop when people choose inappropriate perceptions of being treated unfairly to hide, distance them-selves from responsibility, avoid pain, or excuse their own negative behav-iors. These imagined issues of unfairness occur in part because we have lost the ability to be disappointed and we have lost the ability to not "win."

1. Disappointment

   Disappointment is not something we handle particularly well. When we experience disappointment, we want someone to "pay" when things do not go our way.

   > A promotional opportunity for a new supervisor arises in our department, and five employees approach the department head announcing their interest in the job and their desire to be promoted. All five employees are top performers, and all have demonstrated strong leadership qualities. The decision can be difficult because there is little, if any, difference between the five applicants being con- ❧ sidered, and any one of the five would do an excellent job. However, only one of the five can be selected.

The successful candidate will be very happy and will probably say very nice things about the boss. "The boss made the right decision. She did what was fair and made the best decision possible. After considering all of the candidates, she promoted me! Three cheers for the boss's good judgment." The other four candidates will perceive they were treated unfairly and will see the decision as a personal issue between themselves and the boss. They will question whether she has an IQ above freezing. They may subjectively assume favoritism, dishonesty, collusion, or conspiracy (substantiation is not necessary). While the four unsuccessful candidates will be angry at their boss, they will likely take out their revenge on the *successful* candidate. They may punish the person who got the job they feel rightfully belonged to them by refusing to support the new supervisor. They may become a hindrance or barrier to the new supervisor and may even attempt to contribute to their failure. It is not uncommon for unsuccessful promotional candidates to be gone from an organization within eighteen months. They may become angry enough to quit immediately after the promotion is announced, or their performance slips so badly they may have to be placed into the disciplinary process, and ultimate separation can result. We just don't know how to deal well with disappointment.

Is it possible the decision of promotion was based on favoritism or other unfairness? Sure. But in reality, there were five good horses in the race, and one of them won by a nose. It doesn't mean that the four unsuccessful candidates were passed over for promotion or treated unfairly. Going into the decision they had only a 1 in 5 chance of being successful.

Why does this perception of unfairness happen so frequently? Because we have lost the ability to be disappointed! We do not know how to look in the mirror and say, "This one did not go my way; I will work hard to make sure the next one does." Looking in the mirror can be very painful.

> ◗ **Clinging to unfair resentment results in a self-imposed lifetime sentence of today. There will be no growth or development, just perpetuation of current conditions.**

Effective communication is the key to overcoming many of these issues of unfairness. The department head should meet with the four unsuccessful candidates and explain to them why the decision was not made in their favor. Their value and strengths should be emphasized, along with specific comments on the growth or changes necessary to win successful promotion in the future. The candidates do not have to agree with the explanation; however, they will have some positive input to balance their view of unfair treatment. In the absence of this communication, the perception of unfairness will be rampant.

2. Winning

We have elevated winning to such a godlike status that when we do not win we seek to find someone to blame or somewhere else to place responsibility. Make no mistake—winning is very important. Striving to be our best and ultimately winning over our competition are an integral part of success. And as we all know, *in life we do keep score.* It is the narrow and constrained definition of winning that fans the flames of resentment. Winning and success are not necessarily synonymous. We can achieve success and still experience frustration and lack of fulfillment because we have not achieved the restricted platform of exclusive victory. Those who do not win can still be considered successful.

This dichotomy of winning versus not winning is very destructive. Perhaps a good example of this is the advertisement run by the Nike Corporation at the conclusion of the 1996 Olympic Games in Atlanta proclaiming: "You don't win Silver, you lose Gold." The message clearly was "If you are not the best performer in your selected event, you are a loser." Given this mentality, we must be a planet of losers! How many people can ever say they are the very best at what they do? Those who are number two or below, must relegate themselves to the distasteful designation of "loser." This distortion of winning not only feeds resentment, it spawns a win-at-all-costs mentality—rules, honor, ethics, and morals be damned. The ends justify the means. Winning covers all sins, and there can be only one winner. Focusing on success versus winning is a much healthier pursuit.

Those who tend to level judgments of "losers" on people who finish in second place or below are frequently those who only wish they could compete at that level. The people criticizing athletes or teams are those who lie at home on the couch, channel surfing with the remote control, dreaming about what might have been. True competitors have a healthy respect for each other's accomplishments.

▶ **It is easier to criticize than to step up to the plate and risk actual performance.**

■ ■ ■

Now that we've addressed these complex issues of unfairness, we move on to the two other primary contributors to resentment: realistic changes in the workplace and issues of loss or disenfranchisement.

Realistic changes in today's workplace   Another huge contributor to resentment is the changes in the rules governing today's workplace—how we do business, how we treat each other, and the overall factors that influence organizational cultures. Proclaiming that the rules have changed in America is not earth-shattering! In fact, anyone who does not realize the rules have changed dramatically is probably still celebrating "Flat Earth Day." Following are some of the areas where the old rules have been replaced by an entirely new set of rules.

1. Job security

    The old rule was: join our organization, work hard, be productive, stay out of trouble, and you will retire from here if you so choose. Job security was assumed, offered a great amount of stability, and lessened anxieties about the future, economic well-being, retirement, etc. In the past, job security was taken for granted. In many cases, you really had to work at getting fired.

    Today, there are no guarantees. Job security is no longer a given. Jobs are being lost due to downsizing, restructuring, upsizing, etc. Frequently these decisions have nothing to do with an individual's performance, contribution, or value to the organization. Also, now guaranteed security is a two-way street. While the organization can no longer guarantee jobs, employees are no longer guaranteeing long-term commitment. This is especially true among highly creative and productive performers who realize they may not want to make long-term promises of workplace loyalty. Their commitment may be only for the duration of a project or for a specific length of time dedicated to learning and attaining certain skills. Upon successful completion, they may choose to chart their career in a different direction. Security and its accompanying loyalty have been disrupted in both directions.

2. The rule of longevity

    In the past, job security was determined by longevity. Promotions and layoff vulnerability were determined by seniority. Those who lived and breathed the longest on the planet or within the organization had the security, got the promotions, and avoided the layoffs.

Today, longevity is out, productivity is in. In today's workplace, compensation, promotability, and security are increasingly determined by issues of productivity. It is not how long you have been here; it is what you are contributing or producing. To a degree, we are all having to stand for reelection every day. Past laurels have the value of yesterday's newspaper! This is a cataclysmic change for many people as well as entire systems. In many circumstances, we have institutionalized longevity through collective bargaining agreements, civil service protections, tenures, etc. Where these practices are legally institutionalized, the economy, workplace environment, and the law may actually be at cross-purposes. These forces may be on a collision course, and the results are yet to be determined. As America increasingly defines security by productivity (which is necessary to be competitive in this emerging global economy), those whose primary focus is longevity, will rapidly become resentful. We may be facing a period of painful review of laws, common practices, and policies. We are just beginning to see the tip of this iceberg!

3. Promotability

The old rule was: join our organization, be productive, stay out of trouble, put in your time, and take your boss's job. (This does not mean get your boss fired. As bosses move up or out of the organization, you would anticipate rotating into their slot.) It would not be unreasonable to assume that you would spend 25 or 30 years with an organization and receive at least two to three predictable promotions during that time span (more if you were a superstar or well connected)!

In today's workplace, promotions are few and far between! As organizations flatten, there are fewer positions for people to be promoted into. As organizations experience growth, they are less likely to create an extensive layer of supervisory and middle management positions. The competition for promotions is far greater than at any time in our economic history. Many employees can anticipate staying in their current position for the entire duration of their employment (another reason for the disruption of loyalty). People may have to change jobs to move up.

4. Compensation programs

Another old rule was: work hard, stay out of trouble, put in your time, and steady, predictable increases in compensation would be automatic. Consistent 5 to 7% yearly raises were commonplace (10 to 12% in a really good year). In fact, in the past banks would factor your predictable future raises into their home mortgage lending decisions—not anymore!

The era of consistent, predictable, high-percentage pay increases is over. Organizations are finding more productive and creative ways of increasing compensation, including bonuses, gainsharing, and profit sharing. These are based on the overall performance of the organization and allocated on a one-time basis, and are not driven by seniority or longevity. Today many employees' compensation increases are based on the performance of the greater group, not just on individual contributions. Birthday presents are the payoff for longevity, not guaranteed raises!

■ ■ ■

These are just some examples of our significantly changing workplace. The challenge facing all of us is our willingness to adapt to the ever-changing new rules. If we do not embrace the new rules, the result can only be *resentment*. Attempting to play today's game by yesterday's rules can have no other outcome but high levels of resentment with the inevitable resulting "bad attitudes." Why? Because our expectations cannot possibly be met. We subject yesterday's expectations to today's reality, and we spend our time thinking and talking about how things used to be, how things ought to be, how things are not fair anymore, and how we long for the good old days.

▶ **Today's game by today's rules = Success, competitiveness, and productivity. Today's game by yesterday's rules = Resentment, lower productivity, and bad attitudes.**

Our frustration is that in many cases, we know what the old rules *aren't*, but none of us knows what the new rules *are* (management as well as employees). Things are changing at such a swift pace that we may literally be making up the rules as we go along. While this may not be ideal, it is a reality dictated by economic necessity. In the uncertainty of the changing rules, we tend to focus our resentment on the people directly above us (our supervisor, manager, department head, etc.). I'm sure you can readily identify with your employees' perceptions; you are probably experiencing the same thing. The resentment is based in not being told what the new rules are. We may perceive our bosses are holding back information, choosing intentionally not to tell us, and keeping us in the dark at a frustrating disadvantage. However, the truth is

▶ **They don't know what the new rules are either!**

Flexibility is the password, and those lacking it are struggling and will continue to do so. Employees and managers who display high rigidity and low flexibility will probably tumble quickly into the cycle of resentment, bad attitudes, and poor productivity, with high levels of frustration and low levels of success. This is a trap we must all be aware of!

▶ During a consulting/training session, a group of university department heads (academic and administrative) loudly vocalized their resentment toward the school's vice presidents (their superiors). They believed the vice presidents were withholding information and were not honest and forthcoming in telling them what the "new rules" were. Statements such as the following were made:

- "They tell me to do something on Monday, and on Wednesday I am criticized for having done it that way."

- "I am instructed to do something on Monday, and by Friday it is obsolete. I have received multiple e-mail messages, each countering the instructions of the previous message. I am frustrated and confused, and I don't understand why they are doing it."

- "Things change so rapidly around here, I don't know what I am supposed to be doing."

In a subsequent session with the university's vice presidents, this group loudly proclaimed their resentment toward the person directly above them, the university president. Why? Because they believed the president was not accurately communicating the changes in policies and expectations to them. Statements such as the following were made:

- "I'm held accountable for things I don't even know about."

- "I'm asked to handle something that is supposedly a red-hot crisis, so I stop everything else I'm doing to handle the important task. I'm then criticized because I didn't do both the emergency and the normal demands. I just can't keep up with things anymore."

- "I'm being asked to do so much more with so much less, and I don't know what's really important anymore."

As you have probably guessed, in a subsequent session, the president of the university was loudly proclaiming her resentment toward the board of trustees in the state's capital. She proclaimed:

- "I am trying to lead a major university, and the trustees are changing the policies almost on a daily basis."

- "Our goals and mission seem to be changing with every phone call I receive from the board of trustees."

- "I am not sure anyone really knows what's going on, and I am the one that is held accountable."

While resentment toward those above us is very normal and understandable, it is also self-defeating. Just as you may be experiencing these feelings toward your superiors, your people are experiencing them toward you! What good does it do to resent someone for something he or she cannot control? We must develop the flexibility to deal with the cascading change, or we will become consumed by resentment and paralyzed into inactivity. Survival and productivity are not possible in today's workplace without the valuable tool of flexibility. Key questions to be asked are: How flexible are your bad attitude employees? How can you help all your employees become more flexible?

Issues of loss or disenfranchisement   The more we depersonalize the workplace, the more we increase resentment and create a fertile breeding ground for bad attitudes. Depersonalization makes people feel as if they are just a number and not valued as individuals. This is especially true in organizations when

- There is little or no recognition coming from management to the employees.

- There is a huge dichotomy of separation of stature and value between the management and employee levels within the organization. (In some organizations management has their own restrooms, eating facilities, and choice parking spaces.)

- The organization relies solely on management to solve problems with little or no input from employees.

- People are not acknowledged for their intellect or ability to think beyond their current scope of responsibility. One employee voiced these feelings: "I'm not treated as a valuable human being; around here, I'm just a piece of meat with eyes."

Feelings of disenfranchisement are further compounded by our growing disconnectedness from each other. Some examples are

- Our dependence on voice mail or e-mail versus actual human contact

- Employees working in locations away from the organization and coworkers

- Increasing instances of telecommuting
- The organization's disregard for an employee's family life or other non-work-related activities

We must also realize that our own behavior (usually unintended) contributes significantly to this growing type of resentment in a number of ways.

1. Aloofness

   When we position ourselves remotely from our people or create an air of aloofness, this contributes to the depersonalization of the workplace. When we are not available to give our people advice or answer questions because we are always too busy doing other, more important things, this sends a clear message that the employees are not valued. Many of us proclaim an "open door policy." The problem is the door is open—but nobody's home—or people learn there is a price to be paid for darkening the door of their boss or exercising their open door rights!

   Some of us show up in the workplace or assert our presence only when there is a problem. This is a deadly situation for any manager to create. The result is our presence consistently raises anxiety and halts productivity! When employees realize the manager is present, they know it can mean only one thing—there must be trouble! Productivity stops as everyone begins to play C.Y.A. (cover your anatomy), trying to figure out what the problem is and how to distance themselves from blame and responsibility.

2. Public Embarrassment

   In some organizations, employees take significant risk of public embarrassment merely by approaching their manager. They may be subjected to a tirade or questioning of their rights and motives for demanding the valuable time of their boss. Interruptions are punished.

3. Superior Attitude

   Other managers position themselves as socially above their employees (the little people!). They refuse to interact and will not participate in outside activities where employees may be present (company picnics, nights out at the ball park, group volunteer efforts, etc.).

   > ♦ **The greater the distance between us and our employees, the greater the intensity of resentment generated toward us (and the greater the prevalence of bad attitudes).**

4. Disrespect and Disregard

A particularly egregious contributor to feelings of loss and disenfran-chisement is when we demonstrate blatant and callous disregard for past employees, regardless of the conditions of separation (layoff, downsizing, voluntary separation, or termination). When employees who are no longer with the organization are treated with disdain, scapegoated, or terminated in a cold and callous manner, there is resentment among the employees who remain.

> A bank merger took place in the southeast. The larger financial institution, acquiring a significantly smaller group, realized there was significant duplication of effort and service in many of the employees they were absorbing in the merger. Immediately after the change became official, they decided to eliminate the duplications, and a significant down-sizing was announced. Approximately 17% of the smaller organization's employees were given thirty days' notice and an extended two weeks' severance pay until their services were no longer needed. The announcement was abrupt, unan-ticipated by both organizations, and there was no regard for the downsized employees or their families' well being, other than the organization meeting their legal requirements (C.O.B.R.A., for example). There was no outplacement assis-tance offered, no retraining or counseling available to help the severed employees through an obviously difficult time. All of the remaining employees observed the blatant disregard the organization demonstrated for the people involved and realized they could expect the same treatment if and when it became their turn to be downsized.

Blatant managerial disregard for employees nourishes resentment in those who remain. It encourages the survivors to look for other employ-ment to escape the carnivorous culture. (Some organizations resemble species that eat their young.)

Strategies for Avoiding Resentment

What can be done to counter these conditions? There are four critical con-siderations for avoiding resentment:

- Listen
- Eliminate one-dimensional communication and problem solving

- Avoid using punishment to teach
- Don't use the disciplinary process for minor circumstances

Listen   When we demonstrate unwillingness to listen to employees' ideas, recommendations, or concerns, resentment and bad attitudes flourish. There is a lockstep relationship between the listening activities of authority figures and overall morale and bad attitudes within an organization.

Listening is one of the most valuable skills a manager can possess. Unfortunately, listening may be the least practiced management skill in today's workplace.

> ◆ **Many managers do not listen; they just wait impatiently to talk!**

How do we demonstrate unwillingness to listen? When we present ourselves (managers) as being the only people with brains around here or the only ones with the power, influence, and control to get things done, we imply that listening to anyone other than us is merely a waste of time. We are obviously going to do what we think is right anyway! The old mottos in the American workplace were

"Do it because I told you to, and I'm the boss."

"If I want you to have an opinion, I will tell you what that opinion is."

That mindset has been shattered. American workers today are demanding to be listened to. And when they are not listened to, resentment escalates dramatically.

The role of listening is often misunderstood. Many employees voice the criticism: "They ask my opinion, I tell them, and then they do not do it. Why should I bother telling them things when they are not going to do anything about it anyway?" This implies an expectation of obedience. It is important to confront a painful but true reality:

> ◆ **Obedience is not a part of listening.**

When ideas and opinions are shared, it is *not* a realistic expectation to assume they will be automatically carried out just because they were voiced. Let's face it, the ideas may not be valid, realistic, or appropriate. It has been estimated that two out of three employee suggestions cannot be realistically implemented. The reasons vary. The ideas may be too expensive, may not truly solve the problem, may not be possible to implement, or may assume simplistic cures to complex issues. So the expectation that every idea will be listened to and implemented is not realistic. In the real workplace world, expecting to be obeyed is a foolish expectation!

The key issue is that while obedience is not necessary, *feedback* is. The missing component in the listening process for many managers and organizations is the lack of feedback. We do not have to jump through hoops and do everything our employees suggest. However, management is required to provide feedback in a very timely and specific manner. If you do not provide feedback and treat with respect the two ideas you cannot use, you never hear the third idea that just may be the one you have been looking for, and the lack of feedback increases resentment.

> Mike had an idea he thought would cut the order processing time for his department by 10%. He was excited because he felt this would reduce costs and increase the quality of service to customers. He approached his team leader, Randy, and in a twenty-minute discussion, explained his idea and his excitement about the cost and quality implications. Randy listened patiently and said, "Mike, that's a great idea, and it really gives me something to think about it. Let me process it, and I will get back to you." Mike waited and waited and waited and never heard a word from his team leader. The lack of any acknowledgment or follow-up angered Mike, and his resentment rose. He felt that Randy really didn't take him seriously and that he wasn't listened to; he was just handled by the team leader. He became indignant when he considered the company was always harping about saving money and increasing quality, yet when he has a great idea to actually accomplish those things, nobody cares. Mike's resentment toward Randy continued to grow, he began to take less pride in the quality of his work, and he vowed to keep his mouth shut and never share another idea, no matter how useful he thought it would be.

Consider the possible different outcome if Randy had come to Mike within an appropriate period of time (48–72 hours would be the norm), had given him some feedback on his idea, and provided a reason for not being able to implement it. While Mike would not necessarily be happy or agree with the rejection of his idea, he does know it was taken seriously and that he was listened to. His intellect was obviously valued, and his ideas were not just dismissed out of hand. Just as Randy's obedience is not necessary, neither is Mike's agreement. The important thing is that all parties in this communication process were treated with respect and had both the opportunity for input and the value of an explanation. All people want to be honored for their intellect, and listening provides the best avenue for bestowing such honor. Failure to provide appropriate feedback leaves employees feeling ignored and stupid for believing they would be listened to in the first place.

> ▶ **Being listened to raises people's value.**

Eliminate one-dimensional communication and problem solving   "Do it because I told you to and I'm the boss" is a resentment escalator of unparalleled proportions. It indicates a climate of assumed obedience versus partnership and collaboration. It denies employees any input into decisions and ignores their right to make an intellectual contribution to the process. In today's workplace employees are no longer willing to take blind orders or just to be told what to do. The "my way or the highway" managerial mentality is obsolete, counterproductive, and actually a tacit admission that "I do not possess the depth of skills necessary to influence your behavior, so I have no option other than ordering you around or trying to intimidate you." It is a management style of weakness, not strength. The result is a message of disregard and disrespect, and resentment runs high.

As we have changed and matured as a people, our need to have an overall understanding of what is going on around us has also increased. We want to know *why* we are being asked to do the things we are being asked to do. We are much more productive when we have an understanding of the tasks at hand.

> ▶ **People are motivated by doing what makes sense to them.**

Productivity is significantly enhanced when someone explains the what, the why, the when, and the projected result. Whether they agree with the assignment is not relevant. (None of us has to agree with everything we are being asked to do.) However, we must understand our challenges or resentment runs very high and quality suffers.

> ▶ **Agreement is not necessary—understanding is.**

Providing opportunities for employees to ask questions concerning their assignments, challenges, projects, and so on creates a valuable two-way communication. Questioning does not mean challenging their assignments; it is inquiring specifically to understand, clarify, and discover the key elements of what they are being asked to do. An atmosphere of safe two-way communication encourages people to seek the necessary relevant information to help them understand and achieve success.

It is very simple to understand why resentment runs so high in environments where communication and explanation are lacking. In the real world,

> ▶ **In the absence of explanation, people will work it out for themselves negatively.**

And we suffer the consequences of the inevitable resulting bad attitudes.

The need to provide proper explanations is often misunderstood and resisted by management. The following statements from managers are commonplace:

- "Why don't people just do what they are told?"
- "I don't have time to explain everything I want people to do."
- "They shouldn't have to be told everything; they should just do it."
- "Why should I have to explain every little thing I want them to do?"

In truth, you do *not* have time to explain everything you are asking people to do. It should *not* be unrealistic to expect people to just do what they are requested to do. It adds to the already great burden of supervisors, managers, and leaders to have to initiate frequent and ongoing explanations. However, in order to achieve successful results, *explanation is not optional*—it is necessary. We have all heard the adage (ad nauseam), "There's never enough time to do it right, but we always find the time to do it over." If we take the time to offer appropriate explanations in the beginning, we will lower costs, reduce bad attitudes, experience higher quality, and lessen overall pressure on time demands.

▶ "Pay me now or pay me later."

Avoid using punishment to teach   While there are exceptions to everything in life, punishment is not a good teacher. It engenders fear and promotes intimidation and resentment, not learning. When we punish past behavior or past results, our goal (or personal agenda), unfortunately, is usually to extract a pound of flesh, coerce an acknowledgment of past "sins," or elicit some level of remorse from the offender. It may be understandably human to pursue these outcomes, but they do not yield positive results or increased productivity. The appropriate response is to acknowledge *what* happened, fix future behaviors, and use mistakes as a learning opportunity.

In reality, we can never change what has already happened. While it may be possible to correct the mistake, we cannot eliminate the fact that it happened. There is no eraser big enough to erase history! Rather than focus on the historical past, focus on the fixable future and address the questions, "What will we do differently next time?" and "How will we avoid allowing this to happen again?" A major component of learning is the alteration of future behavior. Punishing the past drives resentment. Enabling people to react more positively in the future drives success. People rarely learn anything positive from being punished. They usually just learn to cover their tracks to avoid getting caught or to avoid taking initiative and exposing themselves to risk. People almost always respond positively to being taught successful tactics and strategies for future correction.

Don't use the disciplinary process for minor circumstances   The disciplinary process is a very effective tool; however, when used improperly, it exacerbates resentment. Typical misuse occurs when

- Formal warnings (verbal and/or written) are issued for minor one-time infractions

- Formal letters are entered into permanent employee records for minor incidents

- Witnesses are brought in to observe early counseling conversations to increase pressure on an employee

- Suspensions or terminations are threatened for minor infractions

These and similar reactionary uses of the disciplinary process contribute to feelings of resentment. These reactions create a "police state" mentality. The ultimate result is employees losing respect for the disciplinary process since this reactive use of discipline rarely, if ever, results in actual suspensions or terminations. The initial petty infractions do not warrant such a severe outcome and cannot be justified. Employees react extremely negatively to management by threat and intimidation. This results in resentment of the manager and scorn and ridicule of the entire disciplinary process, both from them and others observing the actions.

The integrity of the disciplinary process must be maintained. It should be implemented only when

- An employee's behavior and performance can be positively impacted by exposure to the disciplinary process.

- The infractions are serious enough or are part of a demonstrated on-going pattern that ultimately warrants severing the employee from the organization if they are not changed significantly.

Turnaround Tools

Additional strategies for illegitimate issues of unfairness, realistic change, and issues of loss will be covered throughout the book, specifically in Chapters 7, 8, 10, and 13. These issues of resentment are a common thread woven throughout the fabric of bad attitudes and poor performance.

■   ■   ■

We have identified the six primary root causes of bad attitudes and outlined some of your managerial options to create positive outcomes. It is "Pollyanna-ish" to believe we can always make lemonade out of lemons; however, there are frequently more opportunities for success than we realize. We spent a significant amount of time discussing low self-esteem and resentment as these are two of the most pervasive factors you face with your employees. Unresolved conflict and the inability to accept change are significant and complex enough to warrant specific discussion in their own chapters. Now, let's move on to the six most influential secondary contributors to bad attitudes.

■ Secondary Contributors to Bad Attitudes

There are many other things that can contribute to employees' bad attitudes. Some issues may be prevalent in one organization and nonexistent in others. Some may be unique or specific to one individual. Some you can control; others may offer you no influence whatsoever.

The following secondary contributors may be the most commonly occurring factors, but they are by no means exclusive.

- Stress/burnout
- Physical conditions
- Past experiences

- Lack of recognition
- Lack of feedback
- Lack of understanding of incremental goals, mission, vision

Stress/burnout

The perception of high levels of negative stress or burnout contributes to bad attitudes. Tolerance to stress is not experienced uniformly in the workplace. While some organizations create higher stress levels than others, there is no such thing as a nonstressful job or place to work. What may cause one employee undue stress does not faze another. The reaction to stress tends to be internalized and personalized with each individual person. Employees' perception of experiencing very high levels of negative stress can be a self-serving position. It allows them to blame the boss or the organization and to distance themselves from responsibility. This perception of stress is subjective.

Burnout is a very serious emotional situation. Unfortunately, the term "burnout" has been trivialized in today's workplace. It is not uncommon for someone who is tired to describe the fatigue as burnout. High levels of boredom are often described as burnout. Low levels of interest and commitment can also be misinterpreted as burnout. Being burned out is trendy! In some cases, employees use the excuse of the organization "burning them out" as justification for low levels of performance. Burnout is not a trivial circumstance, and when it occurs, it must be addressed effectively and immediately. It is very serious. Burnout is physical and/or mental exhaustion caused by excessive demands (real or imagined) on emotions, energy, time, and other resources.

Symptoms   The early signs of burnout are generally considered to be

- Significant energy depletion
- Irritability
- Feelings of self-pity
- Significant conflict of being torn between work and home

  The intermediate signs of burnout are

- High levels of frustration
- Depression
- Sleep disturbance
- Inconsistencies in paying attention
- Physical manifestations (headaches, back pain, etc.)

As these symptoms escalate $\longrightarrow$	They may lead to
• Extreme depression	• Substance abuse
• Escapist thoughts	• Mental breakdown
• Advanced sleep disturbance	• Self-destruction
• Lessening self-confidence/ increased insecurity	• Thoughts of suicide

Turnaround tools   While every individual is responsible for maintaining his or her own positive well-being, it is important for managers to monitor the telltale signs of high stress/burnout and to offer training or other appropriate interventions to help employees manage these real life circumstances.

Stress management training, if properly done, can reduce the levels of stress and bad attitudes. Stress management training allows employees to deal with the demands of their job in a positive, healthy manner. It also emphasizes their value to the organization and how their personal well-being is highly regarded. While it is not uncommon for employees to expect to have the stress-inducing factors changed, in most organizations this is not a realistic alternative—teaching people how to successfully deal with the day-to-day workplace stress is. Effective stress management also equips them with very valuable transferable skills to help them in their personal lives and relationships as well.

Physical Conditions

Bad attitudes can result from negative physical conditions. These can range in intensity from severe physical pain, substance abuse, and sleep deprivation (legitimate sleep disorders) to low levels of energy due to weight problems, poor nutrition, or lack of exercise. In these circumstances, your options are few and may be limited to raising employee awareness and providing education. Offering training programs on wellness, nutrition, and health may alleviate some of the problems.

Past Experiences

Employees will often bring the baggage of their negative past experiences with them into the workplace. If they have been treated unfairly (real or imagined), they may carry resentment from past employment experiences and apply it to their current situation. You cannot change or erase people's past experiences. What you can do is help them close the book on those chapters and move ahead. Help them to see their current job as distinct and unrelated to their negative past experiences and to confront the choice of continuing to live in the past or to move ahead to their future. *It's their choice.* For employees to punish you or the organization for unrelated events of the past is an extreme demonstration of unfairness, bordering on absurdity. They are holding you accountable for crimes you never committed and problems you do not have the power to fix. However, for them it is safe, and it gives them something or someone to blame—it comfortably distances them from responsibility.

If the identification with past experiences is significantly disruptive, professional counseling recommendations may be appropriate.

Lack of Understanding of Incremental Goals, Mission, Vision

Earlier we addressed the importance of people understanding why they are being asked to change or accomplish a specific task. This also applies to more global issues as well. When employees do not understand the goals, mission, or vision of the organization, or where their contribution fits into the big picture, this leads to frustration and feelings of being disconnected and left in the dark. Bad attitudes can be a defensive mechanism in response to this lack of knowledge and information. Unfortunately, many employees truly do not have a clear understanding of the goals and objectives of their organization. At best, they understand their individual piece of the puzzle, but they do not fully comprehend how it fits into the entire picture. These are issues of communication, which we will discuss in more depth in subsequent chapters.

Lack of Feedback

We discussed the importance of feedback in communication, but it is also critical for employees to be given appropriate feedback concerning their performance, growth, and development. The absence of this ongoing, meaningful information will lead to bad attitudes. Employees do not function well in a vacuum of information. Feedback is necessary in areas, including

- Individual task achievement
- Overall performance evaluation
- Future growth and development
- Overall organizational performance (not just knowing the goals, but truly being aware of whether the goals are being achieved)

It is painfully true that many employees truthfully do not know where they stand, or how they are viewed by their manager or the organization. Everyone wants to be "in the loop," especially about their own performance and circumstances. Receiving appropriate feedback helps people to feel they are informed and are important enough to be kept current. It is worth the manager or the organization investing the time to make sure employees have the appropriate information to do their job successfully.

Lack of Recognition

Here it comes again! The importance of recognition cannot be overstated or overemphasized.

- When people do not feel appreciated, they develop bad attitudes.
- When people perceive they are being taken for granted, they develop bad attitudes.
- When people perceive they are told only when things are wrong, never when things are right, they develop bad attitudes.
- When people are being asked to constantly improve, and they are not recognized for the level of performance they have already achieved, they develop bad attitudes.

Let's move on to a closer look at management's contributions to bad attitudes and poor performance.

Self-Assessment:
A Look in the Mirror

We have identified the primary causes of and secondary contributors to, employees' bad attitudes. In later chapters, we will discuss techniques to deal successfully with specific bad attitude behaviors and poor performance challenges. In this chapter, we are going to focus on the unilateral issues, the adjustments you can make, and the actions you can implement, totally on your own, to create an environment conducive to the reduction of bad attitudes and the increase of overall performance. This will be a "look in the mirror." We are going to consider

- Your real world managerial limitations—what you can and cannot influence and how to know the difference
- Your management style and how it is a help or hindrance in dealing with attitude and performance issues
- Your culture creation—the positive and negative contribution you and the total organization make to the greater work environment

■ Limitations

A stark reality of today's managerial life is that there are the many factors influencing your employees and their performance, over which you have no control whatsoever.

♦ You can influence only that which you have influence over.

There are legal impediments and ethical constraints. You must acknowledge that there are some factors over which you have no control. These factors were discussed in the previous chapter, and include:

- Habitual low self-esteem
- Health/addictions
- Previous life and work experiences
- The impact of previous decisions
- Lack of preparation

These are just a few examples of circumstances where you lack control or influence. Regardless of the conditions, every employee is required to meet the standards, expectations, and objectives of the organization and the specific job—nothing alters that responsibility.

While it is important to realistically acknowledge the existence of factors over which you have little or no control, it is more productive to target the conditions and variables over which you *can* exert considerable influence. These are your management style and the organizational environment created by you and others in leadership.

■ Management Style

Your style of management has significant influence over the attitudes and performance of your employees. The old authoritarian management style that was successful for many years in our economic history is no longer productive. Continued use of this style (known as command-and-control management) is rapidly becoming obsolete and counterproductive.

> ◗ **Authoritarian and autocratic management is a major contributor to bad attitudes and poor performance.**

Authoritarian Management

Highly authoritarian management is becoming ineffective for a number of reasons.

The maturing of the American worker   As a people, we have matured and are no longer responsive to a management style that devalues us or treats us as less than equal. In highly authoritarian environments, creative and productive people tend to leave in search of better employment circumstances, more appealing to their needs. The people who stay in highly authoritarian environments are those who perceive they have no other options. While there are exceptions to everything in life, these are not the employees who will perform at high levels and make the organization great. Some very productive people do respond well to authoritarian styles; however, their numbers are dwindling dramatically and they are *not* being replenished by the new generations entering the workplace. The people who stay in these environments often have high levels of resentment with bad attitudes and poor performance proliferating.

The focus of motivation has shifted Fear and intimidation are no longer successful motivators. This command-and-control management style makes the flawed and outdated assumption that workers are more highly motivated to avoid loss rather than to achieve gain. In the past workers were inclined to perform well and manage their behavior to keep the boss happy. High performance with strict policy and rule compliance were actually avoidance behaviors (doing good to avoid the bad). The goal was to protect your job, income, benefits, and financial security. Today's workers are motivated by achievement and gain. They perceive authoritarian leadership to be a gatekeeper, or barrier, actually impeding their success. Today's employees are less fearful of what you might do to them and more resentful of what they perceive you haven't done for them. The fear of something being taken away has greatly diminished as the options available to highly creative, productive people have increased. Loss can be recreated. "Take something away from me here, and I can duplicate it somewhere else." We are no longer motivated to avoid loss.

The threat, stated or implied, to dismiss an employee and take away his or her job has an empty ring in today's economic climate because you are not in a position to guarantee that job in the first place. When jobs were secure and employees were confident of long-term employment, threatening to take away jobs and security had a significant impact. In this era of downsizing, rightsizing, and so on, job security has been greatly diminished, and employees are keenly aware that their jobs can no longer be guaranteed longterm.

> ⬩ **You cannot threaten to take away that which you cannot promise or guarantee.**

In her article, "Dissatisfied Workers Hurt Productivity," published in the *Princeton Business Journal,* Lisa Pevtzow quotes a survey by the consulting firm of Kepner-Tregoe. "Only one-third of workers said their supervisors know what motivates them to do their best work. And only 40% reported that they received recognition of a job well done."

Legal protections, awareness of rights, and the litigious nature of our society Workers have much more legal protection today than ever before and are keenly aware of their rights under the law. People know what their boss and the organization can and cannot do, and they are not shy about seeking legal redress when they perceive they have been treated illegally.

Shifts in job satisfaction   Today's job satisfaction is driven by giving employees:

- More influence over their environment
- Input into decision making
- The joy of knowing they are doing something important and providing meaningful outcomes
- Increased connectedness to their job and outcome
- Opportunities to learn new, highly marketable skills

In the previously cited article, Pevtzow states from the survey: "More than 40% of workers reported they do not feel valued by their organizations, and less than half said the people they work with are happy to be employed by their company."

Assessment: Are you an authoritarian manager?   In our book, *No Fear Management: Rebuilding Trust, Performance and Commitment in the New American Workplace*, co-authored by Dr. Robert Craft, we identified fifteen traits of authoritarian fear-based managers. We refer to this management style as "Third Reich Management." I offer the following as a self-assessment tool for you to rate your management style and the organizational environment.

		Rarely	Frequently		Habitually
1. "Telling" workers what to do (issuing orders). Do I/we issue orders to employees with little or no explanation of the issues involved?	**You**	1	2	3 4	5
	The organization	1	2	3 4	5
2. "Demanding" obedience and one-sided loyalty. Do I/we expect employees to do what they are told and to do it because I told them to and I am the boss?	**You**	1	2	3 4	5
	The organization	1	2	3 4	5
3. "Failure to listen." Do I/we deny employees opportunities to influence decisions or express their thoughts, concerns, problems, etc.?	**You**	1	2	3 4	5
	The organization	1	2	3 4	5
4. "Internal competition" is encouraged. Do I/we encourage employees to compete with each other and to achieve success at the expense of others?	**You**	1	2	3 4	5
	The organization	1	2	3 4	5
5. "Suspicion" of employees. Do I/we possess and demonstrate a belief that employees will work productively only when they are monitored closely and that employees in general cannot be trusted? Does this belief influence how employees are treated?	**You**	1	2	3 4	5
	The organization	1	2	3 4	5

	Rarely		Frequently		Habitually

6. "Compartmentalization" of tasks and responsibility. Do I/we assign employees their "turf" and deny them opportunities to exert influence or participate in cross-functional areas?

You	1	2	3	4	5
The organization	1	2	3	4	5

7. "Blaming" employees for mistakes and failure. Do I/we blame employees for problems and distance ourselves from negative responsibility by shifting the blame?

You	1	2	3	4	5
The organization	1	2	3	4	5

8. "Corporate execution" to achieve problem closure. Do I/we find a scapegoat for problems/failures and subject them to the punishment of public embarrassment, sanction, demotion, or dismissal as a means of bringing problems to conclusion?

You	1	2	3	4	5
The organization	1	2	3	4	5

9. "Misalignment" of authority and responsibility. Do I/we hold employees responsible for tasks and outcomes without empowering them with the appropriate authority?

You	1	2	3	4	5
The organization	1	2	3	4	5

10. "Failure to recognize" employees for their contributions. Do I/we fail to extend positive recognition to employees for their achievements and contributions to our overall success?

You	1	2	3	4	5
The organization	1	2	3	4	5

11. "Low tolerance for mistakes" within the organization. Do I/we react negatively to employee mistakes and invoke sanctions or punishments to teach or make the offenders visible examples of what happens to people who commit errors?

You	1	2	3	4	5
The organization	1	2	3	4	5

12. Refusing to share success. Do I/we take credit for the achievements and accomplishments of the people we manage? Do I/we take personal credit for the positive performance of the department?

You	1	2	3	4	5
The organization	1	2	3	4	5

13. Short-term focus: failing to assess the long-term. Do I/we tend to measure performance and success on a daily basis? Are employees only as good as their last performance?

You	1	2	3	4	5
The organization	1	2	3	4	5

14. Recreating ourselves: selecting people in our own image. Do I/we tend to employ and promote people who look like us, act like us, think like us, and talk like us?

You	1	2	3	4	5
The organization	1	2	3	4	5

15. Ethical breaches: highly visible illegal, unethical, or immoral behaviors. Do I/we encourage illegal or unethical behavior by looking the other way or with some form of silent approval, insuring our hands would be clean and involvement untraceable if these acts were discovered?

You	1	2	3	4	5
The organization	1	2	3	4	5

Total   You_____

Total   The organization_____

A score of 3 or above on a particular item indicates a critical area inviting a review of policy style or strategy.

An overall score of 48 or above indicates that an organization or individual manager is utilizing an inappropriate, highly authoritarian style, relying on fear or intimidation as the catalyst for motivation.

Scores in the 43–47 range indicate organizations or individual managers that tend toward a blended style, with heavy a slant toward the authoritarian. The authoritarian style quickly becomes dominant in conditions of stress, pressure, or perceived threat. The knee-jerk reaction to problems is to increase control and fear and to emphasize the consequences of punishment if employees are unresponsive or resistant. An us-against-them mentality probably prevails with organizations or managers scoring in this range.

Scores in the 36–42 range indicate less reliance on authoritarian strategies. Organizations and managers in this range should be experiencing fewer overall bad attitude and poor performing employees. (Individual challenges, yes—overall high incidence, no.) While there may be a tendency to invoke authoritarian, fear-based techniques in more extreme circumstances, this would be the exception.

Scores in the 35 and below range indicate organizations and managers who have successfully moved away from a dominant, authoritarian, fear-based style and have evolved to an appropriate participative environment. They are probably reaping the harvest of bad attitudes and poor performance as only isolated individual occurrences.

> **⚠ Scores below 29 probably indicate an unrealistic assessment, and a second opinion would probably be a great idea. Denial may be an issue to explore!**

Why does this obsolete style continue to be practiced by some managers and organizations today? Because training for American managers has not kept pace with the changes in the workplace. Today, effective management and leadership skills remain largely untaught. In this vacuum of training and development, many managers model the behaviors they believe to have been effective in their past bosses. Thus command-and-control management is perpetuated. The result—yesterday's inappropriate management style is applied to today's revolutionary changing workplace. Why are we surprised when we encounter so many poorly performing bad attitude employees? We frequently use the wrong tool to fix the problem. Hammers are not an all-purpose "wonder implement."

Does authoritarian management ever serve a positive purpose in today's workplace? Yes, it does have limited application, in varying degrees of intensity, with

- Short-term crisis situations. (At the scene of a raging fire, we don't take time for focus groups and surveys!)

- New employees. (A benevolent, authoritarian style is appropriate until the employee is experienced enough to begin to participate.)

- Highly resistant employees. (Use as a *last resort*, when all other turn-around options have been exhausted. Unfortunately, with most managers the authoritarian style is used as the first resort, which serves only to escalate the problem.)

As employees demonstrate intensified bad attitude and poor performance behaviors, our traditional reaction as managers has been to increase authoritarian influence. It isn't working. We are treating the symptoms with the wrong therapy and significantly aggravating the patient's condition. The appropriate "therapy" in today's workplace is to

- Embrace an interactive, participative management style

- Create a culture of high trust, respect, and responsibility

- Hold people responsible for their outcomes

Interactive/Participative Management

An open, interactive, participative style of management creates an environment for defusing existing bad attitudes, preventing their escalation, and increasing overall job satisfaction and performance. This style requires a set of tools I call the manager's interactive tool kit. The tool kit includes

- Listening/feedback

- Partnered decision making

- Communication

- Training

- Recognition

- Closing the past

- Outcome/performance measurement

While these management tools will not eliminate bad attitudes totally, they will reduce them dramatically. The degree to which you can incorporate some or all of these tools into your management style is the same degree in which you will experience an increase in employee satisfaction, longevity, and productivity. Is it possible to adopt a totally interactive style in today's workplace? Probably not. In the real world, a successful style will be a blend of participative and authoritarian style slanted as far away from the authoritarian as realistically possible.

Listening/feedback   The evolutionary growth and maturity of American workers demands they be listened to. They want to be honored and acknowledged for their intellect. They want to make meaningful contributions to their workplace environment and influence the decisions most directly affecting them. Employees are demanding to be a part of the creative process. When they are not listened to, they feel devalued. They perceive they are being taken lightly, dismissed as worker bees or pluggers and chuggers, and not seen as people of value possessing enough intellect to contribute meaningful thought and insight.

> ◆ **Real or imagined, bad attitude employees believe they are not being listened to.**

Authoritarian managers do not listen to people; they tell people what to do. Interactive/participative managers extend to people the dignity of valuing their input. Listening is only a part of the process. Feedback and sincere consideration of employees' contributions are necessary to visibly communicate their value.

Partnered decision making   In an authoritarian environment, decision making is exclusively a management activity. Managers make the decisions and the employees are expected to carry out their directives. In today's workplace, many decisions are actually delegated to workers or teams, while others lend themselves to partnering or shared responsibility. Determining the types of decisions in which to involve employees is always a challenge and frequently misunderstood.

There are three levels of decisions:

- Decisions of management exclusivity
- Employee-driven decisions (individual, departmental, team)
- Partnered decisions (collaborative decisions between management and employees)

Decisions made exclusively by management include what, why, and when. What the organization does, why they do it, and when it must be completed (deadlines) are decisions made exclusively by management. These include establishing missions, goals, standards, objectives, and expectations. Managers are hired to make these decisions and provide appropriate leadership.

Employee-driven decisions usually revolve around the word "how." Once the what, why, and when have been determined, employees should be empowered whenever possible to make decisions of how they are going to make it happen. This invites them into the decision-making process at their level of greatest expertise. They are the ones doing the job on a day-to-day basis. They are in the best position to determine how the goals, objectives, and expectations of the organization can most effectively be achieved. Obviously, decisions of how cannot always be totally influenced by employees, especially in highly regulated environments, but every opportunity should be seized to involve them in these decisions whenever possible.

▶ **There is not a manager in America today who could not do a better job of giving away the "how."**

The X-ray department of a hospital was being relocated to the new wing of the facility. The move had to be completed during a very short, specific period of time, and with as little interruption of service to patients and professional staff as possible. Nancy, the department head, met with her entire department to brainstorm the logistics of the move. She told the staff, "The move will begin at 8:00 p.m. on Thursday, and will be completed by noon on Friday. Service specialists will be here to relocate the X-ray machines, and the rest of the move will be up to us with help with the heavy desks, etc. from the maintenance department." She then turned the discussion to her staff and asked, "How can we make this happen?" The staff brainstormed and recommended a plan that not only accomplished the move in less than the allotted time, but maintained service by keeping two machines operational in the old location until two others had been successfully relocated to the new wing. At no time during the move were they unable to provide X-ray service. The staff was highly motivated to carry out their plan, and there was little resistance to the extra work and hassle. At no time were there comments such as, "I'm an X-ray technician; I wasn't hired to be a mover" or "That's not my job." Nancy acknowledged, "There's no way I could have developed such a successful and efficient plan solely on my own and have the staff embrace it so positively."

Inclusion in the decision-making process reduces feelings of disenfranchisement and lack of control that feed bad attitudes. Organizations are not democracies. Votes are not taken to determine the most popular opinion of the majority. Decisions are not made with the sole intention of making people happy. The vast majority of decisions made in an organization are not employee-driven; however, every opportunity for inclusion should be utilized.

Partnered decisions include decisions where the risk is extremely high; nonpolicy decisions that heavily influence employee morale; and process-oriented problem solving. In circumstances of high risk or high sensitivity to morale, involving employees in the decision-making process considers their creativity and vantage point and gives them exposure to all sides of the issues.

> A service-oriented organization lost a major contract and was suddenly faced with a need to dramatically reduce their operating costs without negatively impacting their remaining customers. Five percent of the staff was laid off, and it was necessary to reduce the compensation package for the remaining employees by 15%. Knowing this circumstance would have a negative impact on employee morale, the CEO held a series of three meetings to inform them of the issue, brainstorm options, and allow them to participate in the decision-making process. After due consideration, the employees decided overwhelmingly to take a reduction in pay and forgo contributions in the pension plan rather than take a reduction in health benefits (management erroneously assumed a different solution would be chosen).

Communication   Communication must be

- Equal
- Inclusive
- Explanation-focused

- Goal-, expectation-, and objective-driven
- Visionary
- Realistic

Everyone in the department or team should be exposed to the same information at the same time. You must invest the time to communicate the what, why, and when to everyone, not just to the favored few. When time is taken to explain effectively why a change is being made, a project begun, or a task assigned, performance increases and bad attitudes decline.

Communicating the vision (where the organization is going) is a critical component of interactive, participative management. As employees are asked to implement changes, undergo constant adjustment, and do more with less, they must be aware of the ultimate vision or reasoning behind the demands placed upon them. If the destination is unclear, the sacrifice of the journey is not worth making. Bad attitude employees frequently fail to comprehend or accept the vision.

Training   Training is the most significant tool available to raise people's value. Training prepares people to perform successfully and meet their individual challenges. It helps them to gain the skills to overcome weaknesses or perceived inadequacies and helps to increase their self-confidence. Unfortunately, training is also one of the significant casualties of downsizing and budget cuts. Interestingly, as we are asking people to do more with less and to assume additional new duties, we simultaneously reduce our training efforts, which would help them achieve success in their new roles.

In most organizations today, training is narrowly perceived to be specific technical development. We train people technically on how to operate the new equipment, how to fill out the proper forms, how to use the new computer program, etc. Technical training is extremely important to success, and most organizations today do a good job of developing technical skills. Our organizations, schools, colleges, and universities all provide good technical training, and we are a technically proficient society.

Our challenge lies in addressing the fact that there are many other critical skills necessary to successfully compete in today's workplace, and these go largely untaught.

> ◗ **Training must be targeted to develop the critical skills of success.**

Organizational skills

- Knowing how to set up a filing system
- Knowing how to manage a desk
- Knowing how to manage paperwork flow
- Knowing how to organize work in an efficient sequence
- Knowing how to plan the day properly
- Knowing how to organize tools or supplies

While all employees are expected to possess these abilities, most are not being properly trained. It has been estimated that only 8 to 12% of employees are actually being taught the important skills of organization. How would you rate your or your organization's efforts in this area? By teaching employees the skills necessary to control their workload successfully, and be less "victimized" by it, you increase their confidence and productivity. Organizational skills are great contributors to reduced stress.

People skills or the skills of interaction

- Communication
- Conflict resolution
- Getting along with others
- Team participation
- Goal setting
- Problem solving
- Being "gotten along with"
- Developing and implementing action plans

People skills (including leadership) are among the least-trained skills in America today! Poorly performing, low self-esteem employees frequently lack appropriate interrelational skills. This reinforces low self-confidence, poor self-image, and frustration. People skills *can* be effectively taught; however, highly authoritarian managers reject such training, perceiving it to be "touchy-feely garbage." In fact, the proper training and development of people skills are what makes an employee or an entire organization great.

> ♦ **Technical skills make us good. The relational people skills we combine with our technical skills make us great!**

We are teaching goodness, not greatness, in the American workplace today.

Training opportunities are not limited to workplace-only skills. Many organizations are providing optional training programs on transferable skills such as:

- Financial planning
- Overcoming negativity
- Step-parenting classes
- Home buying seminars
- Credit counseling

- Budgeting
- Gardening skills
- Auto maintenance and repair
- Self-defense
- Consumer law

These skill development opportunities may be offered to the employees and their families, providing real life skills to assist in meeting their everyday personal challenges.

Recognition   Interactive/participative managers give appropriate recognition for employees' efforts, outcomes, and achievements. The look in the eye and the pat on the back that most employees crave but few receive recognize people for their contributions. Its absence contributes to bad attitudes! Bad attitude employees perceive (perhaps rightly so) that their achievements are never recognized; only their faults are consistently criticized. "Nobody pays any attention when I do something right, but, boy, do they pile it on when I make a mistake."

Closing the past   In an interactive/participative environment, closure is achieved by acknowledging the past and moving to the present and the future. The past can never be changed. We can only prepare ourselves to do things differently in the future.

 A new management team was brought in to lead a facility of a large manufacturing organization. The previous management team, which had been in place for approximately eight years, systematically practiced an abusive management style, heavily dominated by authoritarian behaviors (telling workers what to do, demanding obedience without question, motivating by fear and intimidation).

As the new management team began to introduce a style of interactive/participative management in an attempt to change the environment, they experienced tremendous resistance from the workforce. The residual anger and resentment from the previous management group erected a barrier that the new management team was unable to penetrate. Every new initiative was greeted with an attitude of "Why should we accept or believe this? Management can never be trusted. Look at all the bad things they have done to us in the past."

To help overcome this barrier of anger, resentment, and resistance, a series of venting sessions was held. All employees, in groups of approximately fifteen people, were invited to meet with members of the new management team in open, frank, no-holds-barred discussions. The goal was to air all of the grievances of the past. While much of the venting was done verbally, every employee was asked to list all grievances in writing with as much fact and detail as possible. Legal pads were distributed, and all comments were guaranteed anonymity.

When the venting sessions were completed, a funeral was held to literally bury the issues of the past. A pine box built by a group of employees was placed on a table in the lunchroom. All of the employees approached the table, placed their legal pad inside, paid their respects, and moved on. It was anticipated this would take approximately twenty minutes; however, it actually took over two hours as the exercise took on a hilarious, comical atmosphere. ("Saturday Night Live," on its best night, couldn't hold a candle to the comedy generated during these two hours.) Some employees dressed in black to grieve; others read irreverent eulogies or scripture parodies they created. Sidesplitting, tear-generating, can't-get-your-breath humor poured forth for two solid hours.

At the conclusion of the wake service, the box was carried in procession outside to an area behind the building. A hole had been dug, the box was put inside, and employees took turns shoveling the dirt back in to fill the hole. In a surprise ending, a wooden monument built by the engineering department was carried out and set on top of the freshly dug dirt. The inscription read, "Here lies the past." The new facility manager made some humorous closing remarks, emphasizing that the past, while it was very real, was now *over*. Anyone wishing to cling to the issues of the past now knew where to come to pay their respects. And with that, the entire group of employees turned and walked back into the building. The message of a past closure and a new beginning was very clear.

At last look, the monument was still standing. The organization had begun to move forward, implementing the changes necessary to achieve success and to meet their current challenges. As with any organization, problems and crises continue, but they are current and not toxified by the past.

Outcome/performance measurement　In an interactive/participative management environment, outcomes and performance speak for themselves. While everyone is treated with dignity and respect, people who meet the standards, expectations, and objectives of the organization are recognized and rewarded accordingly; those who do *not* are held *accountable* for their lack of productivity.

Open, accurate, objective measurement of performance is commonplace and necessary. Some employees are uncomfortable with this objective measurement, not wishing to be watched too closely. Many have seen measurement systems used against people in authoritarian environments. Bad attitude employees abhor and avoid measurement more than most.

♦ Objective measurement brings accountability and responsibility.

Performance issues will be covered in detail in Chapter 11.

■ Corporate Culture

Let's address the style of the entire organization. Just as individual managers develop a style that sets the tone for the environments they influence, entire organizations have distinct styles that create the overall culture. This culture is strongly influenced from the top, permeates all levels of the organization, and reflects the attitudes and behaviors of the leaders themselves and the actions and behaviors they encourage or tolerate in others.

Bad Attitude Creators and Culture Destroyers

What are the predictable management and organizational behaviors that create the breeding ponds for the mosquitoes of bad attitudes to grow and flourish? Following are nine of the most significant contributing organizational behaviors. If we are being honest, we will all see ourselves and our organization to some degree in at least a few of these. Where do you see yourself or your organization accurately described?

Ethical, moral, or legal violations   When organizations systematically and openly engage in unethical behavior, it contributes to the deterioration of the entire organizational culture. This behavior may range from offering bribes to customers or regulatory officials, and encouraging illegal harassment or abuse of employees, to falsifying records, stealing retirement funds, and encouraging the padding of expense accounts. The obvious flaunting of laws, rules, or procedures creates an environment of high disregard for conventional norms or order, and bad attitudes are bound to proliferate.

Practicing vague dishonesty   By design, many organizations intentionally communicate in vague terms that can be denied, reinterpreted, or disputed later if it is expedient to do so. Promising a customer that you will "do whatever it takes to make them happy" and then refusing to honor commitments lowers trust and destroys goodwill throughout the entire workplace. Telling employees that "things will be worked out at a later date" or promising "to take care of them when the time comes" and then doing nothing or conveniently forgetting the commitment or denying the comments, eats away at loyalty and feeds distrust and skepticism. Systematically creating wiggle room through vague, blurred communication may be considered an effective technique by some, but it encourages bad attitudes to multiply.

Consistently valuing dollars over people or quality   There must be a balance in any organization between

- Financial concerns
- Employee issues
- Customer/quality commitments

At any given moment, this balance may be unevenly slanted toward any of these issues to the detriment of others. However, long term, the balance must be seen as an equal consideration of all three. Bad attitudes proliferate when employee issues are consistently ignored in favor of the others.

Refusing to invest in adequate safety equipment and continuously exposing employees to unsafe conditions sends a clear message of callous disregard. Reacting to problems only when they begin to cost the organization money, emphasizes what the company considers truly important.

> The owner of a service organization hired an executive vice president who was talented and highly regarded industrywide with great experience and excellent credentials. The vice president was

very productive and contributed almost immediately to increased revenue, enhancing the value of the corporation. He also demonstrated a disturbing pattern of verbally abusing people and a willingness to openly intimidate others to get his way. His behavior bordered on sexual harassment with some female staff members. When employees complained to the owner about this behavior, he listened sympathetically but did nothing. At best, he would issue a mild verbal reprimand to the offending vice president. The complaining employees then absorbed the wrath of the vice president and learned not to risk exposing themselves in the future. With each episode, the behavior worsened. As long as the profits were flowing from the vice president's efforts, the owner was willing to continue to expose the employees to the abusive, perhaps illegal behavior. He offered only lip service, at best, to the affected employees.

However, when the vice president was found to be consistently lying on his expense account and cheating the organization out of hundreds of dollars each month, the owner responded decisively by firing the vice president. The clear message was, "I am willing to tolerate abuse and harassment of our employees, but when it comes to my bottom line, I won't tolerate any abuse whatsoever." One employee stated, "When it begins to cost him money, he takes action; when it's just our dignity and well-being on the line, he could care less." Enter bad attitudes and employee defections.

Favoritism/unfairness   Whether real or imagined, when individuals or groups of employees are perceived to be receiving special treatment, bad attitudes explode and organizational culture deteriorates. How are these perceptions nourished in your organization?

- Is the workload assigned equally?
- Are the rules waived for the boss's buddies?
- Do the favored few take long lunches with the boss?
- Is everyone held to the same performance standards?
- Do some sit around drinking coffee while others do their work?
- Is compensation equal? (Are some paid more money for less work?)
- Are policies such as absenteeism/tardiness applied equally to everyone?

Many managers do not realize the negative impact of even the *illusion* of favoritism. Also, managers lose control over the actions of the favored few in their absence. They don't know what the privileged ones are doing or saying to exploit their special status when they are not around. When privilege, perks, or promotions are based on the likes or dislikes of the boss, bad attitudes abound. Organizational support or toleration of any unfairness escalates employee resentment.

Breaches of confidence   Inappropriate sharing of confidential information of any nature negatively affects organizational culture. While people may relish hearing information on subjects they may normally not be privy to, the information is a double-edged sword. It proves to them that any confidential information they share may well be open to others.

How many conversations in your organization begin with, "Don't tell anyone I told you this . . ."? Employees are not stupid; they know their turn for tabloid exposure will come. Divulging privileged information does not build bridges or curry favor; it creates canyons of wariness and separation.

Inappropriate compensation   People (including you) are never paid what they believe themselves to be worth. While this is human nature, serious consideration must be given to the issues of employee compensation.

- Is the compensation package you are offering consistent with industry standards?

- Is it in the range an employee could duplicate somewhere else if he or she went to another organization?

- Do you allow internal inequities to exist (lower pay for equal work— same pay for less performance or quality)?

If we are dramatically underpaying by being significantly below industry standards, why are we surprised when feelings of resentment run high? Stability is disrupted by the turnover of people leaving to make more money elsewhere. The short-term cost savings of underpaying people usually results in significantly higher long-term costs of the continuous recruiting, rehiring, training cycle repeated over and over again.

Compensation, while always an issue, generally boils over only when groups or individuals perceive unfairness. While pay rates and compensation packages may be rigid and inflexible, any toleration, encouragement, or active prolongation of inequitable compensation programs by the organization invites the deepening of resentment and resulting destructive attitudes and behaviors.

Rewarding negative behavior   When we provide payoffs for poor performance or disruptive behaviors, we obviously are encouraging their continuation. These payoffs are usually unintentional and the significance of their impact is rarely considered when we allow them to happen.

> Keith is a consistent whiner and complainer. He is constantly vocalizing his perceptions of being overworked and over-stressed, and when he is asked to do anything new or in addition to his job description, he goes into his standard tirade. "Poor me, I'll have to work overtime or take work home with me. Nobody cares. It isn't fair." After his tirade, he usually elects to take some downtime to recompose himself, which further depletes his productivity. Keith's perception of his workload and negative circumstance is not shared by his boss, Tanya, or his coworkers. However, they have listened to Keith and dealt with his reactions for so long, they just accept putting up with him as a condition of employment. Consequently, when Tanya is faced with a crisis or a task to delegate, she doesn't turn to Keith. To avoid Keith's predictable reaction, she will do the task her-self or assign it to others in the department. Unknowingly, she is rein-forcing Keith's behavior and allowing him to control a portion of her activities and decisions. Because of his actions, Keith is actually asked to do less work than his coworkers. Also, if Keith submits com-pleted work that is mediocre or unacceptable, Tanya rarely asks him to correct it. She will make the corrections herself or assign it to another employee to meet the standards of acceptability. Again, Keith's negative behavior has paid off. He is not held to the same standards because no one, including his boss, wants to invoke his mantra of self-pity. His behavior will continue until he perceives it to be ineffective, but at this point, he thinks it's working fine.

Passive punishment   Bad attitudes flourish when employees are pun-ished passively for their actions. Overt action is not taken, but covert things are done in organizational retaliation. This is management's version of passive-aggressive paybacks. If an employee who reports a safety viola-tion is then assigned a distasteful job or a task everyone else is avoiding, this sends a very subtle message.

> John's company instituted an "Employee Suggestion Program." He put serious thought into some ideas and submitted sugges-tions in three specific areas in which he felt the company needed to improve. Nothing was ever done with his ideas, and the suggestion program died the usual slow death of "flavor of the month" type ini-

tiatives. John found out much later that the employees who participated in the program (especially him) were viewed by upper-level management as disgruntled troublemakers who needed to be watched closely. What do you think happened to John's attitude? It also explained why he was excluded from three successive, highly visible projects with substantial bonus opportunities.

These passive punishments can rarely be proven, and while linkage is blurred, employees clearly understand the message. "Keep your mouth shut and do it my way if you want to stay out of trouble."

♦ Passive punishments escalate employees' passive-aggressive behavior.

Initial negative response   A consistent, knee-jerk negative response to bad news or negative circumstances is a common occurrence and creates an unhealthy organizational culture. Many organizations are well known for shooting the messenger. Some managers have such a high negative emotional response to problems or bad news, their employees learn to avoid their manager in times of trouble or crisis. This is a deadly organizational circumstance because information that frequently could serve to eliminate a problem or stop a small crisis from escalation isn't shared up the ladder, as lower-level employees refuse to expose themselves to the inevitable wrath. The price the organization pays for allowing this negative culture is incalculable. This style of initial negative response demonstrates the manager's and organization's lack of regard for anyone but upper-level management. As long as their emotional needs of the moment are met, they don't care about the damage they do to anyone else. This is one of the most flagrant demonstrations of selfishness in the workplace today. Teaching managers to suppress their initial negative response and reducing or eliminating the "shoot the messenger" mentality establish a healthy, nonthreatening environment.

These nine organizational traits, while not intended to be totally inclusive, are examples of overall organizational behaviors that create fertile breeding grounds for bad attitudes to flourish. How would you rate your organization's culture?

5 The Role of Conflict in Influencing Bad Attitudes

U nresolved conflict was identified as one of the six primary root causes of bad attitudes. Conflict is inevitable. Most of us are not skilled at
resolving conflict, and this inability, coupled with the unwillingness of bad
attitude employees to resolve conflict, puts them at an even greater disadvantage. They are repeatedly mishandling incidents that are a predictable
part of organizational life and are allowing them to escalate unnecessarily
into conflict situations. Their inflexibility, or avoidance behavior, has
short-term payoff (distancing them from responsibility and providing
someone to blame). However, there is a complex, long-term downside.
Conflicts become prolonged, and, of course, bad attitude employees
believe it is the other person's responsibility to resolve the conflict, not
theirs. The ongoing costs of their behavior can be overwhelming.

In this chapter we are going to address the following:

- Why employees with bad attitudes typically react negatively to conflict

- How and why conflict escalates

- The three typical negative behavioral responses to conflict

- The significant impediments to resolving conflict

- The critical foundations of successful conflict resolution

■ Conflict and Bad Attitude Employees

Bad attitude employees tend to have higher incidents and intensities of
conflict than others. They often experience higher levels of ongoing, escalating, and unresolved conflict. Some actually perceive perpetual unresolved conflict to be an effective strategy to avoid facing and resolving
problems. Perpetuating conflict can become a way of life.

Whether by choice or inability, bad attitude employees struggle with issues of conflict for many reasons.

Bad Attitude Employees Lack Conflict Resolution Skills

Conflict resolution skills, while highly relevant to success in today's workplace, are part of the people/relational skills that are poorly taught. People are expected to possess these important skills, but they are not being trained to develop them. Expectations and accountability are high; preparation is very low.

Bad Attitude Employees Are Mistrustful

Bad attitude employees generally have little or no trust of management or peers. Many see conspiracies where none exist. Conflict situations affirm these perceptions of low trust.

Trust is a complex issue. It is very subjective and can be selectively extended or rescinded at will. Because trust is an intangible, bad attitude employees are never held accountable for their unwillingness to extend trust, and they use the granting or withholding of trust effectively as a manipulative tool. When it suits their purpose, they choose not to trust. They can mistrust someone merely because they *want* to. Mistrust is at the core of bad attitude employees' perceptions and beliefs. It is an issue over which they have total control, and they use it effectively to avoid commitment and accountability. Whether the lack of trust is rational and fact-based is of little consequence. Bad attitude employees' negative goals are served by the manipulation of trust.

Bad Attitude Employees Tend to Personalize Conflict

Conflicts are seen as personal issues. Bad attitude employees do not focus on what the conflict is about but choose instead to concentrate on who they are in conflict with. It becomes a personal battle.

> ▶ Charley wanted to use one of the company's trucks to move some furniture on Saturday. He went in to see his boss to ask permission. The boss told Charley that their insurance coverage prohibited using the trucks for any nontraditional business usage. It also barred anyone who had not received a minimum of twenty hours of safe driver training in that particular type of vehicle from using the trucks. Charley became incensed. He knew that other employees had used company equipment in the past, and he challenged his boss, saying, "That's not fair. I remember I helped John move a couple of years ago, and he was using the company truck all weekend. I just

want to use it for a couple of hours." The boss responded, "This may well have been true in the past, but the policy dictated by our insurance coverage had been in place for about eighteen months." Charley replied, "That's nonsense. You just don't want me to use the truck." He thought to himself, "Just because I'm not one of your favorites, and not a brownnoser around here, you're not letting me use the truck. You just don't like me. I'll bet if somebody else walked in here right now and asked permission, you'd give it to him." As Charley's anger grew, he turned and stormed out.

To bad attitude employees like Charley, conflict is seen as a win-lose challenge. There will be a victor and a vanquished. They tend to see their personal value or self-image challenged in conflict situations, and winning or losing takes on additional important dimensions. When they perceive they have not won the conflict, they vow to get even and expend considerable thought and energy trying to redeem their honor. Their conflicts are not about things or issues; their conflicts are about them and you. Charley immediately personalized this conflict with his boss.

Bad Attitude Employees Are Not Solution-oriented

They are very good at telling you what is wrong; however, they are not oriented to proposing *realistic* solutions. Their solutions are unrealistic overreactions based on giving them everything they want and usually entail fixing you or the other individuals involved. (It is never the bad attitude employee who needs to be fixed; it is everyone else!)

For bad attitude employees, problem identification is easy. It is a very low-risk behavior. They have all of the rights of free speech and personal observation with none of the obligations of intellectual process or responsibility. They want to tell you about all the problems, and they want *you* to be responsible for fixing them. That's why they constantly harp or replay problems over and over. Theirs is not to fix—theirs is merely to identify.

Bad Attitude Employees Bring Historical Perspective to Conflict

For bad attitude employees, conflicts are not seen as separate, individual occurrences. They are an ongoing continuum. "One more straw to break the camel's back." These employees resist closure of past events or compartmentalization of current incidents. In their perception, everything is connected. An event causing conflict today is somehow linked to something else that happened last year (or somewhere in the deep, dark past).

▶ With bad attitude employees, conflict is never current events, it's always a history lesson.

Closure is a personal choice. Choosing not to get over past events is a way of perpetuating self-righteousness and offers a self-perceived, legitimate basis to blame or not trust someone. Choosing not to achieve closure keeps conflict and negative emotion alive. Closure equals accountability, and bad attitude employees are very good at avoiding the "A" word.

Bad Attitude Employees' Conflict is Emotion-based, Not Content-based

Immediate and emotional responses of anger, resentment, hostility, and pain are frequently the bad attitude employee's knee-jerk reaction to conflict situations. Objectivity is long gone. When emotion is high, conflict becomes irrational. Charley's reaction was hair-trigger and degenerated immediately to pure personalized emotion. Successfully introducing facts and data can quell or lessen emotions; however, such objective reasoning and appeals are ineffective with someone whose perception is subjective. Charley refused to accept his boss's rational statement of the facts surrounding the truck-use policy change, and his rejection further fueled his negative emotions. Emotion-based conflict can at best be neutralized; it is never resolved.

Emotions escalate (perhaps yours as well as theirs) and result in

- An "ugly incident" (perhaps including violence).

- Abandonment (throwing up your hands in surrender and walking away in frustration, while blaming the other).

- A focus on neutralizing or reducing the emotion, which is usually accomplished at the expense of resolving the real issues. Bad attitude employees hope you will give in and let them have their way just to calm them down. If they are successful, they usually increase their anger with each conflict. (See section on rewarding negative behaviors in Chapter 4.)

All three of the above are unproductive, and *none* results in the successful resolution of the conflict (although neutralization of emotion is a necessary first step, it is not an end result). All insure the conflict will resurface again with even greater emotional intensity, and when it does, it feeds their perception of the interconnectedness of past conflicts (the history lesson).

▶ The serious mistake we make is believing the reduction of emotion is somehow a resolution of the conflict.

Mary, the customer service representative, was angry when her recommendations were ignored by Jeff, her regional manager. "Jeff, I just found out you totally disregarded my recommendations for handling the Kerr account. I can't believe this. You never listen to me. You always override every decision I make. I don't know why I even bother trying to do my job. If I were a guy, you would pay attention. You just don't think women are capable of making decisions." Jeff decided he'd had enough of Mary's bad attitude and declared, "Mary, you are just a spoiled brat who is all bent out of shape because she didn't get her way. You're acting stupid, and if a guy acted the same way, I'd overrule him, too." Mary said, "I'm sick and tired of being treated this way and maybe I should just quit." Jeff said, "Fine," and they parted on that note.

After calming down a short time later, Jeff called Mary to his office and said, "I feel badly about the shouting match we had this morning. I said some things I shouldn't have. I apologize for the way I talked and for being disrespectful." Mary replied, "I've been thinking about it, too, and I know I reacted badly. I should not have said the things I did, and I really don't want to quit my job over this." They both agreed they had acted childishly and decided to show their willingness to bury the hatchet by going to lunch together. They chatted at lunch about family, friends, vacations, etc., and it was obvious that neither bore any hard feelings toward the other. The result was the negative emotions were gone, but the real core issues of the conflict were not addressed.

Why didn't Jeff accept her recommendation?

Why does Mary feel that all of her recommendations must be accepted with no room for alternative decisions?

Why does Jeff think Mary acts like a spoiled brat?

Why does Mary think Jeff has a gender bias?

What can be done to eliminate these circumstances in the future?

When the negative emotion of conflict is successfully calmed, a sense of accomplishment prevails, and victory is celebrated. In reality, *nothing* is actually resolved. Accept a temporary cease-fire, and the hostilities are bound to recommence. It is just a matter of time until this same conflict again rears its ugly head. A boomerang has just been lofted in the air, and it will be back.

▶ **Do not confuse emotional neutralization with conflict resolution.**

Bad Attitude Employees May Perceive They Have a Stake in Prolonging the Conflict

As conflict is prolonged, all parties involved continue in the comfort of being right. Successful resolution generally means a rethinking of hardened positions with a willingness to soften positions or to meet in the middle. Continuing the conflict avoids the necessity of such introspection and does not threaten the righteousness of their position. Resentment continues to be fed (as discussed extensively in Chapter 3). Accountability and responsibility are avoided by keeping the conflict alive while the other parties can conveniently be blamed for the lack of resolution.

■ The Bad Attitude Emotional Conflict Cascade

The following deterioration, or cascading, of emotions typically occurs in conflict situations with bad attitude employees. One step leads to the next, and reactions escalate to negative behaviors.

1. Event (real or imagined)
2. Blaming
3. Generalized and pervasive feelings
4. Perceived threat escalation
5. Selective victimization
6. Behavioral responses

Event

In general, workplace conflict starts with one or more circumstances, including:

- An action taken is perceived to be detrimental or irritating to someone else.

- Expectations are not met (yours or others'—somebody doesn't get what he or she wants).

- Management implements a policy or plan believed by some to be contrary to their best interests (or to the greater interest of the organization, customers, etc.).

- Management confronts someone about unacceptable actions or poor performance.

▶ **Conflict is the difference between what you expect to happen and what really happens.**

Let's take another look at Charley and the truck episode. Charley was denied use of a vehicle, which means he isn't getting what he wants and his expectations aren't being met. It's also possible he has made commitments to others that he will now have difficulty keeping. He will face his own embarrassment as well as their negative reaction. His initial response is not to solve the dilemma, but to blame someone (his boss) for the situation.

Blaming

Typically, bad attitude employees quickly identify someone to blame for the conflict. They focus on "who" as the root cause.

- Who did it to them?
- Who doesn't like what they're doing?
- Who is not giving them what they want?
- Who confronted them about their behavior?

This knee-jerk tendency to identify "who" (which Charley did very well) immediately personalizes the conflict. Quickly the guilt of others and the innocence of themselves become crystal clear. Bad attitude employees readily absolve themselves of all responsibility (spraying themselves with instant Teflon and proclaiming the problem and solution to be the sole responsibility of others).

Coupled with blaming comes personal distortions of information. These distortions include the following:

- Selective listening (Charley's disregard for the policy change and the insurance company's restrictions).
- Self-serving interpretations ("John used the truck to move, so I should get the truck, too").
- Denial or disregard of any contending information (Charley said, "That's not true," basically calling his boss a liar!).

The distortions, or cover-ups, are necessary to reinforce the perception of external blame and internal innocence.

Generalized and Pervasive Feelings

Common statements are

- "Here we go again."
- "Nobody cares about me."
- "This always happens to me."
- "They are always trying to blame me for everything."

- "I never get credit for the good things. They only criticize the bad."

Charley walked away from the incident feeling, "That's just like management around here. Anybody who caves in and does what they want gets all the breaks. People like me who stand up to management are told no. It's really unfair and everybody knows it. *Everybody* in the lunchroom talks about how unfair management treats us. I can't wait to tell this to the people in my department it happened again. They will all agree with me about how management stinks and how they do this to us all the time."

These feelings of generalization and pervasive persecution support the bad attitude employee's perception of the linkage or continuation of bad events. The conflict moves from a single, easily managed, individual incident to part of a much greater, overwhelming, ongoing problem.

Perceived Threat Escalation

As emotions increase, the threat seems to escalate. The stakes rise considerably. The need to protect one's self-interest intensifies, and the fear of reactions or attacks from others becomes paramount. Two predictable reactions occur at this stage: alignments of inclusion/exclusion and management of information (the active, intentional distortion of information to others).

The bad attitude employee assesses

- Who are friends and supporters
- Who can be trusted
- Who are foes
- Whom do we have reason to suspect

Charley's thought process probably goes something like this: "This just proves that I'm not one of the boss's pets like John. John always seems to get what he wants, but not me. He's part of the first shift, and everybody on the first shift always gets the breaks. This company just dumps all over those of us who work on the second shift. I'll bet if the layoffs I've been hearing about really happen, it will be me and everybody on the second shift who's going to be laid off. That's not fair. We have to do something to make sure that doesn't happen. I can't wait to tell everyone that because I'm not one of the boss's pets, I didn't get to use the truck." (The policy change and insurance information will be conveniently omitted from his comments.) "We all need to stay away from those suck-ups on the first shift. They don't care about us anyway." Management, John, and the entire first shift are becoming the enemy, and the layoffs are the weapon or threat to be used against them.

This can be equated to circling of the wagons. Support and affirmation for self-serving perceptions are sought from others. Anyone not in active agreement is seen as an enemy to be excluded. You are either with me (us) or against me (us). (Further examples of conflict being who-, not what-based.)

Formal or informal codes of conduct emerge for protection and non-exposure. The group is to be protected at all costs. You never rat on a member of your alliance. Blame is for the other guys. ("We need to stay away from those first-shift suck-ups." Perhaps anyone maintaining first-shift friendships will be scorned as a traitor to the cause.)

Information is managed in the best interests of the individual or group. Pertinent facts may be withheld (in extreme cases, documents are altered or lies are told). Charley may not tell his peers the factual reason he was denied use of the truck.

Management of who knows what and when they know it becomes very important. This can escalate to some people (including the boss) being set up by supplying false information or intentionally withholding important data. Planting of stories or rumors becomes an acceptable way of managing information. Protecting the information you possess and exposing and exploiting the information of others become all-encompassing, and the end justifies the means.

Selective Victimization

This is where bad attitude employees choose to see themselves as being perpetually victimized by management or the system. They brood about how badly they are being treated. They catalog or inventory the litany of all the bad things that are being done to them, now as well as in the past. Resentment flares and the reaction leads to vows of fighting back or getting even or, in some cases, just giving in and proclaiming, "What's the use? I'll never win. This always happens to me" (victimization and helplessness).

Charley's thought process of selective victimization continues. "This is just another example of how bad things are around here. I don't get to use the truck. We didn't get a big enough raise. They took away our shift differential. We don't get hot food in the cafeteria like the first shift. We have to eat out of the vending machines. The first shift always leaves the problems for us to fix; we're always cleaning up their mess."

Behavioral Responses

Charley intends to fight back by inflicting pain and extracting a price and doing so covertly, not overtly. "I need to do something about this. I'm not working any more overtime. If any extra work needs to be done, let the first shift do it. I'm not cleaning up my work area anymore; I'm going to leave it for somebody else. I'm not doing any more work on any special projects, and I'm sure not going to the company picnic. I'm going to see what we have to do to get a union in here. I'm going to have a meeting at my house next week for all the people on second shift to talk about what we ought to do to pay them back for everything they do to us." All of this because Charley didn't get to use the truck.

■ Negative Responses

Bad attitude employees respond with three primary, negative methods in conflict resolution: avoidance, winning at all costs, and capitulation.

Avoidance

This has become the style of choice for many people in the American workplace, not just for bad attitude employees. Conflict is not confronted and resolved face-to-face. Instead it is avoided, and we brood internally about the issues and harp about them to people who cannot help correct the problem. Conflict is taken underground and acted out in many ways that are damaging and destructive.

If John and Susan are experiencing workplace conflict, they do not sit down and say to each other, "It appears we have some issues of disagreement. Let's see if we can't work them out." Instead they turn to their various internal support groups to vent and seek affirmation. John goes to his friends and tells them how frustrated he is with Susan—how she is difficult to get along with and how she purposely does things to aggravate him. Susan goes to her friends telling them how intolerable John is and how she just cannot stand working with him. Most of the people in their internal support group listen politely without comment. While some actually may agree, most are, in fact, either neutral or in disagreement; however, they choose to express their neutrality or disagreement with silence. Both John and Susan perceive this silence to be agreement, and this only helps to escalate the emotion and deepen the "cold war." John and Susan end up avoiding each other and choosing not to communicate. They resort to memos, faxes, or e-mail, even though they sit side by side in the office. Workplace cliques and factions begin to develop. Additional conflict breaks out if someone from one side talks to someone on the other side or vice versa. (Although it sounds childish, it is *very real* in the workplace today.)

As this avoided conflict escalates, it sucks others into its web. It negatively affects morale and ultimately threatens the quality of work. When questioned, both John and Susan will predictably blame each other for their failure to resolve the conflict.

Susan says, "If it were up to me, I would sit down with John and discuss his problem. That's the kind of person I am, but you just can't talk to John. I'm not the only one who feels that way—everybody knows how difficult he is. John says, "Everybody in this office knows how easy I am to get along with. Anybody who can't get along with me must have a real problem, and no matter what I do, I can't get Susan to be civil. She has a chip on her shoulder. I'd like to work it out, but you just can't talk to Susan; she is just that kind of a person."

This blaming is a comfortable way to distance themselves from any responsibility, affirms their righteousness, and avoids accountability for unresolved issues. This avoidance strategy is one of weakness, not strength. It may be an expression of fear or a perceived lack of skill or confidence in bad attitude employees' ability to communicate or resolve problems. They choose not to risk resolution (they get to be right!). The reality is people can exist and be at least marginally productive and successful (but probably significantly unhappy) without the cooperation and support of the people around them. Abandoning relationships and "going it alone" can be an acceptable alternative to actually taking the risk (or first step) in resolving conflict.

Avoidance is an attractive alternative, especially to bad attitude employees.

Winning at All Costs

This conflict resolution style is predicated on the belief that every conflict must be won. There is little or no regard for the feelings or issues of the other parties involved. No matter how large or small, important or unimportant, all conflict must be won. Aggression and intimidation are perfectly acceptable and may actually be the preferred tactics of choice. Not only must bad attitude employees win every conflict, but it is also very important that someone else must lose. Demonstrated dominance is a huge issue.

Charley was becoming committed to outward avoidance, but covert winning at all costs in our example. Not only did he want to win, he wanted to inflict pain and suffering on his boss and the entire organization along the way.

The flaws in this style are

- Winning is *not* successful conflict resolution.

- There is no assessment or prioritizing of issues. Every conflict is treated with the same intensity. Bad attitude employees do not differentiate between a four-alarm blazing fire and a burned marshmallow—all conflict must be won at all costs.

- Collaboration and cooperation are alien concepts. There is no consideration for the issues of other parties.

- Winning results in others being intimidated, and while this may appear to be one of the fruits of victory, it actually invites the defeated ones to fight back covertly with passive-aggressive retaliation. Because others no longer stand up to them, they think they have won. In reality, the escalated passive-aggressive behaviors they will face will further provoke them into more intensified winning behaviors. This is a self-perpetuating cycle with no end in sight (*and no winners*).

- If the conflict is not won, aggression intensifies significantly. Bad attitude employees create additional conflict to provide more opportunities for ultimate victory. ("I didn't win the first time, so I'll keep playing until I do!") Charley didn't win initially with his boss, so he went underground to manipulate his victory.

While this may appear to some to be a style of strength, it is truly a style of weakness. It's an admission of "I have no other way to influence you other than to defeat or dominate you." Bad attitude employees truly do not believe they have any options other than to win. They do not have the ability to negotiate or compromise. They do not have the confidence or skill to create alternative solutions acceptable to everyone involved.

Capitulation

People who capitulate practice "surrenderization." For some, conflict resolution means giving in at all costs.

- Always let them win.
- Always accept the blame.
- Always be the one to lose.
- Always be the one to make the concession.
- Always be the one to take the responsibility for fixing it.

This style creates lose-win conflict resolution. Capitulators are very willing to lose at the slightest provocation. Their motto is "Give in early." It is not just glorified avoidance; it is surrender and acceptance of whatever terms are extended. It reflects their perceived lack of options or alternatives.

- "Nobody listens to me."
- "My issues are not important."
- "I can't possibly prevail in this conflict."
- "It's easier to give in than face the hassle."
- "I can't communicate my issues successfully."

Capitulation is seizing the path of least resistance. It is a style that reeks of perceived low self-worth, lack of confidence, and victimization. Every conflict merely reinforces this negative belief system. In the long term there are serious consequences attached to this resolution style. People who frequently capitulate become overloaded by all of the accommodations they are making. They stuff all of this inside and risk an eventual explosion. They make so many concessions to so many people, they may not be able to accomplish them all realistically. When they do not deliver, this causes more conflict, which breeds more concession. It becomes a never-ending downward spiral. Rather than disagree over who is going to do something, they willingly assume the responsibility. Without anybody realizing it, they may be working extended hours, through lunch, or taking work home on the weekends just to keep up. They may become the perpetual stepsister from the Cinderella story—always left behind to do the work while others enjoy the freedom and good times. They work diligently to meet their commitments just to avoid further conflict. Giving up may seem easy, but the frustration and resentment can build to dangerous levels. When overload results, resentment mounts, and there may be an eruption.

> Woody was a capitulator. When the organization cut expenses and canceled the contract for the cleaning service, his peers were grumbling about having to do chores they weren't being paid to do. Woody decided to commit to coming in an hour early each day to empty wastebaskets, clean the coffeepot, and so on. Everyone thought Woody was a great guy. When the project he and Amanda were working on was rejected by their boss, they were instructed to work late to fix it. Amanda was upset because she had a very important meeting to attend that evening. Woody said, "Don't miss your meeting. I'll stay tonight and finish the job. I'll stay as long as is necessary."

When a charity appeal was announced, nobody wanted to chair the project. Everybody hated begging for money. Woody volunteered and promised he wouldn't work on it during company time. He also promised to stay late on Wednesdays to help Jill learn the new computer program. Do you think Woody is headed for some trouble?

All three of the preceding responses to conflict are unhealthy and problematic. The conflict will eventually have to be dealt with—it's only a question of time.

■ Impediments to Resolution

Two critical barriers to resolving conflict for bad attitude employees are inflexibility and emotional barriers.

Inflexibility

There are three primary contributors to inflexibility.

Preconceived conditions   These are conditions predetermined and formulated *before* any attempt at resolution begins. They are very damaging to the resolution process, and the employee erroneously believes they are the *only* acceptable basis for satisfactory resolution. These conditions evolve from the premise of "Here's what I want—the only way to resolve this problem is to give me what I want, and I won't be happy unless I get it!" Charley's preconceived condition was that the company truck was his only alternative and that he had to have it—his position excluded any other alternatives.

> ● **Preconceived conditions result in inflexibility.**

Unilateral ethics (Because I want it, it's right.)   Unilateral ethics are a narrow, self-serving perception of what is fair or unfair, right or wrong, honest or dishonest. This distorted perception is based solely on what is best for the individual. Everyone sees things in his or her own best interest.

- "What is right is what is right for *me.* "
- "What is best is what is best for *me.*"
- "What is fair is whatever is in *my* best interest."

Unilateral ethics contribute to people being driven to get what they believe they are entitled to and also contribute to conflicts becoming issues of principle. "It's not just using the truck. It's the principle of the thing. It's unfair to give it to John and not to me." This self-serving perception of what is ethical or deserved demonstrates itself in many unique ways in the workplace.

> ▶ Judy doesn't come to work until noon on Wednesday. Without any notification, she comes in half a day late. When confronted about her tardiness, Judy flares up and says, "Well, I saved the company $10,000 on Monday by solving that accounts receivable problem, and I deserve to take a morning off once in a while." She justifies her actions by what she unilaterally perceives she deserves.

■ ■ ■

> ▶ When David was confronted about his unapproved personal use of the petty cash fund, he responded, "I work hard around here. I should be able to use that cash when I'm short of money.

Besides, I always pay it back, and everybody else does it, so why shouldn't I?" He is willing to excuse himself from adhering to company policy by his self-serving perception.

Unilateral ethics are self-serving interpretations of the rules of life (organizational or personal). These interpretations may be in direct opposition to written policies, procedures, and laws. It is the prevailing attitude that "the rules don't apply to me." It seems that many of us (not just our employees) are very willing to excuse our behavior or make self-serving exceptions in circumstances where we hold others to rigid compliance. Whether they are traffic laws, parking zones, daily starting times, performance standards, or considerations of tact, they are for everyone else, but not for me (and that's how it should be!).

Negative historical reference   As previously discussed, historical reference is the continuation or connection of negative events. It is consistently seeing current situations as interconnected with incidents of the past. This accumulation of incidents contributes to an overall mindset of "I've had enough. I can't take this anymore, and I'm going to dig in my heels and not give in to them." Every event is filtered through a negative interpretation of the past. Have you ever noticed that bad attitude employees never let anyone out of jail? If they perceive you have done the crime, guilt and punishment are eternal. You are always suspected of having done it again! Every incident becomes a mere continuation of past sins.

The negative historical reference is debilitating for bad attitude employees because it truly inhibits them from moving forward. Because they cannot let go of past events and move on, they perpetually live in the past. Conflict issues are difficult to resolve because you are not just dealing with the current issue, you are dealing with the entire litany of their interpretation of all the things that have happened in the past.

Emotional Barriers

These barriers increase negative emotions, and they frequently prohibit clear thought and reduce our willingness to negotiate positive outcomes. The three major contributors to negative emotional barriers include negative projections, personalization, and perceived option deprivation.

Negative projections   Negative projections are beliefs or interpretations concerning the intentions and motives of the other people involved in the conflict. Bad attitude employees see their intentions and motives as pure, right, innocent, and high-minded. They see others' intentions as evil, dishonest, and selfish, possessing ulterior motives that are not in their best interests. Bad attitude employees assume they know what is driving others' actions and behaviors. They assume others are driven by the vilest motives and intentions. Usually these assumptions are self-serving and profoundly negative.

> Tyrone wanted his boss to approve his request to attend a three-day seminar on Just In Time (J.I.T.) purchasing programs. His boss refused the request. Tyrone fumed and stewed. He said to himself, "The boss is too stupid to see how this will benefit the entire organization if I go to this seminar. I know why he didn't approve my request. He sees me as a threat. He is afraid that if I successfully implement a J.I.T. program, I will save us so much money I'll take his job. He doesn't want anyone to get ahead but himself. He is the most selfish and self-centered man I have ever met."
>
> In reality, the request was turned down because the seminar was scheduled during year-end inventory. Tyrone played an active role in coordinating the entire organization's inventory efforts, and he was needed. He could attend the next J.I.T. seminar being offered in three months with minimal disruption. Sound familiar?

These negative assumptions contribute to a hardening of preconceived conditions. Bad attitude employees' attempts to analyze positions from a very narrow, self-serving, negative vantage point not only devalues them, but creates highly critical, antagonistic emotions within others. They become their own worst enemy (inflexible). Not wanting to give in, they become angrier and more resentful. They believe others are motivated by disrespect for them, their own selfishness, and are seeking only their personal gain. Is it any wonder conflict resolution is such a significant challenge?

Personalization   We have discussed personalization previously, and it also plays a significant role here. Bad attitude employees do not separate the "what" from the "who" in the conflicts they experience. They see conflict as personal issues between themselves and the other person. This is the us-against-them mentality.

The personalization of conflict increases negative emotional barriers. Conflict-producing situations tend to perpetuate because conflict is never resolved; it is only won or lost. For bad attitude employees, their interpretation of their own self-worth may hinge on whether they win or lose.

Perceived option deprivation

A huge emotional barrier is created when people in conflict perceive they have no options for resolution. They either fight or give in; they don't resolve. Resolution is perceived to be inflicted upon them, and they have no platform for being heard or for seeking redress. As we have discussed, people who win at all costs or capitulate perceive they have no other option; these are the only things they know how to do. Lack of options equals victimization. This constraint or helplessness contributes significantly to negative emotions. Resentment, fear, and diminished self-esteem prevail. When Charley was denied use of the truck, his perception of no other options drove his anger and embarrassment.

■ Foundations of Successful Conflict Resolution

Conflicts can be resolved successfully. You can be an asset to your bad attitude employees by teaching and collaborating with them to create these foundations and conditions.

Create Conditions of Flexibility

Flexibility provides opportunities to brainstorm creative solutions that are acceptable to all parties. We stumble headlong into rigidity when we assume that each party has the same positions and that all parties cannot be satisfied simultaneously. Here are the keys to enhancing flexibility.

Commonality of interests and outcomes   In conflict, we usually emphasize our points of disagreement. Flexibility is increased when we identify our areas of agreement as well. "We agree on all of these points. We disagree in just this one area. Let's see what we can do to work it out."

In his book, *The 7 Habits of Highly Successful People,* Dr. Stephen Covey cites as his second habit, "Start with the end in mind." Flexibility in resolving conflict starts with identifying the successful outcome all parties want to achieve.

- "We both want to do what's best for our customers."

- "We all want to make this a better place to work."

- "You and I both want you to succeed."

Once we identify and agree on where we are going, resolving how we get there becomes less of a challenge.

Charley assumed an inflexible position that using that particular truck was his only option. Had he and his boss focused on the intended outcome, the actual vehicle used to accomplish the move would not matter. Charley focused on the truck; he would have been better served by asking for ideas on accomplishing a successful move. Charley's boss had no issue at all with his intended outcome; however, he was not willing to violate company policy or risk an insurance problem.

Could there have been other alternatives?

- Could borrowing the boss's personal pickup truck been at least a start?

- Could other employees be enticed to help out?

- Could Charley rent a truck at a significantly reduced rate by going through the company?

- Could a friendly supplier, anxious to build a relationship by going the extra mile, have provided one of their vehicles?

Are any or all of these solutions possible? Who knows? But they were never even considered as Charley's inflexibility caused him to storm off when his request was denied.

Broaden the shared field of vision   Acknowledge that the parties involved may have totally different perceptions of the conflict. Validate the right of everyone to have his or her perceptions—correct or incorrect, rational or irrational—it doesn't matter. Legitimize the perceptions by giving everyone an equal opportunity to state his or her interpretation. Seeing the view from the other party's perspective may shed an entirely new light on the conflict.

> ◆ **"I am willing to listen to your side of the story; will you be willing to listen to mine?"**

Emphasize shared responsibility and participation   Establish very clearly that successful resolution and outcomes are the responsibility of *all* parties involved. Resolution does not have to be inflicted; it can be negotiated. Everyone involved has a responsibility for an ultimate successful outcome. Flexibility and commitment are enhanced when shared responsibility is emphasized and accepted. Successful resolution is a collaborative effort.

Avoid distancing yourself from responsibility   Weak managers resolve conflicts by blaming others. They may blame higher-ups for unpopular decisions rather than accept and defend the validity of their position.

- "I don't agree with this either, but this is what the big boss says we have to do."

- "I wish I didn't have to do this, but this is what corporate says we have to do."

- "I agree this is probably a mistake, but this is what we have to do."

- "Don't blame me; this wasn't my idea."

▶ Blaming higher authority is weakness.

Blaming is an easy way to deflect the heat for unpopular decisions. While it distances you from responsibility and sets someone else up to be the bad guy, it also makes you appear weak and lacking in influence and control. (Short-term gain—maybe. Long-term downside—guaranteed!) This results in employees disrespecting both you and your management efforts. It invites challenges of insubordination in the face of your obvious weakness or lack of influence. Be willing to accept responsibility in conflict situations. Do not retreat to safety by making someone else the bad guy.

Resolution remorse　People may make agreements and, upon reflection, begin to feel uncomfortable with their commitment or begin to regret the manner in which the conflict was resolved. This is not unlike buyer's/seller's remorse that sets in with the purchase or sale of any significant item or possession (house, land, car, business). Nagging questions may emerge: "Did I do the right thing? Did I make the right decision? Did I really look at this objectively? Did I allow myself to be taken advantage of?" Post-resolution remorse is not uncommon. Just as state legislators enact buyer's remorse laws to protect consumers from making impulsive and emotional decisions, it is prudent to build in remorse contingencies for your resolution agreements.

> Earl was a contract employee providing computer skills training on as as-needed basis for the company's remote field offices around the country. He became frustrated and disenchanted with what he perceived to be the company's violation of housing and travel arrangement agreements. He notified the company of his unhappiness and his unwillingness to fulfill his next assignment scheduled thirty days later. While the company was disappointed and reluctant to waive his obligation, they realized the risk of having a disgruntled contractor interacting with their employees. They agreed to excuse Earl from his contract if he would pay the additional $600 cost of bringing in another trainer on short notice. Initially Earl agreed enthusiastically (he would do anything to sever his relationship with the company). However, as he pondered his agreement, remorse set in and he regretted his decision. He felt he had been taken advantage of and decided to re-open the discussion and counteroffer with a reduced dollar figure. He stated, "I am not attempting to avoid liability; however, I would like to reconsider the settlement." The company listened to his reasoning and accepted his reduced offer. His reasoning was sound, and the settlement avoided any costs of legal

action and insured Earl's cooperation in debriefing the replacement trainer. He pledged to give the company good future references for other contractors.

Flexibility is increased when remorse contingencies are factored into your resolution agreements. They encourage people to reach agreement more quickly and to consider creative alternatives. When they realize their agreement is subject to further consideration, there is much less pressure to prolong the conflict and far less fear in its resolution. What is an appropriate period for reconsideration? Depending upon the intensity of the conflict, a maximum of twenty-four hours is considered appropriate. Actual reconsiderations, while not uncommon, occur more infrequently than you might expect. The elation, or satisfaction, of a successful agreement tends to raise everyone's comfort with the outcome. Dealing with remorse issues in the resolution process avoids a delayed backlash of resentment and the onslaught of passive-aggressive retaliatory behaviors.

Defuse Emotional Barriers

As previously discussed, emotional barriers inhibit positive conflict resolutions. When negative emotions run high, irrationality prevails. There are specific steps to neutralizing these roadblocks.

Maintain mutual dignity and respect   As all parties explain their perceptions, under no circumstances will any disrespectful displays be tolerated. Respect and dignity are two-way streets. Zapping, editorializing, and personal attacks are unacceptable. There is zero tolerance for either side talking about the other's "momma"!

- Acceptable: "I disagree with your decision."
- Unacceptable: "That's the stupidest decision I've ever heard."

Break the linkage of past issues   While acknowledging past conflicts, cite concrete examples of any interim successes.

> Colin was very upset because his request to work on a new project team was denied. He confronted Sandra, his boss, and stated that he was angry because she did it to him again. Previously, a similar request was denied. Sandra acknowledged his issue and said, "I understand your disappointment and I really appreciate your bringing the issue to my attention instead of just stewing about it. My perception is you were appointed to three special project teams at your request since the last time I said no. I don't see a pattern here at all, and I can't always give you the assignments you want."

If specific past wounds are still open and active, it may be appropriate to deal with the issues head on.

> ▶ "Colin, I know we have had problems with work assignments in the past, especially the water works project in '96. How can we get past that? It's over; we can't do anything about it. What can we do to deal with each current event without always having to relive that problem?"

Help the employee to see the current issue as separate and distinct from previous occurrences. There is no common thread. Each conflict is a whole new garment.

Neutralize the win-lose issue (lower the stakes)   Take the antagonistic "me versus you" out of the conflict equation.

- "I'm not trying to win this conflict (argument, disagreement, etc.)."
- "I'm not trying to be right. I want us to do what's best."
- "I don't see you as being wrong or the bad guy. I just think we have a different opinion."
- "We disagree. That doesn't make us enemies."

Focus on the "what" and not the "who"

- "This is not about you."
- "We are talking about a problem here, an issue that is not about either one of us personally."
- "This is about what happened, not who did it."

Use time as a tool   Properly used, time can reduce negative emotions effectively. Time can be used to establish

- Moratoriums
- Cooling-off periods
- Processing or reflection opportunities (to consider the circumstances)
- Effective information gathering (facts, witnesses, observations, etc.)

Declaring that you need time to think before reacting to a problem actually validates the importance of the other party's position. It recognizes the depth of their thought process. It also impresses them with your reluctance to just wing it by taking an action or position before you consider it in-depth (sacrificing quality consideration for expediency). "What you have raised is too important for me to just make a snap decision. I want to think, not react impulsively. How about if we both consider it further and get back together (specific time)?"

▶ **The key to using time as a tool is the *deadline*.**

Deadlines are necessary, and the shorter the better. Time becomes a tool of avoidance without a specific deadline. As deadlines lengthen indefinitely, we lapse into avoidance by default or inaction.

> **Time is a tool, not a crutch; nor is it a weapon to be used against an employee.**

Some managers use time as a means of provoking fear or raising an employee's anxiety.

> Bruce's boss approached him at 4:59 P.M. on a Friday afternoon declaring, "I'm really unhappy with what you have done. You've really screwed up this time. I want you in my office first thing Monday morning to discuss your future with the company." This left Bruce twisting in the wind and the timing was abusive, to say the least. Just as fire is beneficial or destructive, time can reduce or fortify emotional barriers.

What should Bruce's boss have done? Take the weekend to reconsider strategies for correction and waited to approach Bruce until Monday morning (or meet with him at 4:59 Friday, if it just couldn't wait). The meeting would still be held; the difference is Bruce's anxiety and ruined weekend.

Clearly Identify the Problem/Cause

Successful conflict resolution is impossible without first establishing a clear understanding of the problem. Lack of clear problem identification leads to reacting to symptoms or indicators rather than actual root causes. When we fail to look beyond the surface observations, we are inclined to make cosmetic adjustments to reduce the friction of the moment. This only perpetuates the actual conflict issues.

Frequently in our attempts to be decisive and project an aura of competence and control, we prematurely respond to symptoms. You may be familiar with this description of American management: Ready! Fire! Aim!

▶ **It is not uncommon for us to blaze away before we really know what our target is!**

▶ Babette had been the only employee in the order processing department for ten years. Her performance had always been excellent until recently, when the labels and picking tickets she generated became increasingly illegible. This resulted in a huge increase of shipping and delivery errors and an explosion of customer complaints. Her boss criticized her work, telling her she must do better, and she experienced significant conflict with many people in the departments who processed her work. Babette maintained she was doing nothing differently and bristled at the complaints and criticisms. Her boss was ready to fire her, and she was ready to quit when the human resource department intervened in an attempt to avoid a serious problem. The resulting dialogue and investigation yielded an interesting discovery. The purchasing department, in their well-intentioned attempts to save operating costs, had made a change in their supplier of shipping forms and labels. These lower quality materials produced blurred copies due to cheaper, inefficient carbon paper inserts.

The symptom was blurred labels, and the blame was directed at Babette. The actual root cause was the new form and a purchasing agent's well-intended but problematic decision. The resolution wasn't found in fixing Babette; it was achieved by reverting back to the former supplier.

The only way to clearly identify problems and their root causes is to communicate honestly and openly and to mutually commit to objective evaluation, targeting the true discovery of why the conflict is occurring.

Communicate Effectively

It has been estimated that only 7% of total communication is verbal. 93% of communication is determined by tone of voice and nonverbal messages.

▶ It's not what you say; it's the way you say it.

A verbal claim of cooperation or intent to resolve conflict is ineffective if not supported by a positive tone of voice and body language. It is not enough to *say* that you want to solve a problem. A positive message is totally aligned and sincerely communicated with the words supported by a conciliatory tone and nonverbal demonstrations of attention, interest, and commitment.

In every conflict situation, ask yourself repeatedly, "What nonverbal and voice inflection messages am I sending?" We spread considerably more conflict with our tone of voice and nonverbals than with our actual words. You know how it looks and sounds from others—you're sending the same messages.

Communication style

1. Focus exclusively on the employee during discussions.

   Do *not* fit him or her in while you do two or three other things at the same time.

   Do *not* assure him or her that everything will be all right while you are talking to someone else on the telephone.

   Do *not* talk with him or her while keeping an eye on other activities in your field of vision.

   ▶ **If you cannot give the employee your undivided attention, do not address the conflict until you can.**

   Nothing is more infuriating than knowing someone is not willing to give you undivided attention.

2. Avoid aggressive "you-based" messages. Concentrate on "I-" and "we-based" messages of inclusion. You-based messages are accusatory and exclusionary and project blame. They imply negative motive or intent.

Unacceptable	*Acceptable*
"You did this."	"Here's what I think happened."
"You shouldn't have done that."	"Here's how I think it should have been handled."
"You didn't do what I asked you to do. Why?"	"I don't perceive our agreements were carried out. Help me understand why."

   I- and we-based communication keeps the discussion focused on content, *not* emotion. Successful conflict resolution is impossible until the negative emotion can be neutralized.

3. Separate fact from opinion. In conflict situations, opinions are often communicated as facts. Opinions are perceptions and not reality. Facts can be verified while opinions remain conjecture until they are proven by data, measurement, or experience.

   In conflict situations, be wary of the word "is." The use of the word "is" implies the statements following actually contain fact.

Negative statements:

- "This *is* what happened." (Not really—it's probably what they perceive happened.)

- "John *is* wrong." (I think John is wrong.)

- "Susan *is* stupid." (I think Susan is stupid.)

Positive alternatives:

- "Here is what I believe happened."

- "Here is my perception."

- "This is what allegedly took place."

- "This is how I see it."

All of these statements acknowledge that perception is not fact.

Avoid falling prey to "factual future predictions." It is not uncommon for people to use their current perceptions to predict future outcomes, especially when emotions or perceived threat is high. "If this keeps up, here *is* what will happen." (Perception presented as certainty.) While opinions of future outcomes may be presented as facts, there are no facts about the future. Even using accurately measured current trends to predict the future is merely conjecture based on assumptions that nothing will change or be done to alter or disrupt current patterns. Predictions of future outcomes may be valuable; however, anything future-based is perception and must not be accepted as guarantees.

4. Avoid verbal communication barriers. Avoid the use of the words "but" and "however" in conflict situations. These words are cancelers and render the statements that precede them invalid. They prepare the listener for the negative communication that is about to follow.

   - "I know you think you did the right thing, *but* here's what you should have done."

     (Translation—*you were wrong!*)

   - "I know you completed the task, *but* there were a couple of things you forgot to do."

     (Translation—*you really failed.*)

Using "but" and "however" in your responses escalates conflict.

Statement: "I did what you asked me to do."

The inappropriate, escalating response: "But/However you didn't do everything that I requested."

Your effective response: "*And* there are some additional things to be completed."

♦ But/however = "You are wrong."

There is never a time when "and" cannot be substituted for "but," unless the "but" has two t's!

5. Listening. When you talk, it's about you. When you listen, it's about the person talking to you. Not listening devalues others. Fewer actions contribute more to relationships than effective listening, and fewer actions deteriorate relationships more than demonstrating poor listening skills.

Some effective listening tools:

- Listen from their perspective. (Try to process it from their point of view. How would you see it if you were in their shoes? This doesn't mean you agree with their perspective, merely that you acknowledge it.)

- Respect their silence. (If they pause to think, let them. Don't take away their right to restart the conversation by seizing the opportunity to talk yourself. Silence is a component of thought, not always a void to be filled. Frequently we are so anxious to talk, we seize the conversation when they pause to take a breath.)

- Ask short clarifying questions. ("I want to be sure that I'm clear on that particular point . . . Did you say that . . . ?")

- Clarify ambiguities. ("Help me understand what . . . means.")

- Take notes. ("What you have to say is very important, and I want to be sure I understand it correctly. Do you mind if I take some notes?") If the other person is threatened or intimidated by your taking notes, don't do it. Taking notes forces you to be a more complete, focused listener. You have to listen in order to have something to write. It also impresses them with the obvious importance you attach to their statements. (This is an excellent technique to help you stay focused in phone conversations as well.)

In order to test your listening skills and reinforce your commitment to the discussion, restate to the employee your understanding of what was said. The restatement must be assertive (I and we) as opposed to aggressive (you). It must be void of emotion, negative judgment, rejection, or critical comment of any kind. The restatement

- Proves to the employee you are listening intently to what he or she says.

- Insures accuracy. If your restatement is accurate, the employee agrees. If it is not, he or she will correct it. The result is an acknowledged, clear understanding of the statements and perception.

- Reduces the influence of emotion. When either party hears his or her statements repeated back to them, the absence of emotion tends to minimize the intensity of the issue and helps it sound much more reasonable and fixable. When it is said initially, there may be high negative emotional content. When it is repeated, it does not sound nearly as intense or insurmountable.

In our next chapter we will address the varying degrees of conflict intensity and specific successful strategies for working through conflict.

6 Positive Conflict Resolution

In Chapter 5 we identified the impediments or barriers to resolving conflicts successfully and the foundations for positive resolution. In this chapter, we will identify the various degrees of conflict, learn to evaluate the progression of the intensity, and select the appropriate resolution response. Not all conflict is bad, and we will learn to intervene effectively to make conflict a healthy, creative dynamic not inherently destructive. We will address the interrelational skills and successful strategies for dealing with conflict in a positive manner. The chapter will conclude with a discussion of mediating the conflict of others and the difference between mediation and arbitration.

We begin with the four critical points of successful conflict resolution. There have been many excellent studies on the varying intensities and levels of conflict, and many models for effective resolution. All of these studies and models concerning conflict are helpful. In truth, a *bad* model for resolution is better than *no* model for resolution. For our discussion, we will approach conflict from three degrees or levels. These degrees vary in intensity, frequency, and the appropriate resolution strategy.

Bad attitude employees tend to see conflict as second and first degree.

Degree of Conflict	Level of Intensity	Occurs	Challenge of Resolution	Strategies
Third-degree	low	frequently/ ongoing	low to moderate degree of difficulty	1. Coping 2. Interactive communication
Second-degree	medium to high	less frequently	medium to high degree of difficulty	1. Interactive communication 2. Mediation
First-degree	extremely high	infrequent in healthy organizations; higher frequency in author- itarian organizations	extremely high degree of difficulty	1. Mediation 2. Arbitration

▶ **The greater the number of bad attitude employees, the greater the number of second- and first-degree conflicts.**

In considering the degrees of conflict and successful resolution strategies, be aware of ten undeniable, inescapable, real-world conflict truths:

1. Ineffective or unresolved conflict escalates.

2. Conflict may actually surface at the first- or second-degree levels.

3. Conflict, if unresolved, may steadily escalate upward from third to second to first or skip from third to first.

4. The self-perpetuating cycle: conflict escalates as concern for self increases, and concern for self increases as conflict intensity escalates.

5. As concern for self and conflict intensity increases, the desire to win escalates along with the desire to inflict loss.

6. As conflict intensity increases, saving face and protecting oneself from loss increases proportionately.

7. Reasonable, rational people become harmful to others and more intent on extracting retribution as conflict intensity increases.

8. People may be at different degree levels in the same conflict.

9. The degree and intensity of conflict determines the successful resolution strategies.

10. Strategies effective in resolving conflict at one degree may be counterproductive or harmful at another degree.

■ Third-Degree Conflict

Third-degree conflict is low intensity conflict and is generally issue-focused. These are things everyone has to deal with on a day-to-day basis, including

- Misunderstandings
- Irrational behaviors
- Unintended slights
- Differences of opinions
- Irritations
- Minor miscommunications
- Inconveniences
- Disagreement on the interpretation of facts and data

Typically, in third-degree conflict there is a high level of separation of problem from people. If addressed properly, there is usually a high willingness to discuss and resolve problems and to avoid personalization.

Strategies for Addressing Third-Degree Conflict

Third-degree conflict is readily resolvable; there are two effective options for ensuring that the conflict does not escalate:

Coping skills Coping skills are unilateral behaviors of conscious choice. They are not interactive; they are one-dimensional responses that are implemented solely on your own and can be an appropriate, effective response for dealing with many minor issues of conflict and day-to-day irritations.

The three primary coping skills are tolerance, delay, and accommodation.

1. Tolerance is choosing to put up with the source of the conflict. It is a healthy response if you actually make a conscious decision to tolerate the behavior of others. While this is probably the most frequently used coping strategy, it is also the most misused strategy. We tolerate the behavior of others when it just isn't worth trying to correct the problem or fight the battle. (On a scale of 1 to 10, it is not a 10.) Proper use of this strategy and the decision to tolerate low levels of irritation or improper behavior apply if they are rare, one-time occurrences (not ongoing patterns), if there is little or no disruption to others, and if they have no impact on personal or overall productivity.

   Tolerance is counterproductive and dysfunctional when we choose to tolerate while simultaneously continuing to harbor resentment about the circumstance. Toleration without letting go is called avoidance!

   ◆ **Avoidance is *not* a coping skill.**

2. To delay is to set a specific time when some form of resolution will be pursued. The difference between avoidance and delay is a timeline.

   ◆ **Avoidance is ongoing. Delay is planned inaction for a specific period of time.**

   Delay is an excellent strategy when

   - There is reason to believe the problem may correct itself if given enough time.
   - There is a significant impediment to confronting the problem at this moment.
   - A little more experience or on-the-job seasoning will correct the problem.
   - Extenuating circumstances exist (when an employee is approaching retirement, a transfer is pending, or there is a short duration of exposure through short-term contract, temporary assignment, etc.).

When *not* responding will allow the problem to continue, then delay becomes unacceptable avoidance. Continuation of the problem will only escalate the intensity. Interactive communication is necessary.

Frequently when delay is chosen as a tactic, the approaching deadline is continually extended, which becomes just another form of avoidance.

3. Accommodations are decisions to give in; they allow the other person to have his or her way. While this is a unilateral action, it has some elements of interaction as it is important to communicate to the other party your decision to accommodate. Accommodation may keep things moving without disruption, and it may be appropriate for a later trade-off. It also helps you to feel good about yourself and your willingness to give people something that they want. You can celebrate your magnanimity!

> Sam is the supervisor in the shipping department. His crew is a group of young people who do a good job and are willing to work hard. Things are going well. The work environment permits a radio to be played throughout the department, and Sam's workers have come to an agreement among themselves on a music selection compromise—country music until 10:00 A.M., rap until 1:00 P.M., and rock the rest of the day. Sam prefers talk radio and finds the music selection annoying and occasionally nerve-racking.

Sam has three options for coping with this situation.

- Tolerance. It just doesn't matter. These folks do a good job, and it just isn't worth a morale problem battling over such a small thing. When his nerves get raw, he focuses on their productivity and his potential performance bonus check. All in all, a little bit of bad music is worth it!

- Delay. The company is in its peak season, and these folks are going at full speed. Now is not the time to pick a fight over the radio. Since demand slows considerably in about six weeks, he'll address the radio issue then. Just knowing he had a plan for addressing the problem helped make the music a little less annoying.

- Accommodation. The music is an aggravation, but it seems to mean a lot more to them than it does to Sam. He will let them know that this old guy is not such a fuddy duddy, and he's willing to let them have their way with the radio. In a meeting Sam told the group, "As you all know, this isn't my kind of music, but I'm willing to let you guys listen to whatever you want to. I'll remind you of this when I need your help during peak season."

Coping responses are appropriate if

- You willingly, consciously choose to respond in a specific manner.
- You do not continue to hold the other person responsible for your decision.
- You do not continue to keep score or log into your memory bank every time the other person demonstrates the tolerated behavior.
- You do not continue to harbor negative, accumulating emotion toward the other party.

If these conditions are not met, you are not coping; you are just loading up and preparing yourself to do battle at the next level.

! **Coping is a deadly management mistake if the offender's behavior is disruptive, hinders productivity, or displays disrespect.**

If coping skills are not effective in dealing with third-degree conflict, interactive communication is.

Interactive communication   When coping is no longer successful or you are dealing with significant differences of opinion or disagreements on relevant facts and data, interactive communication is necessary. Failing to communicate only escalates the intensity of the conflict. The conflict will not go away, and the sooner it is addressed at the lowest degree, the greater the chances for success. Why wait?

Interactive communication strategies with third-degree conflict situations are relatively simple and straightforward.

1. Depersonalize the conflict. Make sure everyone understands this is a "what" issue, not a personal "who" issue.

2. Focus only on current events. Do not entertain past unresolved grievances. Do not link current issues to past events.

3. Communicate inclusively.

   - Everyone communicates equally. Everyone listens and restates his or her understanding.

   - Clearly analyze commonality and identify areas of contention.

   - Resolve through brainstorming, creative problem solving, and emphasizing shared responsibility. (Accommodation may actually surface as an acceptable solution.)

▶ Lisa and Ann worked together in the payroll processing department. They are friends, have a good working relationship, and are reluctant to raise any issues that might put a ding in their relationship. Lisa has an attendance problem. She is eligible to take seventeen days off each year with pay in addition to traditional holidays (ten working days of vacation, seven sick days). Lisa used her seventeen days by April. Ann's problem is Lisa's attendance is very unpredictable, and it is difficult to schedule work flow and maintain coverage in Lisa's absence. Ann believed the problem wasn't going to get better. In the past when Lisa exhausted her approved number of days, she willingly took days without pay. Ann was bewildered as to why management allowed this condition to exist.

Ann's strategy so far has been to tolerate Lisa's behavior and just write it off to Lisa being Lisa. However, the problem was beginning to affect their performance, and Ann was developing some feelings of resentment based upon a disproportionate amount of work falling to her.

What are Ann's options for handling this situation?

1. She can continue to put up with the situation and say nothing. Her resentment will build, the relationship will suffer, and the deterioration in the performance of both women will probably bring an eventual reaction from management, probably leveled equally at both of them. To allow this to happen would be unacceptable.

2. She can confront Lisa, share her perceptions, and attempt to find a common ground for improvement. Ann knows she is taking a risk but feels there is going to be a problem anyway, and it's better to deal with it now when it's small than to wait until it becomes big.

Ann approaches Lisa and says, "I'm having a problem, and I think that we can work it out. This is not about you and me; it's about managing our workload and making sure that we aren't putting ourselves in a position to be criticized by management for a slippage in our productivity. The key question for me is how to manage the workload and anticipate how to get everything done when I am frequently here by myself. When days off are taken isn't my issue; it's how to keep things on track when neither of us is here. Tell me what your thoughts are."

▶ Lisa predictably responded with "I'm entitled to all of my days off, and if I take too many days, I don't get paid for them. I'm taking only what I'm entitled to." Ann's response was "This is not about how many days you take off; it's about the two of us managing our workload and getting the job done."

The result of their discussion was an agreement that Lisa would try to avoid Monday absences when their workload was heaviest. She now had a better understanding of how her absenteeism was affecting Ann. She had never really considered that Ann paid a price when she wasn't there.

Bad Attitude Employees and Third-Degree Conflict

For the most part, bad attitude employees do not address third-degree conflict well. Some activate their win-at-all-costs reactionary behavior and literally declare war at the slightest provocation (which immediately escalates this low-level conflict to the next degree). Most choose to avoid the issue and allow each incident to build up in intensity.

This is the typical tolerating pattern of bad attitude employees. They tolerate rather than confront the problem, yet still hold the other party responsible. This is unfair and destructive because their resentment prohibits them from letting go. Their resentment builds, and they tolerate until they erupt. The other party typically responds by saying, "Why didn't you tell me about this sooner?"

Bad attitude employees allow the irritation to remain active, and absorb the pain and damage. Eventually, they erupt. Instead of dealing with conflict when it is small and insignificant, they avoid it until it becomes disruptive and damaging.

A final thought on third-degree conflict. In Chapter 5 we described capitulation as an inappropriate response to conflict. People who capitulate tend to do so early at the third-degree conflict level. They appear never to allow conflict to go beyond this low-level stage. This is deceiving. In reality, while they appear to accommodate quickly, they are actually building increased levels of resentment toward themselves and the other party because they had to give in. Capitulation (giving in at all times, at all cost) is *not* a healthy strategy for dealing with any degree of conflict. It is going to erupt sooner or later.

Let's address the next level.

■ Second-Degree Conflict

Second-degree conflict ranges from medium to high intensity and can be more difficult to resolve than third-degree conflict. The causes tend to be more significant and frequently become personalized. Typical sources of second-degree conflict (ranging from lowest to highest intensity) include the following:

- Unresolved, escalated third degree conflict.

- Methodology. (We agree on what we are going to do; we disagree on how we are going to do it.) Conflict over the methods to be used to attain desired outcomes. Each party wants to do it his or her way. Generally, both parties cannot prevail. Compromise can be very difficult, and frequently those with more power win and inflict their resolution on the other party. (This should be the resolution strategy of last resort, not first.)

- Mission/Objective. (What we are going to do.) We disagree on the goals and priorities of the group, team, department, or overall organization. Conflicts concerning goals and priorities are very serious for individuals and organizations. They reflect disagreement regarding the very core of the organization and what it is all about. This is disagreement on what is valued and deemed important and has serious consequences if not resolved successfully.

▶ If you do not agree on where you are going, does anything else really matter?

Symptoms

Following are typical signs of second-degree conflict:

- Emotion/anger is visible
- Negative projection becomes the norm
- Personalization of conflict is high
- Personal opinion is embraced as fact
- Trust erodes
- Fear of punishment or retribution increases
- Passive aggressive behaviors may begin or intensify
- Winning and saving face gain importance and may become the dominant issue
- Distorted communication begins to occur (use of words such as "always," "never," "everyone," etc.)

▶ Intensity increases significantly in second-degree conflict.

In second-degree conflict, it is not uncommon for people to become more resistant or withdrawn rather than openly addressing the conflict-causing issues. (They begin to dig their trenches.) Employees frequently begin to take their case to others who have no power to successfully influence the outcome. They seek support and affirmation of their perspective instead of resolution. Cliques begin to form and alignments crystallize.

Suspicion and doubt intensify. Sarcasm and innuendo emerge in emotionally charged communication. Alliances are formed around whether someone is a friend or foe.

- "Are you with me (us) or against me (us)?"
- "What will you do with this information?"
- "Whom will you tell?"
- "How do I know you won't tell someone you shouldn't?"

Strategies for Addressing Second-Degree Conflict

There are two strategies for successfully resolving second-degree conflict. As a leader, your skills in helping to resolve conflict at this level and your ability to teach those skills to others will be crucial in eliminating escalation.

> **!** Any form of coping strategies are inappropriate with second-degree conflict.

Interactive communication   Second-degree interactive communication is much more complex than it is in the third-degree. Intensity is higher, conflict is deeper, and there is much more at stake. Following is a set of eight guidelines to establish and facilitate interactive communication.

1. Increase trust and reduce fear. Invite punishment-free communication. This means that *no* topic is off limits and there will be no retaliation. Punishment-free communication does not absolve anyone of the responsibility to be tactful or to consider others' feelings. It is not a license to abuse. Dignity and respect must be maintained at all times for all parties involved (including those not in attendance). Communications and actions attacking dignity and respect are common with this degree of conflict as things heat up considerably. Correct these actions early. Maintain zero tolerance for disrespectful behavior.

    ▶ **Encourage disagreement—reject disrespect.**

    Keeping agreements and maintaining confidentiality are crucial in building trust. Typically, bad attitude employees make agreements insincerely to avoid issues and then dismiss those commitments later. That's dishonest and destroys trust. The conflict will not be resolved until trust is either created or restored and fear is diminished.

2. Gather as much relevant and accurate data as possible. Take whatever time is necessary to ensure that everyone has the same information and that all information is accurate. Facts and figures should be double

checked, statements verified, witnesses requestioned. Positive resolutions are impossible with inaccurate, incomplete, or unshared (hoarded) data.

3. Establish shared responsibility. Neither party assumes the entire burden for resolving the conflict. Involve everyone in finding a satisfactory, creative resolution. Those who are not included in the resolution process will typically

   - Reject resolution efforts later on

   - Harbor negative feelings of exclusion

   - Choose to see the resolution as being inflicted upon them, which intensifies resentment and escalates passive-aggressive responses

4. Two-way communication is vital. Listen and ensure that everyone is heard. Ineffective listening only increases resentment and further exacerbates and aggravates the conflict. Restatement of communication is critical. There is a big difference between hearing and listening, and at this degree of conflict, hearing will get you into big trouble. Restating helps you to identify the root cause of the problem as well as clear up any misperceptions or misunderstandings on either part.

! **If two-way communication is not established or is allowed to break down, the conflict will quickly escalate to the first-degree.**

5. Acknowledge emotions and anger. Do not criticize or ridicule people for being angry or emotional. Calm them, do not judge them. Acknowledge the emotions and anger as very real and understandable. "I understand there is a lot of emotion in this for you. I'd like for us to work through the emotion and fix the problem."

6. Identify commonality. Build momentum by emphasizing areas of agreement. Rarely in conflict situations are there absolutely *no* issues of agreement. Regardless of the intensity of the conflict, there are some issues held in common. Identify those quickly and gain acknowledgment. When the points of agreement are identified, momentum is gained, and the contentious issues may begin to look less ominous.

7. Negotiate resolution agreements. Be very flexible on how you are going to achieve resolution. Be willing to allow the other side to win the "how," and save face. Allow yourself to be satisfied with the conclusion. Focus on the ultimate arrival at an acceptable outcome and be less concerned about the journey that gets you there.

8. Clarify agreements. Misunderstandings of resolution agreements can be deadly at this level, and selective listening, unfortunately, is very common (we tend to hear what we want to hear). Disagreements caused by any misunderstanding of agreements quickly escalate to first-degree conflict. Believing there is a resolution agreement and finding out it is different than we understood it to be obliterates trust, and regardless of the innocence of the misunderstanding, the results may be irreversible. Take whatever time is necessary to insure all parties have the same accurate understanding of the resolution agreement. (Put it in writing, and ask people to initial it.)

Mediation If interactive communication between the parties is not effective in resolving second-degree conflict, mediation becomes necessary. Mediation is the active involvement of an *objective* third party who is respected and perceived to be neutral by all parties involved. The role of the mediator is not to resolve the conflict but to stimulate and guide the parties through the process of resolution. The mediator is the tour guide through the rocks and whitewater of the river. The mediator does not paddle the boat but ensures that everyone arrives safely *and* enjoys the trip!

In the mediation process the mediator

- Balances the prevailing subjectivity with rational objectivity
- Manages the communication process
- Facilitates specific identification of the problem
- Helps to create resolution alternatives
- Develops the vision of what's next

Mediation is process-, not content-oriented. The mediator helps the parties in conflict to reach their own resolutions and agreements. Mediators suggest; they do not impose. Mediators facilitate; they do not control. Mediators unite; they do not divide.

Following are signs that mediation is necessary:

- Civility breaks down.
- Flexibility erodes (or is never established).
- A few major issues appear to separate the parties.
- Mutually acceptable resolutions appear to be impossible.
- Cliques or alignments become a major issue in the conflict.
- The parties are unable to reach an agreement on their own.
- The mutual willingness to resolve the solution appears to be threatened.

- The cause (subjectivity) begins to prevail over the substance (objective reasoning).

- The ongoing, unresolved conflict begins to have a negative impact on others, the organization, and/or overall productivity.

You will probably be called upon to mediate the conflict of others— perhaps your direct employees, your peers, or other people in the organization. Becoming an effective mediator certainly doesn't hurt your career development; it raises your visibility and provides a valuable service to the organization and everyone in it. The following guidelines assist in successful mediation. Some of these guidelines mirror those in the preceding section on interactive communication.

> ▶ **The role of a mediator is to stimulate the resolution process and not to dictate resolution.**

1. Establish and maintain your objectivity. You will not be an effective mediator if you are perceived to be an advocate or adversary of any party involved in the conflict.

2. Be willing to invest the time necessary to actively mediate the conflict. If any party senses you are not investing your full energy or are uncommitted to dedicating the appropriate amount of time, your efforts will be resented. Haphazard or disinterested mediation demeans the process and everyone involved in it. The participants will believe you are not taking the process seriously.

   Unfortunately, for many managers mediation is merely chastising employees and giving the problem back to them, saying: "You need to work this out for yourselves. Be adults and find some way to get over this. I'll get into it if you want me to, but no one will be happy if I do." That is *not* mediation; it is a threat of execution! Mediation requires active involvement, not implied threats or "tinkering" from a distance.

3. Invite all parties to identify their perceptions clearly in an acceptable manner.

   - Maintain dignity and respect at all times.

   - Separate opinion from fact.

   - Focus on one issue at a time.

   - Maintain present focus, give no history lessons.

   - Ask appropriate, clarifying questions for your own depth of understanding.

- Restate to each party their perception as you understand it. (Your restatement of the issues is extremely important because it allows all parties to hear the perceptions presented in a very clear, neutral, concise, emotionless delivery.) Frequently the mediator's restatement allows all parties to recognize they are really not very far apart. Helping to remove subjectivity and neutralizing the emotional content of everyone's perceptions are the most important tasks of the mediator.

- Check all facts and details. (Take nothing at face value. Your own independent verification is critical.)

Three key issues are to

- Verify the facts
- Verify the facts
- Verify the facts

Are you getting the message?

4. Identify all areas of commonality in agreement. Regardless of how inconsequential any points of agreement are, stress their importance. Inflate their value, if necessary, to clearly demonstrate the existence of common ground. Positive momentum is gained as agreements build. Capitalize on any success.

▶ **Creating commonality = successful mediation.**

5. Clearly identify the points of contention. State them in concise, unemotional terms. Minimize the number of points if at all possible. (Link closely related multiple points into one issue; this reduces the number of issues to be resolved.) Continually state your confidence that the points of contention can be successfully resolved. Compliment all parties on their depth of thought and their positive intent and motivation. (Avoid implying any negative judgment.) Acknowledge the value and equality of all parties involved.

6. Actively seek and expand resolution options. Do not allow discussions to narrow too early on any predetermined conditions of either party. Identify as many options as possible. While avoiding the absurd, encourage even the least likely options—there is strength in numbers. Brainstorm, insuring active and equal participation by all sides. Suggest your own creative options. Keep in mind you are not *imposing* your will; however, you are contributing your creativity.

At the beginning of the search for resolutions, yours may be the only options forthcoming. As momentum builds, participation will increase.

◆ Patience is a virtue.

An impatient mediator shuts down the resolution process very quickly. Be willing to take the appropriate time and show no frustration with the people or process.

7. Begin to narrow the focus of realistic options. Do not free-fall from multiple options to just one. You should manage the deletion of options through the process of elimination. Reassure all sides that you are still in discussion at this point. Nothing is cast in stone (but the concrete is starting to harden). They may react negatively if they perceive their favorable options are suffering early elimination. As you discard a favorable option of one side, it may be prudent to begin to dismiss an option favorable to the other side. If one side perceives unfair deterioration of their position, you may have a revolution on your hands!

8. Simultaneously identify the best option and outline the next step or segment of the journey. This is a balancing act for any mediator.

◆ The resolution should be seen as a beginning, not an ending.

If anyone leaves the mediation with the thought of "Oh well, it's over," the mediator has not done his or her job. Everyone must leave saying, "Okay, here is what I'm going to do next to make this happen. . . ."

Coupling the resolution to the next step lessens the blow to those who may be perceived to be losing or at least experiencing a less favorable outcome. It also helps those needing to save face.

9. Determine how agreements are to be monitored. Agree to serve as the watchdog of the agreement. (It is probably not wise to ask the contending parties to police each other.) Meet regularly to assess compliance and review results. Find something positive and celebrate it. Continually compliment and give positive recognition to all parties for their openness and willingness to seek resolution and to make it successful—it's their success, not yours.

Bad Attitude Employees and Second-Degree Conflict

This is an extremely critical level of conflict when dealing with bad attitude employees because most actually start conflict at this level. Those who demonstrate a must-win style of resolution go immediately to stage two. Not only must they win, but the other side must be defeated. When those who avoid and capitulate reach their limits, they explode the conflict into second degree (or higher). The goal is to contain the conflict here and not allow it to escalate.

▸ **Your skills at managing second-degree conflict are crucial to your success with bad attitude employees.**

The inability, or unwillingness, of bad attitude employees to differentiate between insignificant issues and those demanding attention assures that all conflict will be at least second degree. (There are no small fires, just four-alarm, raging infernos.)

Let's return to the example of Ann and Lisa on pages 111–112. If Ann and Lisa had not addressed their third-degree issues successfully, the conflict would have escalated and become more intense. Ann's feelings of anger and being taken advantage of would have grown. Her negative projections toward Lisa would have gotten progressively worse. "She is just a selfish and uncaring person. She doesn't care what she does to anyone else. She doesn't care how hard I have to work when she's not here. She doesn't care that people's paychecks may be delayed because she doesn't come to work." Fear of negative reaction by Lisa would begin to mount. "I can't say anything to her. If I do, she'll just do even less. She'll take more time off, and she won't do anything when she's here. I'll have to do it all. This just isn't fair. She's getting paid as much as I am, and I'm doing all of the work." Typically Ann would then begin to take the conflict to others. She would seek out people sympathetic to her cause, and criticize Lisa to them. (They can't possibly do anything about the conflict. Their silence or agreement would tend only to affirm Ann's position and she would become more deeply embedded in the second-degree conflict.) She would tell others, "Lisa's a bad person. You can't trust her. I may have to quit my job because of her. I just can't deal with her. She's really unfair. . . ."

Lisa, sensing a change in Ann, can't figure out what's going on. She realizes Ann is angry and knows their communication is breaking down; they aren't as close as they once were. She then takes the conflict to others telling them, "Ann used to be such a nice person; now she has changed. I can't talk with her any more. She is always angry. She is difficult to get along with. I dread coming to work because Ann has become so difficult. . . ." Factions begin to develop. We end up with Ann's side of the lunchroom and Lisa's side of the lunchroom, and tensions mount if one side is too friendly to the other.

They would develop an uneasy tolerance of each other that flares up at the slightest incident. They would begin to fight back with each other with petty responses like not communicating phone messages (especially personal ones), refusing to help each other on special tasks, not meeting the other person's deadlines, and so on.

Welcome to the world of second-degree conflict.

First-Degree Conflict

First-degree conflict is to be prevented at all costs. The best protection against the escalation to first-degree conflict is to deal effectively with second-degree conflict. (Avoiding second-degree conflict is a deadly managerial behavior.) If conflict reaches the first-degree stage, it must be dealt with immediately. Every minute it exists, it does irreparable damage to the organization and the people involved. Although the ultimate outcome may be bad, it is better to absorb the damage and move on than to allow the out-of-control buzzsaw to continue to inflict internal destruction.

First-degree conflict is very serious for two reasons. First, it is extremely difficult to resolve and probably demands influence from a third party. Second, the stakes are extremely high. The ultimate result may be one side separating from the organization. Frequently, all remaining parties take on an "enemy for life" mentality for the duration of their tenure.

The goals of the parties involved in first-degree conflict also shift and compound dramatically. Winning is no longer a singular issue. Winning now exists in tandem with the desire to hurt the other party. Self-interest takes on the righteous fervor of what is morally right. What is best for me (us) is what is best for the company (or the world). The merit of issues becomes lost in the principle of the thing or the bigger picture. "We are not dealing with a minor incident that took place in our department. We are dealing with what's right in the eyes of God!"

First-degree conflicts are frequently prolonged over an extended period of time. If not dealt with effectively, they do untold damage to the organization. They may result in the emergence of an underground negative culture. They inflict terminal damage on trust and commitment. Quality and service frequently become undeniable casualties, and performance takes a free-fall. Coming to work to do the job becomes secondary. Coming to work to inflict punishment to the other side becomes the primary daily motivation.

Symptoms

The hallmarks of first-degree conflict are

- Low potential for successful resolution due to escalation
- Lack of intention or skills to resolve the conflict

- The need for retribution and punishment overriding considerations of resolution

- Individuals or groups having a significant stake in prolonging the conflict

- Required third-party intervention

Emotions run high in first-degree conflict. However, they are highly controlled (not suppressed) and akin more to white heat than red heat. (White heat is hotter and much calmer.) The subjective nature of the positions taken in first-degree conflict tend to be totally emotion-based.

Strategies for Addressing First-Degree Conflict

Both strategies for successfully dealing with first-degree conflict, mediation and arbitration, have one thing in common—the involvement of an objective third party. The cardinal rule of first-degree conflict—get help!

Mediation   Mediation is usually a predictable necessity in any successful conclusion of first-degree conflict. There are two additional critical components to the mediation process at this level:

1. Lower the stakes. Acknowledge the conflict while reducing the ultimate consequence. "Let's acknowledge that we have a disagreement, and let's also realize this does not have to end with someone leaving the organization. This doesn't have to be that serious." By effectively lowering the stakes, the conflict may possibly diminish to second-degree. If those involved are anxious to avoid the ultimate worst case scenario, this may quickly calm the intensity.

2. Create the next step. In first-degree conflict, the conflictors tend to see resolution of the issues as an end. If the conflict is to have any possibility of ongoing positive solution, all parties involved must view resolution as a next logical step in a process; it must be seen as a beginning or interim step, not as a closing or ending. All parties (especially those who are perceived to have lost) must have a specific action plan for future activity. The mediator must make sure the conflictors leave the resolution with a clear understanding of what they do next. If this is not clear, they will brood over the results (or perhaps gloat or celebrate too exuberantly). If this beginning or continuation of journey can be instilled in the conflictors, it is possible to avoid ongoing resentment and passive-aggressive retaliation.

Arbitration   If efforts to mediate are not successful, arbitration becomes necessary. In arbitration the decisions of resolution are made by a third-party and imposed upon the parties involved. Obviously, the difference between mediation and arbitration is significant. Mediation utilizes guidance; arbitration turns the decision over to the third-party. (Marriage counseling is mediation—divorce court is arbitration.)

For arbitration to be successful, all sides must commit to the arbitration process and agree up front to accept the arbitrator's decision. In reality, this is rarely the case. The actual commitment tends to be, "I'll agree with the process if I win. If I don't win, I will view it as unfair." (The arbitrator becomes a traitor!) By its very nature, arbitration creates losers. There is a polarizing decision in favor of one or the other, and it takes real maturity to lose in arbitration and to continue to move forward with positive intentions.

Arbitration always brings surface resolution to the conflict. Whether the conflict is truly ended or the passive-aggressive, covert, underground activity explodes in escalation is always the critical question.

! **If you are involved in a first-degree conflict, do *not* attempt self-arbitration. If for no other reason, your lack of objectivity and obvious subjective perception may result in an unwise decision that may have future negative ramifications (if you make a dumb decision, you might get sued!).**

When managers are party to a first-degree conflict, by power of their authority, they may attempt to become both party to and ultimate arbitrator of the conflict. Typically, they look at all sides of the issue, theirs as well as the other parties' involved, and they objectively decide in their own favor. This is the equivalent of going to court and finding out the party you are in contention with is also the judge who will make the final decision. Do you think there might be some feelings of helplessness here? Do you think the employee may feel set up, not listened to, or exploited?

One simple rule of arbitration and mediation: They both require an objective third-party.

Bad Attitude Employees and First-Degree Conflict

♦ In first-degree conflict, everyone becomes a bad attitude employee.

Even people who are traditionally positive and willing to interact become disruptive and highly resistant at this stage. Typically, bad attitude employees achieve first-degree status much more quickly and may, in fact, actually begin conflict here.

Bad attitude employees' penchant for the personalization of conflict and the pervasiveness of the us against them (management or the world) mindset allows them to flourish and revel in first-degree conflict. They actively pursue alignments and engage in constant agitation to keep first-degree conflict alive. They realize (or fear) that resolution of such conflict could be detrimental to them, so they may prolong the agony to avoid the threatening conclusion.

The building resentment harbored by bad attitude employees and their tendency to avoid third-degree conflict often allows conflict to actually erupt or emerge at the first-degree stage. Remember, conflict does not have to escalate from third to second to first degrees, it can be "born" in the first-degree or leapfrog. While bad attitude employees may lack the skills or instincts to deal with third- and second-degree conflict, they instinctively possess the skills to escalate and manipulate first-degree conflict. Active prolongation is an appealing way for bad attitude employees to fight back against the manager or the organization. While they may take their activities underground in second-degree conflict, they overtly display their antagonisms in the first degree. There may be little or no attempt to even camouflage their activities at the first-degree level. They put their "stuff" right out on front street frequently. They enjoy the exposure!

Bad attitude employees may be content to stay at first-degree conflict indefinitely. Mediation or arbitration forces them out and presents opportunities for a successful outcome.

■ Conflict Assessment Checklist

How can you determine the degree of the conflict you are facing? Here is a quick assessment tool to help. Two or more affirmative responses indicate the conflict has probably escalated to the higher degree.

Third-degree conflict

1. Does the conflict appear to be workplace-driven and not influenced by issues from outside?   _____

2. Are individuals willing to discuss their perceptions and evaluate facts?   _____

3. Are individuals able to separate the "what" from the "who"?   _____

4. Are individuals focused on current events not historical issues?   _____

5. Is the communication in specific terms as opposed to general summarizations?   _____

6. Are all individuals willing to negotiate a solution?   _____

Second-degree conflict

1. Are individuals more competitive than cooperative? _____

2. Is there more emphasis on the "who" than the "what"? _____

3. Are individuals focused on winning as opposed to
   resolving? _____

4. Do individuals demonstrate a higher regard for personal issues than objective resolution? _____

5. Is the conflict beginning to spread to other people not
   directly involved? _____

6. Does there appear to be a disintegration of trust? _____

First-degree conflict

1. Has principle become more important than issues? _____

2. Are individuals demonstrating an extremely high regard
   for self and little or no regard for others? _____

3. Are individuals demonstrating an intention to hurt,
   punish, or gain retribution as well as to win the
   conflict? _____

4. Has individual interest become synonymous with what's
   best for the organization? _____

5. Is there a prevailing attitude that the others are enemies? _____

7 Turning Around Bad Attitude-Based Behaviors

In the next two chapters we will identify typical negative behaviors associated with bad attitudes and present specific successful strategies for neutralizing their effectiveness and limiting their influence on others. While this information is not intended to be all-inclusive, we will focus on the most common of these challenging behaviors.

Bad attitude employees have a half-filled glass of water. They *choose* to see it as half empty and then *choose* how to react to their perception. Seeing the glass as half empty validates their overall negative belief system. They selectively punish whoever they believe is responsible for the shortage in their glass.

Bad attitude employees are in total control of both their perceptions and their actions. Bad attitudes can be changed only by altering this inherent belief system, and you cannot change others' beliefs or perceptions. The bad attitude will be there as long as they want it to be!

Focus on the behavior of the bad attitude employees; it is something you *can* influence. You can establish appropriate boundaries and eliminate the perceived "payoffs" for their negative actions. If behavior is changed successfully, it is possible a change of attitude may follow.

In this chapter we look at and consider productive ways of dealing with people who exhibit four specific bad attitude behaviors that may well be the most disruptive of all.

- People who demonstrate hostility, anger, or out-of-control behaviors
- People who demonstrate negative nonverbal communication
- People who are defensive or take criticism very personally
- People who pursue negative confrontations

Do any of these behaviors look or sound familiar to you? Let's see how we can deal successfully with them.

▪ People Who Demonstrate Hostility, Anger, or Out-of-Control Behaviors

This behavior is manifested in various ways. It may be an overreaction to the problem of the moment or a hair-trigger, intense, emotional response intended to intimidate or inflict public embarrassment on the person who evoked the response. The behavior is intended to discourage others' input when they witness the emotional response. For some people, it is a learned behavior, and they use it successfully to achieve what they want. For others, it's an uncontrolled response, which may lend itself to serious incidents and may be indicative of significant personal problems.

It is important for you to deal with this anger and hostility effectively to reduce its frequency and intensity and to establish acceptable boundaries of workplace behavior. Left uncorrected, these responses tend to escalate in seriousness and unacceptability.

Symptoms

Early warning signs of escalating anger and hostility can be seen in three areas:

Physical
- Facial or neck muscles become rigid
- Posture becomes extremely erect
- Eyes dart quickly back and forth and then become extremely focused
- Face becomes flushed
- Teeth are clenched
- Fists clench and unclench

Auditory
- Speech becomes rapid-fire delivery or may become very slow and deliberate
- Voice becomes louder or may actually drop in intensity as anger mounts

Behavioral
- Moods abruptly change/hair-trigger
- There is pacing or physical agitation

- Aggressive nonverbal behaviors (slamming, pounding of fists on the desk, kicking inanimate objects, etc.) are acted out

> Robin works in an inbound call telemarketing center. The policy is that whoever takes the incoming call and writes the order gets credit for the sale and receives the commission. Robin perceives that even if she talked to a prospect six months ago, she should receive credit for the order no matter who writes it or when it is written. She surreptitiously reviews the sales logs to discover orders being stolen from her. Every time she finds a previous contact who has finally purchased, she explodes in anger at the person who wrote the order. She contends the circumstance, calls the salesperson a liar and a cheat, and demands credit for the order. (She denies looking through the sales log and alleges that she just happened to overhear the transaction.) She believes she is routinely being cheated out of sales credit and recites all of the previous questionable orders over the last five years every time she has a conversation with her boss to prove her point. Her peers are afraid of her, and people have quit to avoid having to deal with her behavior. She is always out-of-sorts and very distrustful and broods over everyone trying to cheat her. If someone asks for her help, she angrily refuses because of an order they stole two years ago—she holds grudges!
>
> Behaviors such as Robin's are a major issue, not only because of the frequency of their occurrence, but because of the potential seriousness of the outcome. While the causes for Robin's reactions may be numerous, deep, complex, and far beyond the scope of this book and your role as a manager to diagnose, the effective turnaround strategy applies regardless of where the anger and hostility come from.

Turnaround Strategy

The five-tiered strategy for dealing with people's anger and hostility is

- Acknowledge their perceptions and avoid personal, emotional involvement
- Neutralize their emotion
- Identify and diagnose the real problem
- Identify multiple options
- Agree on future actions (including possible consequences of repetitive incidents)

Acknowledge their perceptions and avoid personal emotional involvement   The first step is to gain control of the situation. Failure to control it early on only invites escalation and the potential for serious consequences. To gain control effectively, you must

- Acknowledge their perceptions

- Position yourself as a partner (or at least neutral)

- Avoid any immediate adversarial positions

- Keep your emotions under control

Your challenge is to accomplish these simultaneously!

Let's consider Robin and her behavioral response to orders being stolen. Since her peers have been unsuccessful in dealing with her, her boss must intervene. In this situation the initial response could be

- "I understand you're angry. Let's go somewhere and talk about it."

- "I can see that you're frustrated. Let's see if I can help you."

- "Obviously you are upset; let's talk about it."

> **!**   **Avoid at all costs any statements implying negative judgment or an adversarial relationship.**

Do not use statements such as

- "Stop acting that way. It's very childish."

- "You're wrong."

- "Just shut up and listen to me."

- "You don't understand what's happening here."

To maintain control you need to control your internal communication (monitor what *you* say to *you*). Frequently this is easier said than done. Position your own thoughts by saying to yourself

- "I'll calm this down now and deal with my issues later."

- "I'm not going to let them control me by matching their anger."

- "There is no statute of limitations on anger. I'll deal with mine later."

Do not let employees' behavior provoke your anger. Avoid responding in kind.

It is also important to control your physical response (monitor how you appear to them). Remember, when your anger flares, even if you don't show it, your body reacts physically. You experience what is commonly known as the "fight or flight" syndrome. You literally prepare yourself physically to respond. You may notice your body experiencing the same signs of escalating anger and hostility mentioned previously.

One excellent technique to defeat the physical reaction of "fight or flight" syndrome in yourself is to concentrate on controlling your breathing. Breathe through your nose as deeply as possible, expanding your chest while maintaining an upright posture. Exhale slowly through your mouth and repeat this process a minimum of five times. Done correctly, the person you are dealing with has no realization you are even manipulating your breathing. Done ineffectively, you take on the appearance of a panting dog! These simple techniques of positive internal communication and controlled breathing will help you to maintain physical and emotional control.

You also need to be aware of your physical proximity. Position yourself as close to the employee as possible while maintaining a comfortable, non-threatening distance. (Rule of thumb: no closer than eighteen inches and *no touching*).

▶ **Avoid any implication of physical threat or intimidation.**

Neutralize their emotion　After gaining initial control and moving the hostile person to a neutral location, begin to calm his or her emotions. Allow the person's response to subside. Do not attempt to reason while emotions remain high. Keep in mind that the person's anger is totally subjective. Objective reasoning from you will be meaningless and probably provocative.

! **Do not present this as a parent putting a child in time-out.**

Take Robin to your office, the conference room, or maybe outside for a walk. Distance her from the location of the event and the others involved; isolate her from an audience.

Say to Robin, "You obviously have a lot of feelings and energy wrapped up in this. Let's take a couple of minutes and see if we can't put things in perspective." Offer her a drink of water or coffee or just allow her a few moments to regain her composure. If appropriate, do this in private. However, keep bad attitude employees in the neutral location. If anyone is going to leave temporarily, it is you. Give them their privacy but stay close by. Do not allow them to revisit the site of the incident.

The appropriate response is to implement the communication techniques discussed earlier.

▶ **Put the fire *out* first; then address cause, responsibility, and future prevention.**

1. Demonstrate active verbal and nonverbal listening behaviors.

2. Maintain acceptable communication boundaries. Say to Robin, "I understand you're upset. I am anxious to help you, and we will treat each other and those not here to defend themselves with respect."

3. As the bad attitude employee expounds, ask short, nonthreatening questions for clarification. "Robin, are you sure your last contact with the customer was actually the first contact with us? Could someone else have actually talked with the customer before you?"

4. Summarize the bad attitude employee's statements.

Identify and diagnose the real problem   You cannot begin to propose alternatives or solutions until you know what is perceived to be the real problem. Even if you think you know what the problem is (as is probably the case with Robin), continue the dialogue until everyone agrees on the true issue.

There are three very important points to remember:

1. At this point, stay focused on issues. Do not allow yourself to be side-tracked by bad attitude employees' antics. Their behavior may be intended to distract or confuse you. (Robin will *not* want to discuss how she discovered the orders in question.)

2. The source of the problem may well be misperception of unmet expectations. The employee expected something to happen and when it didn't, he or she reacted. Was this expectation realistic? Was this expectation clear to the other people involved? Was this expectation actually unmet—could it have been met in a form different than what was anticipated? (Robin's problem is not really the stolen orders—it is her perception that the policy of how orders are credited is unfair to her. Her anger is misplaced on the other sales representative who stole her order! Her problem is with her boss and the policy.)

3. Break the bond of past events. Bad attitude employees' anger may be based on their perception of an accumulation and continuation of negative experiences. This current event is just one more straw on the camel's back, and the constant piling on is a major contributor to their escalating anger, hostility, and rage. Help them to see events as distinct and disconnected to past incidents. (Each order is a separate and distinct circumstance. The orders are not a link in a chain of conspiracy!)

Identify multiple options   Help employees move from their focus on an event to considering options for a solution. Keep in mind, they are problem identifiers, not problem solvers. The solution may be helping Robin and the other salespeople understand the significance of making their contacts aware of the importance of asking for them personally when they call to place an order, no matter when that might be.

◆ **Past focus feeds anger. Future focus increases control.**

The traps to avoid:
- **Focusing on only one option as a solution**
- **Fixing the problem for employees**
- **Blaming or criticizing employees for the current situation**

As we discussed in the chapter on conflict resolution, it is imperative to move bad attitude employees from conditions or fixed preconceived positions to considering successful outcomes. Their anger and hostility drives inflexibility. If possible, help them to identify at least three options. Avoid narrowing to only one option too early. Use questions such as

- "What would fix this for you?"
- "What would be an acceptable solution for you?"
- "What's the best thing/worst thing that could happen?"

Another effective alternative is to play the hypotheticals.

- "In a perfect world, what would the perfect solution be?"
- "If you had a magic wand, what solution would be best for you or everyone involved?"
- "If there were no impediments at all to solving this—no budget, time considerations, etc.—what would the ideal solution be?"

These questions are intended to stimulate the thought process and challenge creativity. It would be appropriate to ask Robin, "How can we avoid this happening in the future?"

You can also invite bad attitude employees to identify the impediments or barriers to the solution.

- "What do you see standing in the way of a solution?"
- "What makes this difficult to resolve?"
- "What has to change before we can work this out?"

Once you have identified multiple options, begin the process of elimination to identify the one most realistic, doable solution that serves everyone's needs. A very simple pro/con exercise for each solution may be helpful.

Solution Option #1 (Identify the solution)

Pros	*Cons*
1. _____	1. _____
2. _____	2. _____
3. _____	3. _____
4. _____	4. _____
5. _____	5. _____

It will probably be necessary for you to be very active here. The angry, hostile person will undoubtedly be focused on the con side. He or she will be able to tell you why something won't work. It will be up to you to show the upside. The exception to this will be the option that best accomplishes the employee's immediate needs. He or she will be able to list many pros and no cons to that option. You may have to help to identify the actual cons. The employee may be so emotionally attached to this option, he or she is unable to legitimately view any downside.

Once the process of elimination is completed, implement the result and move forward.

Agree on future actions   Agree on the specifics and logistics of the selected option.

- Who
- When
- What
- "How will we know?"
- Where

Agree on future corrections to avoid any repeat incidents of extreme anger and hostility. What are you going to do differently? This may include agreements for Robin to come to you first before displaying her anger to her peers, to seek counseling, or to use a conflict-resolution model with others to avoid the escalation to anger.

Clearly agree on established future behavior boundaries and consequences. Clearly identify the behavior that is and is not considered acceptable. Identify legitimate expressions of disagreement versus unacceptable demonstrations of anger and hostility. Emphasize to Robin that reviewing the sales logs without management approval is *not acceptable* and she will be held accountable if she continues to do so. There will be a consequence.

Escalating anger

What should you do when anger/hostility erupts out of control or presents potential danger?

> **Extreme hostility and rage can result in a physical attack on managers or coworkers. When the escalation reaches infuriation/aggression, take action to avoid further eruption. Do not attempt problem solving or resolution. Your only intent is to defuse the emotion and calm the agitation. However, once calmed, the behavior must be addressed and corrected, and the boundaries of unacceptability must be clearly defined. Delay or avoidance in dealing with the substantive issues results in further escalation and a detonation of this emotional time bomb.**

The following figure shows the steps of escalating anger, from signs of irritation and annoyance at the lowest step, all the way to hostility and rage at the top of the steps.

What should you do when the potential for danger flares? Along with the techniques described earlier, if the person's reaction intensifies to a level of threatening safety or security,

- Distance the person from others; move him or her to a neutral environment, or move observers or others involved out of the area. *Note:* If necessary, have one or two people remain to assist you. If the situation becomes physically threatening, call for security immediately.

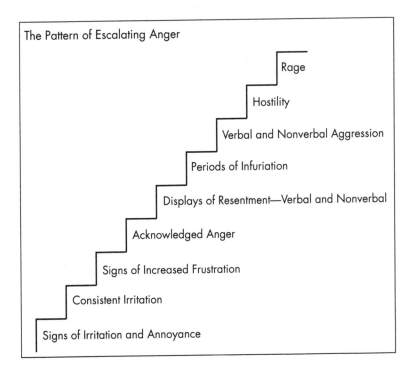

The Pattern of Escalating Anger

Rage

Hostility

Verbal and Nonverbal Aggression

Periods of Infuriation

Displays of Resentment—Verbal and Nonverbal

Acknowledged Anger

Signs of Increased Frustration

Consistent Irritation

Signs of Irritation and Annoyance

- Change posture. If standing, both of you sit. If stationary, begin to walk (outside if possible, not in populated areas).

- Concentrate on not showing anger or fear in your facial expression or body language. Make no sudden or threatening gestures.

- Avoid the person's physical space. (Increase your physical distance to a minimum of 24 inches with people who are potentially dangerous. *No touching.*) Do no allow the person to move menacingly close to you.

- Use a nonthreatening, conciliatory tone of voice. Lower your voice; don't raise it.

- Choose words that will not be perceived as threatening or provoking.

- Agree with the person as much as possible. Ignore any potentially antagonistic statements. Do not respond to any provocation.

- Maintain your personal control at all times.

Threats

Threats can be an issue with employees who are demonstrating anger and hostility.

Workplace threats are to be taken very seriously. Threats run the gamut from passive references of quitting to allusions of sabotage to statements of impending physical violence.

▶ **Regardless of the nature, threats are not to be tolerated.**

In general, there are two types of threats:

- Benign threats, insinuating passive behavioral responses (quitting, refusing overtime, slowing production, etc.)

- Activating threats implying physical threats to people, process (sabotage), or facilities

Benign threats   Benign threats tend to take two forms—direct or implied.

1. Direct

    - "I'll quit if I don't get my raise."

    - "If you are not going to accept my recommendations, I might as well transfer to another facility."

    Confront direct threats immediately—call the employee's bluff. Your response:

    - "Should I assume that you are officially giving your two-week notice? If so, I regretfully accept."

- "Should I assume that this is a request for transfer? As you know, I don't make those decisions. However, I will help you begin the paperwork process."

2. Implied

   The threat is unclear and open-ended. Implied threats are intended to be ominous.

   - "If I don't get my raise, I'll really have to reconsider my future here with the company."
   - "If I don't get the lead position on that project, I'll really have to decide whether all my hard work and dedication is worth continuing."

   Challenge these implied threats. Flush them out by insisting on clarification. They will either escalate to direct threats or be rescinded. Your response:

   - "Tell me what 'you'll have to reconsider your position' means. Is that a threat to quit?"
   - "Tell me what 'you'll have to reconsider your hard work and dedication' means. Are you implying less future effort or less quality?"

If the threat becomes direct, respond immediately. If the statement is rescinded, establish future boundaries: "I'm glad we cleared that up so we won't have any misunderstandings. Please be aware that I take threats very seriously. In the future, I will treat any such threat as an actual statement of intent and will act accordingly."

▶ **Benign threats, avoided, ignored, or unchallenged, become organizational malignancies.**

Activating threats   There are three types of activating threats:

1. Direct

   - "I'll be sure that you never do that to me or anyone else again."
   - "You'll be the sorriest person on earth for what you just did."

2. Third party (threats made through another person)

   - "He will be sorry he ever did that to me."
   - "I'll get even with her if it's the last thing I do."

3. Controlling (intended to influence pending decisions and actions) and epitomized by "If you do, I'll do."

   - "If you do that, I may put you out of business."

- "If you do that, something terrible just might happen to the production line."

Activating threats are very serious and must be reacted to immediately. The possibility of such threats is to be anticipated by the organization with a well thought-out, pre-existing policy formulated and officially put in place. It is not uncommon for such activating threats to result in the implementation of the disciplinary process or immediate dismissal (depending upon the seriousness of the threat). Such a policy

- Must be a combined effort with integrated influence from all levels of management, human resource professionals, organizational psychologists, security specialists, etc.

- Must clearly state the organization's unequivocal reaction to activating threats and the consequence to any employee making such threats.

- Must be in writing, distributed to all employees, and updated and redistributed on a yearly basis.

- Must be made part of the hiring orientation. It is presented along with other important policies regarding weapons, drugs or alcohol, and conditions of employment such as attendance, sick leave, vacation time, etc.

■ People Who Demonstrate Negative Nonverbal Communication

Communication is not just verbal. It is estimated that words and voice inflection comprise less than 50% of the actual communications people send. Most of the messages we communicate are actually nonverbal. Whether it is to ask someone to pass the salt, pour a cup of coffee, sign a document, or to indicate you cannot hear what a person is saying, communication can be very effective without using words at all.

Symptoms
Disruptive behaviors and resistance are frequently communicated through nonverbal gestures.

- Rolling the eyes
- Looks of contempt
- Gestures of disgust
- Slamming doors
- Kicking wastebaskets
- Punching walls

These gestures are effective, cannot be proven, and can always be denied. For many people who cannot easily articulate their feelings, nonverbal communication becomes a great equalizer. We all say things nonverbally that we would not or could not say verbally. Negative nonverbal communication is safe. Teenagers make an art form out of expressing their displeasures and rejections nonverbally. In the workplace, people often abuse their peers or their boss nonverbally. If you do not know how to effectively deal with this communication, these attacks go unanswered and uncorrected—they continue and intensify.

> Tanya has a pattern of acting out her frustrations nonverbally. When she is unhappy about being asked to do something or to correct an error, she doesn't say anything but she begins her "slammin' and jammin'" routine. Books, pads, and doors are slammed, drawers jammed closed, wastebaskets kicked, and her facial expressions show extreme contempt (eyes rolling, mouth snarling, etc.). When asked what's wrong, she responds, "Oh, *nothing* is wrong; everything is just *fine*." She wants the world to know she is unhappy, but she won't risk verbalizing whatever she is unhappy about.

Turnaround Strategy

How can you effectively address this barrage of negative nonverbal communication? There is a very specific three step technique.

- Use the positive confronting statement
- Describe the behavior
- Summarize the perceived conclusion

Use the positive confronting statement   "Tell me what it means when . . ." (If this sounds too aggressive, use the alternative phrase, "Help me understand what it means when . . .")

Describe the behavior   Give bad attitude employees a factual summary of your observations. This should not be done in a sarcastic, condescending, or mimicking manner. "Tanya, help me understand what it means when I ask you to . . . , and I observe rolling of the eyes, slamming of a legal pad, and stomping out." Please note: This is *description,* not an *attack.* You are describing your observation; you are not accusing.

At this point, it is the bad attitude employee's turn to respond. He or she may deny, explain, or apologize. How the other person responds really doesn't matter. The response is something out of your control. You cannot influence or control it, so don't hold yourself responsible for it. Don't worry about the response. Contrary to what you might assume, a very high percentage of the time the response contains an apology or explanation. The reason is very simple—the person just got caught! He or she may not have been aware of the nonverbal message, and even if it was intentional, the person isn't very comfortable with verbalizing it, or it would have been said to begin with. People who intentionally communicate this way want to send the message without being held accountable. Your use of this assertive positive confrontation technique lets them know their communication was received loud and clear.

Tanya's response might be

- "I guess I'm just feeling frustrated, and that's how I show it."
- "I don't know what you're talking about. I didn't do any of that."
- "I didn't realize I did that, and if I did, I probably shouldn't have."
- "It means I'm tired of constantly being interrupted and asked to do other things and then criticized because I don't complete my original tasks."

Regardless of the response, move to part three of this technique.

Summarize the perceived conclusion   Let the employee know the conclusion you could have drawn from the nonverbal communication. Let him or her know the impact of the messages being sent without actually accusing.

Your response: "Tanya, I'm really glad I asked. I could have assumed that you were resistant to doing what I asked or that we were having a problem I wasn't aware of. I might have assumed you don't think the problem is important enough to help correct. Since none of these are accurate, I'm glad we avoided any misunderstanding."

Effective use of this technique:

- Invites discussion/exploration as opposed to defensiveness
- Focuses the discussion on content and not emotion
- Raises employees' awareness of their nonverbal communication
- Indicates to employees that their behavior is not an acceptable way to communicate and will be brought to their attention when it is witnessed (You are establishing limits and boundaries.)

Avoid statements such as

- "Well you acted like you didn't know how to do it."
- "You react as if you don't think it's very important."
- "You were offended by my asking you to do it."
- "You hurt my feelings with your response."

All of these statements are accusatory. Your accusations can be denied—your summaries cannot.

! **Using this technique one time only will not yield long-lasting behavior change. However, consistent effective application will result in employees'**

self-monitoring and self-awareness of their nonverbal communication. If for no other reason, Tanya will modify her nonverbals just to avoid hearing "tell me what it means" from her boss!

When should this technique be used?   If the behavior is occasional or is a one-time occurrence, you are probably wise to allow it to go unnoticed. (Everyone is allowed to have a bad day.) If it is an emerging or established pattern, allowing the behavior to go unchallenged only invites it to intensify and spread to others. Your lack of response signals to everyone that you accept and are willing to tolerate the negative behavior. If you avoid using this technique because you're afraid of a negative or intimidating response from your employees, you are giving them permission to be disrespectful.

> **Consistent, negative nonverbals are visible signs of disrespect.**

■ People Who Are Defensive

People with bad attitudes are experts at demonstrating defensive behaviors. They tend to take any comments or questions about their behavior or performance as a personal attack. Even the most innocent statement on your part is perceived by them to be personal criticism.

Symptoms

Typical defensive behaviors include

- Blaming other things and other people
- Justifying or rationalizing their action
- Denying responsibility
- Personal attacks
- Pleading innocent to crimes they haven't been charged with

> Whenever Billy is asked about a problem or when any attempt is made to discuss his performance, he becomes very defensive. He starts blaming others and denying responsibility before his boss even finishes talking. "It's not my fault, it was John who started the problem." Typically he begins to accuse his boss of picking on him. "I've seen you and Andy and everybody else around here doing this same thing. Why are you picking just on me? It's not fair." Any attempts to talk to Billy end up in his going off on tangents and getting upset; nothing ever gets resolved. He frequently pouts when the conversation is over and does even less work than usual. His boss is so frustrated with his behavior, she avoids any kind of discussion that might set him off.

When Billy is approached about an incomplete or poorly done task, he becomes "righteously indignant." He proclaims how hard he works, all the years of service he has put in, and how he is the first one there in the morning and the last one to go home at night. He challenges you to name one person who works harder than he does. The question about the task becomes lost in his sea of denial, indignation, and bobbing and weaving. The Billys of the world are experts at blurring the lines of accountability and distorted defensive reasoning. You are asking him about something he didn't do, and he is pleading innocent to other crimes you haven't accused him of. Your question has nothing to do with how hard he thinks he works or how many hours he puts in, but that's where he leads the discussion.

These and many other of Billy's defensive behaviors are mere *tactics* in the pursuit of one overall grand strategy.

▶ **The grand strategy of all defensive people is to "change the agenda."**

When defensive people are not comfortable with the current topic of discussion, they will do whatever they can to change the agenda. Billy doesn't want to talk about the uncompleted task, so he takes the discussion elsewhere. It is an effective way of deflecting responsibility, accountability, and acknowledgment.

Causes

Why do we experience so much defensive behavior in the workplace today? Why are there so many Billys? While the reasons are probably too numerous to summarize, consider the following:

- People respond defensively when they perceive they are being attacked.

- Low self-esteem contributes to feelings or perceptions of weakness, and defensive behavior helps to keep these weaknesses undercover.

- Fear of exposure or disclosure. People react defensively when they sense their weaknesses are about to be uncovered. They do not want people to see on the outside what they believe to be the truth about themselves on the inside.

Defensive behavior is intended to distort others' perceptions of bad attitude employees. First let's discuss what you *cannot* do with defensive people, and then let's consider an effective turnaround technique.

! **Three things you *cannot* do with defensive people when they are attempting to change the agenda—agree, disagree, or ignore.**

1. You cannot *agree* with the issues they raise. If you agree with their statements, the discussion is obviously over and they have won. Interestingly, their behavior is not really intended to elicit your agreement. Billy doesn't expect you to agree with his response, but he will accept the agreement if you will give it to him.

2. You cannot *disagree* with their issues. You cannot argue, discredit, or tell them they are wrong, and that's exactly what their behavior is designed to elicit from you. They are trying to provoke you (and most of them are very good at it). Defensive people actually *want* the argument. Billy wants you to defend yourself or dispute his hard work or number of hours. Why? Once you begin to argue or disagree with him, the agenda has been successfully changed. You are now talking about *his* issues, not yours. Billy will debate you all day as long as the discussion is not centered on the issue where he senses vulnerability.

   Disagreeing, arguing, or contending with the defensive person is the trap most managers fall into. We allow them to distract us and change the agenda. How many times has this happened with your version of Billy?

3. You cannot *ignore* the issues of defensive people. If you ignore what they say, they first assume you did not hear them, and they will then restate their positions louder or even more forcefully. If you ignore their issues a second time, they know they've got you! For some reason, you are ducking them, and they will continue to pound you until they force you to react.

Turnaround Strategy

The key to dealing with defensive people is effectively maintaining control of the agenda by *acknowledging and refocusing*. Acknowledge their issues and refocus them on yours: "Billy, if you would like to discuss what John has done, I will be happy to have that discussion with you as soon as we bring this issue to conclusion." Or, "If you believe you are being treated unfairly, I will be happy to have that discussion with you as soon as we determine what we are going to do about this current problem." The purpose of this strategy is to acknowledge the issue without malice or judgment and put the focus back on your issue. You are stating in a powerful way that the employee's issue is real and you are willing to discuss it. However, the issue will become item number two on the agenda; it will never become item number one. The person is skilled at deflecting your issues and inserting his or hers. Effective use of this acknowledge and refocus technique denies the other person the control.

Interestingly, the effective use of this technique extinguishes the defensive behavior rather quickly. When you successfully use this technique two or three separate times in succession, the behavior tends to go away. Defensive people are *not* stupid people. Once Billy realizes his behavior is not working, he stops using it. (He may find some other exotic way to drive you crazy, but he *will* stop acting defensively.)

Once you have satisfactorily addressed your issue, offer to discuss theirs. Rarely do bad attitude employees want to continue the discussion. They really have nothing to talk about—their issues are usually bogus. They were intended to distract you, and when they weren't successful, there was nothing to discuss!

A word of caution: The first few times you try it, the acknowledge and refocus technique will probably be unsuccessful. You are a beginner; Billy has been doing this his whole life. He is better at it than you are! Do not be concerned about your initial lack of success. Practice on him. If your initial attempts at dealing with this behavior are unsuccessful, who cares? What you have been doing so far hasn't been successful, so what's a few more losses? Practice makes perfect! This technique requires practice and patience. It is simple and effective but not necessarily easy.

■ People Who Pursue Negative Confrontations

These bad attitude employees seem to have a perpetual chip on their shoulder. They believe they have a right to say anything they want, and no one, especially their boss, has any right to stop them. These people believe the constitutional guarantee of freedom of speech has their name on it, but woe to anyone who talks back to them in the same way. People such as this frequently absolve themselves of any responsibility to treat others with dignity or respect. Personal attack is their forte.

Symptoms
These employees frequently preface their statements with a qualifying statement such as

- "I'm just an honest person."
- "I just like to tell it like it is."
- "I'm only telling you this for your own good."

These qualifying statements are perceived to make it okay to devastate others with personal attack or criticism. Disrespect and disregard for others are habitual, common occurrences.

Like many other bad attitude employees, these people are quick to inflict public embarrassment on others, sometimes even believing that to do so is cute or entertaining. Their negative confrontations are usually done in front of others.

These bad attitude employees demonstrate an innate inability to prioritize or put things into the proper perspective. If it's important to them, then it should be important to the rest of the world, and they have no regard for the perceptions of others.

Causes

There are a number of factors contributing to this bad attitude-driven behavior.

- These people perceive themselves to be realistic (not negative or possessing a bad attitude) and believe they know what the world is really like. They want others to be sure to see things their way. They may be on a mission to correct the "rose-colored glasses" outlook of all the foolish people around them.

- They may be cruel people who, under the guise of just being honest or telling it like it is, are masquerading their intention to inflict pain.

- They may be demanding attention. The only way to get this attention is by acting out and challenging everyone and everything.

There are similarities between this behavior and a schoolyard bully. These people may be willing to confront things publicly in front of a crowd, but they would not be willing to do so one-on-one. Their willingness to create a scene or public embarrassment is a weapon they use to control others and get what they want. This behavior establishes superiority and borders on intimidation. Other employees refrain from provoking or contending with them to avoid their negative reaction. This controlling behavior can be very effective. Any reluctance to challenge their actions allows them to become more and more disruptive.

The successful teaching and implementation of conflict resolution skills, as discussed in Chapters 5 and 6, will give other employees and managers effective skills and models to use in dealing with this behavior.

Turnaround Strategies

While the strategies for dealing with negative confronters are similar to ones already discussed with other bad attitude behaviors, it is helpful to understand why they are used (similar tactics for different reasons).

It is important to establish barriers and limits with negative confronters.

The Do Nots

- Do not attempt to stifle or silence bad attitude employees. They will howl with indignation at the suppression of their rights.

- Do not subject them to ridicule, derision, or embarrassment; it only escalates the behavior to anger and hostility (violence may not be out of the question). Saving face is of great significance to negative confronters.

- Do not tell them they are wrong.

- Do not fall into the trap of arguing.

The Dos

- Do insist that confrontations be dealt with in private; do not allow them to play to the crowd. They will only become more intense if they feel support, shock, or astonishment from the people around them.

- Do insist that any discussion maintain dignity and respect. Allow no comments to degenerate to personal attack.

- Do insist on the use of assertive I- and we-based communication. Avoid the accusatory, blaming, you-based aggressive communication.

- Do validate their input. Communicate your appreciation (not agreement) of their ideas and the value of their contribution. You are always open to seeing things from a different angle and appreciate their willingness to help you do that.

- Do broaden their communication options and future alternatives. Help them to identify alternative options, other than negative confrontation, for addressing their issues in the future. Teach alternative communication skills.

- Do identify consequences of future confrontational behavior.

Do not hesitate to impose boundaries on behavior; enforce what is acceptable and what "crosses the line."

! If this behavior is *consistently* directed toward management or leadership, it becomes insubordination, which we will address in Chapter 10.

In our next chapter, we broaden our discussion to consider nine additional bad attitude-based behaviors.

8   Turning Around More Bad Attitude-Based Behaviors

Larry consistently criticizes the boss behind his back. He never speaks out in team meetings, but as soon as the meeting is over, he tells everyone what an idiot their team leader is and how none of his ideas will ever work.

Claudette is always afraid that something bad is about to happen. Although there is no basis in fact for any of it, she is convinced that she is about to be fired and her job is about to be eliminated. Things have been going good for too long—it just can't last!

Howard's favorite words are "won't" and "didn't." He has been with the company forever, and any new idea that surfaces will be greeted by his predictable response of, "five reasons why it can't possibly work." He is also quick to point out that there are really *no* new ideas. Everything has already been thought of, tried, and failed, and the only thing that works is his way, "the way we've been doing it for years around here."

Gunther throws temper tantrums. If he doesn't get his way, he yells, bangs his fist on his desk, and accuses everyone of never listening to him or letting him do it his way. (Some people actually swear they have seen his lower lip curl.) If he could take his ball and go home, he would.

Do any of these behaviors seem familiar?

In this chapter, we will address people who exhibit the following nine specific behaviors:

- People who spread the poison of their negative perceptions
- People who communicate in negative, exaggerated patterns
- People who vocalize narrow, personalized, self-serving beliefs
- People who fear the inevitable impending doom
- People who become the "troll" on the highway to change

- People who demonstrate inappropriate emotions
- People who distort reality and facts
- People who pave the "one-way street"
- People who complain

We will present effective responses with a high potential for turning these behaviors around. People using these behaviors will respond positively when you remove the perceived payoff. When the behaviors become ineffective, they diminish dramatically.

■ People Who Spread the Poison of Their Negative Perceptions

Poison spreaders are those who take their issues of anger, distrust, unhappiness, or resentment to others with the intent of spreading the infection or "taking them down" also. People who spread the poison are driven by "I am unhappy; therefore, everyone will be unhappy." They could care less about the effect they have on others. Misery loves company, and they are always looking for company.

Symptoms

Poison spreaders will support, or at least remain neutral on, issues discussed openly in the presence of management (in groups, team meetings, and so on). However, they quickly become adversarial in private discussions with their peers. As a manager, you will often see employees huddled together in quiet conversations that obviously change topics or end abruptly when you appear.

These bad attitude employees covertly build support for their personal issues by linking them to the past toxic issues of others. "The boss won't let me leave early to watch my son play baseball. It's just like last year when you had to work overtime when your relatives were in town. It's just not fair."

Poison spreaders frequently entice others to pick up the standard of battle while continuing to stay in the background themselves. Typically they are seen urging others to go fight. "I'll be right behind you, supporting you by holding your coat." If you have level-headed employees who seem to go off the deep end in pursuing a workplace cause, it's probably a safe bet that a poison spreader is urging them on.

When things seem to be going well but there is an ongoing current of unrest, look to the poison spreaders. It is likely they are keeping things stirred up.

Turnaround Strategies

Dealing with this behavior is very challenging because it cannot always be proven or verified with documented evidence. Poison spreaders frequently operate undercover. How can we shed some light on their activities? One of the best ways is through prevention. There are three levels of prevention.

General prevention   Meet the issue head-on in team or departmental meetings. Acknowledge that people taking their individual issues to others is a very predictable human behavior, and while not necessarily done to harm others intentionally, it has some significant downsides. This general acknowledgment and discussion make the group aware of your knowledge of the talk that's going on. It also emphasizes the negative and selfish motives of the poison spreaders and hopefully makes the group less receptive to their messages.

When employees take their dissatisfaction issues to their peers, it does not result in resolution. Peers are not in a position to help solve the problems or to make changes. It is merely a futile exercise in venting. While blowing off steam is necessary and helpful from time to time, it spreads the poison of discontent to others. Problems can only be fixed by taking them to those who can help solve them. Venting to peers is a low risk and low payoff behavior because it will never result in anything good being accomplished, and there is no accountability or responsibility.

◆ **Venting is problem identification, not problem solving.**

Training   Training your employees to defend themselves from the poison spreader may be one of the most effective actions you can take. Poison spreaders are frequently effective because people do not know how to fend them off. Hikers should be taught what they should do if bitten by a snake in the woods. Employees should be taught what they should do if bitten by a poison spreading snake in the workplace. People typically respond with silence; they just listen politely. The poison spreaders interpret this silence as agreement and intensify their vitriol in response to this perceived encouragement. When employees receive specific training on how to deal assertively with the workplace snake, they can protect themselves individually and stop the spread of the toxin.

> Consider our friend Larry:
> He approaches one of his teammates, Becky, and begins to spread his poison about their boss. "Hey, Becky, how's it going? Let me tell you what our idiot boss did yesterday when you weren't here.

You won't believe how stupid his latest trick was. He forgot to order the replacement parts for the printer, and the whole department was shut down for two hours until the parts could be found. He doesn't have a clue as to how this place should really be run. I can't stand it here. I don't know why I just don't go out and get another job."

How can Becky learn to respond? She can learn a very effective two-step technique called "the deer in the headlights response."

1. Becky uses this phrase:

    "Larry, I don't disagree with everything that you have said." Larry has no idea what this means. He is not sure if Becky agrees or disagrees, if she is a friend or a foe. He will pause momentarily to try to figure it out and will look at Becky with that blank stare of a trembling deer caught in the glaring headlights of an oncoming vehicle. His momentary pause allows Becky to seize control of the conversation.

2. Becky quickly adds her positive response. "And I'm really swamped right now. Let's get together around 4:00. I'll come to your office; we'll get a cup of coffee and talk." While Becky will probably avoid Larry like the plague at 4:00, this technique allows her to fend off his poison before it consumes or disrupts her. It is a successful way to neutralize and silence Larry without breaching her working relationship with him. He eventually learns that when he comes to Becky to vent, there is no receptive audience. He probably thinks she has a problem, but Becky doesn't have to continue to absorb Larry's ever-present toxicity.

Another effective technique is to teach Becky to use assertive I- and we-based responses and to avoid aggressive, negative you-based messages. Becky's intent is to stop the spreading of poison without further escalating Larry's negativity. She can say the following: "Larry, *I'm* having a problem. Sometimes *I* feel that when *we* get together all *we* ever talk about are all of the bad things going on around here. Whether *I* agree with you is really not the issue; *I* am just tired of the problems always being the topic of conversation. *I* need a break. Could *we* agree that *we* will talk about anything other than all of that ongoing garbage? *I* just don't want to continue to stew in those juices."

This assertive message does not blame Larry; it makes him and Becky equal partners in the communication. It also allows her to control the agenda without offending him.

Larry's poison may not always be directed toward management or leadership. He may approach Becky to talk about other employees behind their backs, employees who are not there to defend themselves. He will not address the person he is having a problem with; instead he goes to Becky, and she cannot possibly help or solve the problem. He merely wants to complain, vent, or vilify. Talking the problem over with the person involved would require Larry to shift from problem identification to problem solving, and, to the Larrys of the world, problem solving is like sunshine to a vampire!

Helping employees to learn these techniques equips them with effective self-defense skills to fend off the attacks of poison spreaders.

Personal awareness   If you have reason to believe employees are spreading poison, it is appropriate for you to confront them directly about your perceptions. You will probably have *no* evidence, *no* facts, and *no* corroborative witness willing to cooperate. (Other employees may have come to you concerning the poison spreader, but they are reluctant to serve as actual witnesses.) You will be talking about your perceptions without documentation or proof. Your goal is to make employees aware that you know what is going on and to help them understand how they are being perceived negatively by others.

You may approach Larry yourself. "Sometimes I sense you may be unhappy about something but seem reluctant to bring it to me. Instead I think you may be taking it to other employees. It may be to stir them up or perhaps to get them to support your position. Let me share a couple of things with you. First, they can't help you—only I can. Second, if you are unhappy, please bring your issues to me. I won't guarantee a particular response; however, I will guarantee my willingness to listen and do whatever is reasonable to work things out. Third, don't become a source of negativity to your peers. At any given moment, we all have reasons to be upset about our jobs. There is no such thing as a perfect boss or a perfect place of employment. If we are experiencing an unhappiness of the moment, it doesn't give us the right to take it to other people and bring them down with us. We are very unfair to others when we take our issues to them with no regard for their personal reaction. I would not want others to perceive you to be someone who selfishly brings them down with no concern for them. Nobody wants to have that type of reputation."

Bad attitude employees will probably show no indication of acknowledgment, agreement, or understanding; however, this approach sheds some light on the behaviors they may believe are hidden from your view. It's the proverbial wake-up call!

It may also be appropriate for you to meet privately with the employees on the receiving end of the poison. Without being accusatory, let them know your awareness of what's happening and what's being said. Encourage them to talk. Let them know what options are open to them if the poison becomes disruptive. Just knowing you are aware of the circumstances will encourage them to distance themselves from the poison spreader.

> **!** Do not make employees feel as if you want them to inform or rat on their peers—that puts them in a very difficult no-win situation.

■ People Who Communicate in Negative, Exaggerated Patterns

People with bad attitudes frequently use distorted phrases to communicate. They tend to see things in the absolutes of black and white or hot and cold—there is no middle ground.

Symptoms

The symptoms of this bad attitude are usually heard. These bad attitude employees tend to communicate in phrases such as the following:

- "This *always* happens to me."
- "You *never* say this to anyone else."
- "This company *never* gets things right."
- "This gets screwed up *every* time."

These communicated symptoms generally are unequivocal absolutes, and it is imperative that you challenge them.

Turnaround Strategy

The most effective technique for dealing with distorted communication is to immediately challenge the distortions with whatever factual data is available.

▶ Unchallenged means confirmed.

> **▷** Jack stormed into Sally's office to complain about an error on his paycheck. "My check is wrong *again*," he declared. "This happens *every* week. The payroll department *always* messes up my check. *Everyone* in that department is incompetent. I am sick and tired of my check *constantly* being wrong."
>
> Upon investigation, Sally discovered Jack's check was, in fact, in error. This was the second time in ten weeks that a mistake had been made on his check. Sally was upset to learn there was a 20%

error rate in Jack's compensation. The payroll department was instructed to issue a corrected check immediately, and she returned to meet with Jack to explain the circumstance. "Let me share with you what I have discovered. You are correct; your check is wrong. I have instructed the payroll department to issue a check immediately for the right amount. While we are waiting for the new check, I would like to discuss with you some of the things that were said. This was actually the second time in ten weeks that we have made an error in your check. Under no circumstances is a 20% error rate in your check, or anyone else's, acceptable. We will take the necessary steps to correct that problem. However, two errors in ten checks is not *every* check, and they are not *always* wrong. It does not happen *every* week. In fact, eight out of ten checks were correct, and *everyone* in the payroll department is not incompetent. We will work hard to avoid future errors. However, if they do happen, bring them to my attention immediately, and let's all keep them in the proper perspective."

If Sally had merely corrected the problem, apologized, and sent Jack on his way, he would have continued to vocalize his distortions to others. To remain silent is to imply agreement.

■ People Who Vocalize Narrow, Personalized, Self-Serving Beliefs

Similar to negative exaggerators, these bad attitude employees will frequently vocalize very narrow, me-focused patterns of beliefs or interpretations.

Symptoms

Once again, this behavior is one of communication, and the symptoms are verbal. You hear this in phrases such as the following:

- "You don't like *me*."
- "*I* am treated unfairly."
- "You're just doing that to aggravate *me*."
- "You don't say anything to anyone else but *me*."

Turnaround Strategy

The key to dealing with these negative internal beliefs is to depersonalize their interpretations as much as possible. An effective technique is to "play the hypotheticals" by taking the discussion away from the current personalized issue and focusing on the possibility of other circumstances.

- "I understand that you feel you are being treated unfairly. Is it *possible* there could be another explanation for this other than unfairness?"
- "Is it possible there could be another way to handle this?"
- "Is it possible this is not personally aimed at you?"

Using hypothetical examples to offer alternative ways of seeing things depersonalizes the situation and offers employees an opportunity to broaden their view by at least identifying other possibilities. Employees have total control over how they *choose* to interpret the situation, and using hypotheticals may offer a safe way to get them to acknowledge other possibilities.

With these employees there is the intense personalized perception that policies, actions, and decisions are frequently aimed at them. They may believe management stays awake nights trying to figure out new ways to make them unhappy.

■ People Who Fear the Inevitable Impending Doom

As previously discussed, people with bad attitudes are often very fearful people. They may not know exactly what they fear; they just know that something bad is bound to happen, it is going to be big, it will happen sooner rather than later, and they will somehow pay a price for it.

Symptoms

While these fears take many forms, they tend to evolve around or threaten the things that are most important to individual employees. This attitude of doom dominates their thoughts, actions, and statements. Bad attitude employees believe that bad things in life are inevitable, and they anticipate the worst possible outcomes. Typically you will hear them say

- "I am afraid this decision will put us out of business."
- "I am afraid I will do something to make you fire me."
- "I am afraid the new competitor will eliminate my position."
- "I am afraid my pension money won't be there when I need it."
- "I am afraid we are going to start downsizing, and I am going to lose my job."

  Other symptomatic behaviors may include

- Not seeking promotion because assuming greater responsibility provides greater exposure to failure, criticism, and dismissal.

- Refusing relocation or departmental transfers, fearing change equals layoffs or other doom.

- Tendencies to identify failures and discount success. If they had five positive experiences in one day and one negative or unpleasant experience, these employees will dwell on the latter and attempt to analyze how it will be detrimental to them in the future.

In opening this chapter, we used Claudette, constantly fearful of impending catastrophe, as an example. How can we deal with these disaster-friendly expectations?

Turnaround Strategies

There are two successful techniques for dealing with fearful people—the six-step process and "feel-felt-found."

The six-step process

1. **Identify** the worst-case scenario. Help bad attitude employees to articulate their specific concerns.

   - "What do you fear may happen?"
   - "What is the worst possible thing that could happen?"
   - "If this doesn't work well, what is the worst outcome you could imagine?"

2. **Summarize** their articulated fear back to them. This helps them to "hear" their fear void of emotion and judgment. This demonstrates your interest and insures the accuracy of your understanding.

   - "I understand your fear is that . . . will happen?"
   - "I am hearing you say that you see the potential for . . . happening."
   - "I heard you say that . . . is a real possibility."

3. **Affirm**/compliment their thought process. Acknowledge without agreement or judgment. This aligns you as their partner.

   - "I am glad you told me about this. You have obviously given it a lot of thought."
   - "I would be concerned too if I thought that would happen."
   - "If that really happened, it would be bad for all of us. You're really looking out for everyone's best interests."

4. **Project** the positive "upside." Help them to identify and consider a potential positive outcome.

- "Let's look at the other side. What is the best thing that could happen?"

- "Let's see if we can predict some positive outcomes that might result."

- "If it goes as planned, what do you think the good results would be?"

5. **Minimize** the fear. Help them to see their feared outcome as a highly unlikely reality. (Minimize, do not ridicule.)

   - "For . . . to happen, all of these things would have to go bad at one time." (Outline them.)

   - "For you to lose your job, you would have to do all of these unlikely things." (Develop a complete list.)

   - "Downsizing is not in our future, and before anything like that would happen, we would all get plenty of notice."

   - "I am confident . . . would not happen for all of these reasons . . ." (Present a complete summary.)

6. **Action** plan for avoiding the catastrophe and insuring success. Help to develop options and implement some measure of control.

   - "How would we know if your feared outcome were starting to happen? What would be our early warning sign, and how could we react?"

   - "What can we do to make sure . . . (the bad) doesn't happen and . . . (the good) does?"

   - "How can we avoid allowing . . . (the bad) to become a reality?"

Part of the action plan is following up, and in subsequent conversations continually emphasize the potential positive outcome. Avoid all references to the bad. If employees come to you convinced they actually see the bad starting to develop, make them a part of the solution.

- "Interesting observation. What can we do to fix it?"

- "What can we do to double-check or verify your suspicion?"

- "If your observation is correct, what can we do to make sure we stop it now?"

Feel-Felt-Found   This time-tested, three-step technique is an excellent disarming tool. It acknowledges the validity of employees' fears; it allows you to partner with them by expressing your similar feelings in the past and provides you with the opportunity to focus them on the positive.

- "Claudette, I understand how you *feel*."
- "I have *felt* that way many times myself."
- "Here's what I *found* to be the outcome." (Add your potential positive outcome here.)

! Do not take the Claudette-type of catastrophizers lightly. They may be identifying contingencies you haven't thought of. As frustrating as they may be, their input may be valuable. Listen and develop "what if" reaction plans in case their fears may be accurate. Do not dismiss them out of hand. They may be sounding an early warning.

■ People Who Become the "Troll" on the Highway to Change

This is Howard from the beginning of the chapter. As you move forward with your vision and implementation of change, he erects his little "troll" booth and tells you why it can't be done or that it didn't work before. (He isn't being negative—he is just speaking from experience!)

Symptoms

The most common indicators of troll-like behaviors are the consistent, predictable, negative responses to any new ideas. Typically these responses fall into three categories:

- Been there, done that, it won't work because . . . (Perception based upon the person's wealth of previous experience, which is obviously superior to yours)
- The perception (or desire to create the impression) that the person possesses unique knowledge or inside information concerning the topic at hand
- The perception of being designated devil's advocate—a self-designated role commitment to play it well

While the negative rejections of new ideas and initiatives may be a knee-jerk reflex action, the positions of bad attitude trolls can be well defended. They can cite critical incidents of past experiences to support their perceptions and may have facts and figures to prove their point. Once they stake out a position, they are frequently skilled at marshalling an abundance of supporting material.

Causes of this troll behavior may range from perceiving anything new to be a criticism of them or the way "we have always done it," to being risk-averse or just not wanting to give up the comfort of the known. They may also have an inflated perception of their own intellect and contributions and feel duty-bound to bring everyone else down to their reality.

◆ **Trolls are speed bumps on the highway to the future.**

Turnaround Strategies

Trolls may cause you to slow down, but they will not disrupt your journey. The best way to deal with them is the triple A technique.

- *Acknowledge* their statements.
- *Affirm* their perceptions as possibilities.
- *Assign* them a part of the positive plan of action.

> Tyson, the new production manager, recommended a bonus plan for his department, establishing a threshold quota and giving employees a bonus on production above 105% of that quota. Howard quickly tried to squash the initiative by reminding everyone that we tried something like this six years ago, and while production did increase, we paid a horrible price in lower quality and the corresponding huge increase in customer complaints. We lost customers and money, and when we took the bonus away, the production department almost committed mutiny. He certainly wants *no* part of repeating that fiasco!
>
> The vice president of production (both Howard and Tyson's boss) responded. "Howard, I understand we tried a similar bonus program in the past, and it wasn't successful. It's possible it may not work this time either. It's also possible it was a great idea back then but just wasn't thought through completely or implemented properly. I don't want past failure to inhibit current initiative. Let's learn from the past and put it to work for us now. Here is what we are going to do. I want you, Tyson, Cheryl from quality assurance, and Ralph from finance to recommend a plan that protects our quality and customer issues while increasing production and allowing our people to participate financially in the increased revenue they generate. When can I have your completed recommendation?"

This approach invited Howard to identify the upside solution, not the impending downside. His boss positioned him to actually be part of the positive outcome and to abandon his troll booth.

If you are confident in the employee's ability, make him or her partially responsible for the plan and/or the action. Giving the trolls responsibility for success as opposed to a platform for the prospects of failure puts them in a very challenging position. It causes them to change their thought process from "can't" to "can," and from "what won't work" to "what will work."

> **!** The risk involved here is, if the task, activity, or project is not successful, trolls can always say, "I told you so." Failure allows trolls to be right. If you are dealing with people who are motivated by their achievement and success, this is an effective technique. If you are dealing with people who need to be right, they may have a stake in failure and sabotage the project. Use your judgment on how much influence and responsibility the troll has for the final outcome.

A secondary strategy   Perhaps a more brazen (but effective) way of dealing with Howard is to confront him with participation. In a meeting setting, just as Tyson offered his bonus proposal and before Howard could play his "trollful tune," his boss could have responded by saying, "That's an interesting idea. Before Howard gives us the downside, does anyone else have anything to add to Tyson's suggestion?" Obviously, this exposes the predictability of Howard's responses, and you may find this somewhat aggressive. Use it to your level of comfort.

Being a troll is easy. Being against everything is the path of least resistance. Frequently the troll just wants to be heard. They may not have confidence in their ability to implement so they concentrate on impeding. Do not overreact to them. Do listen, validate their concerns, and give them the opportunity to be part of successful implementation.

■ People Who Demonstrate Inappropriate Emotions

These emotional displays can be verbal or nonverbal, ranging from emotional meltdowns and temper tantrums to helpless withdrawals. The important point is to look for patterns or trends. Appropriate emotional responses to difficult or painful events do *not* make people bad attitude employees. The key question is—are they using these behaviors consistently to manipulate others or gain advantage?

Symptoms

Employees using these behaviors are usually intent on halting a discussion, extracting themselves from an uncomfortable predicament, intimidating others, or gaining expectation-reducing sympathy. It is very important to counter these behaviors by *not* giving into them. If these displays of emotion result in avoidance of accountability, delaying or abandoning the discussion, or lessening expectations, they have succeeded. As a result of this success, they repeat the behavior every time they are in a tight spot. (It works—why not?)

Turnaround Strategies

If an employee begins crying during a discussion, allow the employee to compose him- or herself and continue. It may be appropriate to take a short break (ten to fifteen minutes maximum) or for you to excuse yourself to allow some privacy. The important point is to resume the discussion as soon as possible.

Remember Gunther, who blows up in an intimidating temper tantrum every time he gets into a tight spot? How do you deal with him? There are two options:

- Allow the temper tantrum to run its course. Observe passively, avoiding any visible reaction. When the tantrum subsides, calmly state, "Okay, Gunther, now that that's over, let's continue with our discussion."

- At the onset of the temper tantrum, react and decisively state, "Gunther, this reaction is neither acceptable nor effective. I will give you ____ minutes to regain your control and then we will continue. Outburst like this in the future will be considered insubordination."

When employees realize their inappropriate emotional displays are ineffective, they will quickly abandon them (usually in embarrassment). These are usually learned behaviors or patterns of responses that have worked effectively for them in the past. Don't be manipulated.

▶ **Remove the payoffs for inappropriate emotional responses.**

❗ Continuation of this behavior may indicate emotional problems, and suggestions of psychological counseling or the use of the employee assistance program may well be in order.

■ People Who Distort Reality and Facts

Distortions of reality and facts can be deadly to an organization, and the people who practice distortions are a significant challenge to management. These are the people who play fast and loose with the truth—some innocently, some with severe negative intentions. There are two types of distortion—unintentional and intentional.

Symptoms of Unintentional Distortion

Employees who practice unintentional distortion or exaggeration temporarily create inaccurate perceptions and are a hindrance to evaluation and success. This type of distortion is an ongoing fact of organizational life. Symptoms of unintentional distortion include

- Faulty judgment/observation
- Exaggeration
- Lack of awareness of what to communicate

Turnaround Strategy for Unintentional Distortions

Unintentional distortions can be minimized by providing ongoing training and communication on the criteria for making effective decisions, and discerning the difference between information that is critical to success, and the mountain of "stuff" that is peripheral, at best. Help your employees clearly understand what you perceive to be important.

In fairness to the employee, it is the manager's responsibility to communicate the importance and priority of what information is to be shared. Again, I emphasize the importance of never assuming that employees know what you must be made aware of. These problems frequently can be traced to poor communication by the manager.

Consistently use these phrases:

- "Whom else should I talk with?"
- "What else do I need to know?"
- "What's the worst thing that could happen here?"
- "Is there anyone or anything else involved that I need to know about?"

These questions make it difficult (not impossible) for employees to continue to withhold information effectively. If they are not forthcoming in the face of these questions, they cross over the line to actively lying. If you believe you have an employee with a pattern of intentionally withholding information, temporarily modify the trust you place in him or her and the information until an accurate determination can be made. Always dig a little deeper; you may find a different reality, or you may develop enough evidence to confront the employee. Do not allow your suspicions to build without seeking evidence. Unsubstantiated suspicions become a malignancy.

▶ **A critical management error: Assuming everyone sees things as you do.**

! **Realize that exaggeration is human nature to many; always factor the weight of employees' information against their pattern or tendency to exaggerate. Second opinions are an effective antidote with some employees. You learn over time who calls a light spring rain a "terrible storm," and who calls a hurricane a "slight disturbance."**

Symptoms of Intentional Distortions

Intentional distortions are extremely serious and a form of sabotage that must be dealt with harshly, effectively, and immediately. If serious enough, they may be the basis for immediate dismissal.

There are two kinds of intentional distortion—passive (withholding information) and active (altering facts).

Passive   Most passive intentional distortion is through the withholding of information. The people involved do not alter information; they just do not offer it. "You never asked me" and "I didn't know you wanted/needed this information" are universal expressions of intentional passive distorters. These intentional passive distortions are extremely difficult to document due to their blurriness; however, patterns of such behavior are observable and can be exposed.

Active   The intentional alteration of information is actually lying about an incident (alteration of time cards, expense claims, monthly reports, inaccurate incident/ accident reports). This is a conscious decision to alter facts either to gain an advantage or to avoid a negative reaction.

Turnaround Strategies for Intentional Distortions

Both types of intentional distortions must be confronted decisively.

Passive   Clearly establish with employees that it is their responsibility to communicate complete, all-encompassing information. It is not up to you to ask the right questions—it is their responsibility to tell you what you need to know. Establish the importance of a complete information flow and the potential problems to be encountered when accurate information is not communicated on a timely basis. Clearly establish a linkage of accountability, with employees understanding the consequences of incomplete or withheld information. Employees are as accountable for their information flow as they are for their performance and behavior issues.

> **!** Be aware of any tendency on your part to overreact or shoot the messenger. You may be creating your own problems. While it is a human tendency, it teaches employees to suppress information and delays your initial awareness of problems.

Active The most effective strategy is to hold bad attitude employees accountable for their actions. When intentional distortions can be proven, confront employees immediately. If the incident is serious enough, they may face immediate dismissal. In less critical circumstances, a formal warning or suspension may be enough to turn the problem around. If not, documenting a pattern of ongoing distortion will probably serve as an eventual basis for termination. The key issue here is having the evidence. If you have proof, do not hesitate—move to the disciplinary process. (You have been given a golden opportunity to rid yourself of what probably has been, or is guaranteed to be, a serious problem.)

If it is a one-time incident and the employee corrects the behavior, then we all live happily ever after. If you have suspicions of distortions as yet unproven, begin to document patterns and increase your monitoring. Even the most skilled distorters will eventually leave evidence.

Intentional distortion is frequently symptomatic of deeper-rooted problems, and you are best served by ridding yourself of the source as soon as possible.

▶ **Distortion = Distrust—deadly in today's workplace.**

■ People Who Pave the One-Way Street

These people perceive that life is a one-way street, and it always goes in the direction they choose. They are intolerant of others' ideas. They have probably preplanned their own funeral, insisting that Frank Sinatra's song "My Way" be sung repeatedly as they are lowered into the ground. They have a deeply rooted personal belief that no one can do it as well as "I." If others are asked to participate, all work must be done to their exact specifications and approval. (Obviously, these people do not function well in a team environment.) This behavior is difficult to deal with in employees or peers and can be deadly when displayed by a manager.

Symptoms

Arrogance, selfishness, and intolerance of the ideas of others may actually be a fear that one-way streeters' own ideas and actions may be eclipsed or judged second best. This fear may drive them to actively suppress input from others. They never allow ideas other than their own to see the light of day. "I'm the expert; I know it all" is a frequent refrain. These employees also tend to take credit for other people's ideas and accomplishments—again, a deadly behavior in a manager.

Predictably these people react aggressively or defensively when asked to explain, defend, or sell their ideas. They do not like to be questioned and expect their input and actions to be embraced on face value alone. Driven by a me-against-the-world mentality, they frequently see acceptance of others' ideas and actions as a personal rejection of their own issues and ideas. There is a great deal of personalization with one-way streeters.

- "If he's right, then I'm wrong."

- "If you like Susan's idea, that means you didn't like mine."

- "Accepting their input means you value them more highly than you value me."

Turnaround Strategies

There are a number of tactics you can use in dealing with one-way streeters.

1. Depersonalize the acceptance or rejection of input and ideas. If their ideas are not accepted, give them a wealth of positive recognition for the high quality, well-prepared input they did provide. (These folks are seeking recognition—give it to them.)

2. While stressing the high value you place on their input and ideas, also stress the equally high value (not superior value) of others in the workplace. "I place tremendous value on your input, and it is important that I hear from John/Susan also. I want to give consideration to everyone's ideas in making this decision."

3. Play the hypotheticals on any specific issue on which they perceive they are right and their way is the only way. Any alternatives can be discussed in general, hypothetical terms.

   - "Is it possible that under a different set of circumstances John/Susan's idea would work? What might those circumstances be?"

   - "If we were to accept John/Susan's idea at another time, would that be acceptable?

- "Is it possible there could be other alternatives or options that might work in the future?"

If nothing else, these references to hypothetical situations may prepare them to be more accepting of others' input in the future. It also provides an early warning that in the future you will be seriously considering the input of others (not just theirs). Set up future agreements that are less threatening by saying, "In the future, do you have a problem with our using John/Susan's recommendations?"

■ People Who Complain

Complainers appear to have a need to actively seek something to be unhappy about and feel compelled to share it with as many people as possible.

Symptoms
Complainers try to elicit sympathy for their burdens, and their complaints frequently focus on the "who," not the "what" or the "why." Rather than address problems head-on, complainers take their issues to other people who can do nothing about their complaints except listen. Complainers are the consummate problem identifiers and continue to complain about problems even after they have been fixed. They squawk because the problem occurred in the first place. Their goal is to justify their low expectations of themselves and to lower the expectations of everyone else around them.

> ► Richard is a service engineer in the M.I.S. department. When the company reorganized and three regions were consolidated into one, it required a considerable amount of adjustment for everyone. Richard had to give up his corner office with a view and move to smaller quarters. Others lost their jobs, and some were reassigned into positions of lesser responsibility, but Richard perceived his loss to be the greatest of all. As other office space became available, he was moved to an outside wall with a window, but alas, he never regained the corner office which he deserved!
>
> It was impossible to have a conversation with Richard without having him maneuver the discussion to the loss of his office! He raised the issue at every performance appraisal and, even in light of significant pay increases and promotion, he continued to mourn his loss.

As Richard's manager, how would you deal with his complaint?

Turnaround Strategies

There are numerous ways to turn around the behavior of complainers.

1. Tell Richard to get a life and get over it! Obviously, this is what you would like to do, and there is some merit in helping Richard to move beyond the issue. He seems to be clinging to a life raft. There are more effective ways of confronting Richard's complaining.

2. Use the positive confrontation technique. "Is this information different from the last time we talked? We weren't able to do much about it then. What would be different this time?" This communicates your unwillingness to revisit old territory. If it is new, relevant information, listen. If not, let the complainer know there is nothing to be gained by replaying old tapes.

3. Use positive recognition to change behavior. Complainers such as Richard frequently realize there is no possible resolution to their complaint, but they continue to harp, perhaps hoping that it will somehow gain them an advantage farther down the road. Encourage complainers to get over the issue with positive recognition. "Richard, I want to congratulate you. We just worked through a problem, and not once did I hear comments about your office!"

   Since some complainers have no real interest in seeking solutions, take away their perceived payoff or benefits from continued complaining. Let them know they receive attention and recognition for problem solving and not for problem identification. If an employee wants to complain about his ongoing headaches, give him recognition for making a doctor's appointment. If an employee wants to complain about her children's teacher, principal, or school administrators, give her recognition for making and keeping an appointment with the school officials to begin a dialogue. If an employee wants to complain about a peer, give him recognition for implementing conflict resolution efforts.

4. Collaborate on resolution options. Help complainers to identify what options are realistically available to them for solving the root causes of their complaints. As we have discussed, it is extremely important for you to help them identify their various options of solution, but you do *not* take responsibility for the outcomes or solutions themselves. (They would love for you to assume responsibility for solving all their problems! If you make an appointment for them with your doctor— it will be your fault when the problem isn't solved!)

These four strategies are designed to deny any payoff or positive outcome to complainers. When the strategies are used successfully, the complainers realize their behavior is ineffective, and the aggravation they cause others does not work to their advantage. It encourages them to move away from identification to resolution or abandonment of the issue.

If employees' complaints are fixable but they are refusing to be an active partner in the resolution, consider the use of the following technique.

5. Role clarification.

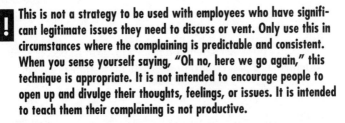

This is not a strategy to be used with employees who have significant legitimate issues they need to discuss or vent. Only use this in circumstances where the complaining is predictable and consistent. When you sense yourself saying, "Oh no, here we go again," this technique is appropriate. It is not intended to encourage people to open up and divulge their thoughts, feelings, or issues. It is intended to teach them their complaining is not productive.

When the complainer approaches and begins his monologue (and it is monologue, not dialogue, they desire), take control of the situation by saying: "Richard, how would you like me to handle this information? What role would you like me to play? Would you like us to focus on a solution, or do you just need someone to listen?"

Richard does *not* really want anything to do with a solution. If you solve the problem, he will have to find something else to complain about. He merely seeks sympathy, affirmation, and a forum to vent. He probably seeks a lessening of expectations. He will probably not acknowledge he just wants to vent, so he will probably dress up his response.

- "I just want you to know what's going on around here."
- "I'm just telling you this for your own good."
- "I want you to know what's happening around here, and I'm not the only one who feels this way."

Somehow he packages the information to appear to be a public service announcement from his radio station. He wants to convince you he is doing it selflessly, only intending to help by making you aware and certainly not selfishly addressing his own negative needs.

Your response: "If you want us to focus on a solution, I will create the time. If you just need someone to listen, while I understand that is important, it is something I can't do right now. I am swamped. Let's try to get together later." (Later may be either a specific time or a general reference.)

Richard is uncomfortable with setting a specific time or formal meeting to communicate his issues. It reeks of formality. It implies an accountability that makes him uncomfortable. He may sense you are trying to solve the problem when, in reality, all he wants to do is talk.

Effective use of this technique teaches him that

- You *are* available for solutions.

- You are *not* available for unending whining and complaining sessions.

- To receive positive recognition from you, he must become solution-oriented, not past critical problem identification-oriented.

■ ■ ■

All of the bad attitude behaviors we have discussed are very common in today's workplace, and you probably identified with each and every one. Not all of them can be effectively turned around—life just isn't that simple. However, using these techniques will afford you a significant amount of success. Don't give in; meet the challenges head-on!

9 Understanding Poor Performance

You cannot have a positive impact on poor performance until you clearly understand where it is coming from. Poor performance falls into two categories: unsatisfactory results by an employee who fails to meet predetermined expectations and standards, and behavior that is not consistent with pre-established policies, procedures, and codes of conduct.

While there have been many attempts to identify and codify the root causes of poor performance, in the final empirical analysis there are five:

- Lack of ability to do the job
- Lack of proper knowledge, training, or information to do the job
- Lack of confidence to do the job
- Performance impediments
- Attitudes of resistance or refusal to do the job

■ Lack of Ability to Do the Job

Obviously, if employees do not possess the innate ability or aptitude (mental or physical) to perform the duties of their jobs, they cannot be successful. This lack of ability does not necessarily speak to someone's intelligence level or his value to the organization. It means that not everyone can do every job. You can easily identify jobs within your own organization, industry, or profession that you could not do effectively. Perhaps you lack the ability or aptitude (relational skills, coordination, technical ability, or small motor skills). These skills and abilities are not distributed equally within the population. We all have strengths and weaknesses. If we employ people in their area of weakness, not strength, they are probably not going to be successful. The "Peter Principle" is alive and well (people are promoted or hired into positions where they are not equipped to be successful). People who are productive and successful in one job may be unproductive and unsuccessful at another.

Accurate assessment of ability and aptitude plays a critical role in these three circumstances:

- The hiring process
- Probationary periods
- Opportunities for reassignment

Assessment during the Hiring Process

Identifying employment candidates' ability to successfully do the job is a critical part of the selection process. Candidates may embellish their qualifications in pursuit of employment, and managers are rarely trained in the skills to identify the degree to which a candidate's skills really match the requirements of the position.

Merely asking candidates whether they possess the ability to do the job is counterproductive. Claiming the ability is easy; demonstrating it is a far more difficult challenge. A compelling question for you and your organization is: How can we successfully determine a candidate's abilities *prior* to employment? Many organizations and managers overlook the opportunity to provide pre-employment screening for ability and aptitude. You invite trouble when you merely accept a candidate's word concerning levels of skill and experience.

> ◆ A common practice in the airline industry when evaluating candidates for customer service positions is to role-play or simulate some typically challenging customer service circumstances. A scenario is developed where a passenger has just missed her connecting flight. She was "promised" that an alternative flight leaving momentarily from a distant gate will be held for her. You accompany her in a rush to the other side of the airport, arriving just in time to see the plane backing away from the gate, leaving the infuriated passenger behind. How do the candidates deal with this situation? Composure, listening skills, and ability to defuse the passenger can be assessed, along with their willingness to fix the problem versus distancing themselves from responsibility by blaming others.

Are such pre-employment skill assessments a common practice in your organization? While ability assessment can be challenging, there are few, if any, circumstances where some measure of proof or demonstration of skill cannot be obtained.

Another key element in the hiring process is the interviewing and assessment skills of the decision makers. While human resource professionals receive extensive training on interviewing and hiring skills, most executives, department heads, or frontline supervisors receive little, if any, training. Their training is usually focused on legal liabilities. While this may help avoid lawsuits, it does not increase hiring quality. Bad hiring decisions result when managers aren't trained in effective hiring skills, there is a rush to fill positions, or there is not a clear understanding of the actual skills, abilities, and aptitudes required. Unfortunately, you end up with candidates who do not have the ability to do the job. Good hiring decisions are the first step in avoiding poor performance and maintaining overall productivity.

▶ The best way to avoid performance problems is not to hire them!

The repetitive cycle of hiring, dismissal, rehiring, dismissal, and so on, that results from poor hiring decisions is extremely costly in dollars, time, and productivity.

Assessment during Probationary Periods

Employees are given a probationary period at the beginning of their employment (30, 60, or 90 days, for example). The purpose is to assess performance before they attain permanent status. Probation addresses the issue of "can or can't" do the job. The decision to release an employee during the probationary period is easily implemented—once an employee achieves permanent status, you play under a whole different set of rules.

In many organizations, managers do not have a clear understanding or agreement of what must be achieved during the probationary period to allow employees to achieve permanent status. Managers tend to make decisions based upon their "gut level hunches," or permanent status is awarded for attendance—if employees show up on the ninety-first day, they get to keep the job! Probationary deadlines are allowed to pass without serious evaluation. Poorly performing probationary employees are permitted to drift into permanent status because impending deadlines and actual performance are not monitored effectively—they slip through the cracks. When this happens, the organization is saddled with a poorly performing *permanent* employee. The cost of these mistakes is astronomical. Not only do these employees perform poorly, they take positions away from those who could be top performers! Has there ever been a case where an employee performed poorly during probation and went on to achieve great success within an organization?

Sure, there are exceptions to everything in life, and the blind squirrel will occasionally find an acorn; however, organizational experience dictates that poorly performing probationary employees do not improve with age. Employees tend to be at their best during the probationary period while they attempt to earn permanent status, and once it is achieved, the pressure to perform often decreases. The probationary period is a safety net constructed to protect the organization from poor hiring decisions. It must be managed effectively and with the proper urgency, and managers must be willing to make tough, perhaps unpopular, decisions. Decisions to allow employees to attain permanent status should *not* be based on the fact that we like them, they are nice people, they are somebody's relative, or we went to school together. These decisions must be based on objective performance evaluation alone—period!

> ◆ **You can't make a silk purse out of a sow's ear, so refuse to allow the sow's ear to become a permanent employee!**

The probationary period is a golden opportunity to "fix" hiring mistakes—use it.

Assessment for Reassignment

When you are considering reassigning employees—either upward in promotion or laterally to new responsibilities—their ability to successfully accomplish the new assignment must be determined *prior* to the official move. *Before* you move people, you must have proof they can successfully accomplish the new tasks you are asking them to do. Just because some people do a good job in one specific area does not guarantee they can do a good job everywhere they go. Just as pre-employment testing and probation are necessary for good hiring decisions, so are pre-promotion or pre-reassignment assessments necessary. This avoids the distasteful, awkward, and sometimes impossible situation of having to move employees back if they do not perform satisfactorily in their new position. The employee experiences embarrassment and loss of face, and the organization suffers the consequences.

One option is assigning candidates for reassignment to temporary or interim positions (with no promise or announcement of permanent status). If they do not produce, they return to their previous job with no surprise or embarrassment involved. The new assignment was perceived to be temporary and the return anticipated. If they perform successfully, they can be rewarded with permanent status. They earn the new position by their performance and there is cause for celebration.

Unfortunately, reassigning people within a company has become, for many managers, the path of least resistance in disposing of poorly performing employees. Employees who are not performing well are frequently packaged, wrapped, and shipped off as a "gift" to another manager in another department. While this solves one manager's immediate problem, it obviously creates a problem for someone else. The organization continues to be punished by prolonging the employment of poorly performing employees and in reality, does a terrible disservice to the employees. They continue to be placed in circumstances where they have little chance of success. Failure is perpetuated, prolonging their frustration and contributing to their bad attitudes!

◗ Reassignment is *not* a cure-all for poor performance.

Too many managers tolerate the performance of people who can't do the job. They give them satisfactory performance appraisal ratings rather than face the hassle of an honest evaluation and then seek opportunities to dump the employee on someone else.

Turnaround Strategies

This one is easy.

◗ Lack of ability cannot be fixed.

No amount of training, experience, or discipline can create abilities and aptitudes that do not exist. "If it's not there, it's not there." When you are dealing with an employee's *lack of ability* to do the job, there are only two options: reassignment or dismissal.

Reassignment   Employees who do not possess the ability to do their current job can be reassigned to another area. While this is a legitimate strategy, it must be carefully considered and not exercised lightly. Before the poorly performing employee is moved to another assignment, the following two conditions must be met:

1. The new job must "exist" within the organization. You cannot create positions for people because they cannot do the job they are currently assigned. This creation of jobs contributes to the ineffective bloating of organizations and may help to create conditions ripe for downsizing. You do not create jobs for people just to give them something to do.

2. Future success must be reasonably guaranteed. You must successfully determine the employee's ability to do the reassigned job. Why should you believe the employee can be successful in something new when he or she hasn't been successful in the current assignment? Make no

mistake, employees *can* move to new assignments and blossom in their performance; however, there must be a compelling reason to believe this will happen. You cannot move people in hopes they will be able to do the new job, allowing them to continue to build up time of service "on a wing and a prayer." The organization suffers badly when you continue to perpetuate poor performance with repetitive reassignments. (However, it's an easy "out" for incompetent managers!)

Dismissal   When reassignment is not a realistic option, the only remaining course of action is to remove employees from the organization. Obviously, any forced separation from the organization must be done legally, ethically, morally, and in compliance with existing organizational policies and procedures. Consistency is the key. However, if you are focusing on measurable results, this is a relatively easy termination to complete. If employees truly do not have the ability and cannot do the job, they obviously cannot be meeting the requirements, expectations, or objectives necessary for continued employment.

As distasteful as it may seem, you can no longer afford to continue the employment of people who lack the ability or aptitude to perform. Not only do you suffer from their low productivity, you send a very clear message to all employees that poor performance is tolerated.

The worst part of dealing effectively with those who lack ability is that they are usually nice people and you really like them. Dismissal is distasteful. (Yes, management is difficult!)

■ Lack of Proper Knowledge, Training, or Information to Do the Job

Poor performance caused by lack of knowledge falls into three categories: knowledge issues, training issues, and communication issues.

Knowledge Issues

Employees may lack the educational background, the experience, or the depth of industry knowledge necessary to successfully accomplish the requirements of the job. This includes appropriate knowledge of organizational policies and procedures.

- An employee responsible for calibrating the settings on a drill press would have to possess the appropriate knowledge of mathematics and weights and measures to effectively do the job.

- A clerk in a doctor's office must have a working knowledge of medical terminology.

- A truck driver must have knowledge of the motor vehicle laws in the states in which he operates.

- An electrician must have knowledge of the laws of electricity to perform effectively and safely.

- An employee in a waste management company must know the organization's procedural requirements for disposing of contaminated products, supplies, and hazardous materials.

Training Issues

Employees must be trained in all of the various skills necessary to do the job.

- A telephone operator must be trained to use the new telephone system.

- An order entry clerk must be trained to use the computer system and the appropriate software program.

- A customer service representative must be taught the skills necessary to deal with difficult customers.

- An emergency medical technician must be taught to use the life support equipment.

Communication Issues

- Employees must understand the goals, visions, mission, and objectives of the organization.

- Employees must clearly comprehend the expectations and standards of performance by which they are being evaluated.

- Employees must be aware of and have access to measurement systems or tools being used to monitor their performance.

■ ■ ■

Many organizations create poor performance situations by hiring "experienced only" employees. It is dangerously assumed that employees bring with them the necessary skills, knowledge, and procedural understanding. This hiring is often done under the pretext of not wanting to waste a lot of time and money on training and orientation. While there is nothing wrong with hiring experienced employees, there are some significant potential pitfalls.

- Employees bring with them their old bad habits as well as their useful experience.

- You assume the employees' experience is superior to your training.

- You assume the employees have been effectively trained. (Why would you assume that another organization was willing to do, and do well, that which you are not willing to do at all—training?)

We also make the dangerous assumption that employees see and understand things exactly the same way we do. Obviously standards, goals, missions, visions, and objectives vary from organization to organization. No matter how much experience an employee has, your organization does things differently. Employees must be trained in the new "differences." When you do not effectively train or communicate with new employees, you send the very clear message that you hired them because of their experience and background. You want them to continue to do it "just the way they have always done it." Have you ever had an employee tell you

- "That's not the way we used to do it over at the ABC Company?"
- "At the XYZ Company we did it another way, and it was much better."
- "That's not how I learned how to do it on my last job."

Although these statements may be aggravating, they could be the employee's way of telling you that you have not trained or communicated effectively. You may not have given the employee anything to replace "the way we have always done it." All he knows is to revert back to his past experience.

No matter how skilled or knowledgeable new employees may be, they must be trained in your

- Policies
- Performance standards
- Procedures
- Mission
- Skill requirements

Please note that it is not enough just to present the training or the communication. Care must be taken to review and ensure that the messages have been comprehended and that the skills have been properly developed and utilized. When training has been completed, follow-up observation is necessary to witness the employee actually using the skills successfully.

▶ Your responsibility for training does not end with the presentation.

Communicating missions, visions, goals, objectives, and standards is only the first part of the transfer of the information process. Assessment must be made to ensure the messages have been accurately received and understood. The most effective way to accomplish this is by asking employees to "feed back" to you their understanding of the communication.

It is important to realize that skills and communications erode over a period of time. Presenting the appropriate training or effectively communicating the standards, goals, missions, visions, and objectives once is not enough. Do not make the dangerous assumption "once in, never out." Ongoing review of basic fundamental training and communication issues is necessary to guard against predictable erosion.

■ Lack of Confidence to Do the Job

In this situation, there are two reasons employees do not believe they can do the job successfully. The first reason is that employees do not believe they personally have the skills, abilities, or knowledge to do the job. This may be an expression of insecurity, lack of confidence, or the low self-esteem we addressed in Chapter 2. This is a critical issue because employees have ultimate control. What they perceive becomes their reality.

> ◆ **"In life, we get to be right."**
> **—Dr. Morris Spear**

Being right is one of the few things we all share equally in life. If employees do not believe they can do the job, they're right—they can't! If they do not believe in themselves, there is a very low probability they will experience success.

Turnaround Strategies

Your influence in overcoming these issues of belief is severely limited. Many times the source of these issues is very deep, perhaps rooted in childhood. There may be many negative things going on in employees' personal lives to effectively reinforce these low self-perceptions. You are not a psychologist, counselor, or personal adviser.

> ◆ **You can influence only that which you have influence over.**

While options may be limited, they do exist. Effective strategies include

- Effective use of positive recognition
- Fixing problems early
- Assigning tasks to employees' strengths

Effective use of positive recognition   As we discussed earlier, positive recognition and reinforcement are essential in helping to build employee confidence. It takes no talent to continually point out what someone is doing wrong. However, it does take high levels of positive leadership skill to identify areas of strength (even in the face of weakness) and give consistent, appropriate, positive feedback. Positive recognition must be very specific and frequent. Avoid telling employees that they have done a good job. While general praising is better than the proverbial sharp stick in the eye, it really doesn't accomplish a whole lot. It is far better to offer specific praising: "Susan, you did an excellent job in dealing with that difficult customer. Not only did you solve the problem, you were able to effectively diffuse his anger and prepare him to listen to your solution."

Specific positive feedback communicates your awareness of employees' individual contributions and "specialness." We all want to be seen as unique, not just one of the herd, and unfortunately, bad attitude employees rarely have their uniqueness acknowledged in a *positive* way. For employees with low self-confidence, positive praising must be ongoing. Seek every opportunity to heap praise upon them. Regardless of what they don't do well—find something positive. When things are not going well, step in to offer encouragement, not criticism. Criticism just reinforces what they already believe to be true, and they tune it out due to its predictability. Help them to see an upside.

Fix problems early   Monitor low confidence employees and react quickly to any significant mistakes they may be making. Your quick reaction is intended to fix the problem, not to criticize or punish. You can effectively influence behavior before bad habits develop and become entrenched.

▶ **It's easier to stop one event from re-occurring than to break a habit.**

This also prevents the employee from digging a deeper hole of poor performance. Fix a problem while it is a mole hill, before it becomes a mountain, or worse, a whole mountain range.

If you do not fix problems early, there are a number of negative consequences.

1. Not reacting quickly and fixing problems early communicates to employees that poor performance is acceptable. The longer you allow poor performance to continue, the more comfortable employees become with their lower level of productivity. You also devalue the employee and the job by not reacting.

2. A clear message is sent to the entire workforce that poor performance is okay. When employees witness a peer's performance decline and see no response from management, they become resentful. (Sound famil-

iar?) In a relatively short period of time they will also reduce their level of performance. "Why should I work so hard when they let the other guy get away with doing nothing?"

3. Not reacting quickly may also create a potentially vulnerable legal situation. You may be establishing a precedent/past practice of accepting poor performance. Once an employee is allowed to maintain a lower level of performance over an extended period of time, that level of performance may be considered a personal standard. If you are going to require one employee to improve, you must demand the same improvement from all employees. Once poor performance becomes acceptable, it is very, very difficult to turn it around. Your inaction legitimizes the lesser contribution. Prolonged acceptance entitles the employee to maintain the current level of performance. The laws concerning this entitlement vary from state to state, and it is important for you to know the laws governing your state.

Assign tasks to employees' strengths   Adding to the discussion in Chapter 2, identify the particular strengths of low confidence employees, and assign tasks that have high potential for success into that strength. Build confidence with a series of "quick wins." When they do something well, help them to do more of it! Generate the momentum of winning and, as their confidence builds, expose them to increasingly more challenging and difficult situations.

> Peggy was Maureen's administrative assistant. She was very good at editing communications for punctuation, sentence structure, grammatical errors, etc. Maureen wanted to broaden Peggy's efforts by asking her to create communications going out under her signature. She hoped to be able to say, "Send Jack a note cancelling Tuesday's meeting, with these two dates as alternatives" and to have Peggy actually write the note. Peggy felt uncomfortable with this responsibility, concerned she would say the wrong thing or not write clearly and concisely. Maureen said, "Peggy, you are so good at grammar and writing skills, and you always fix my letters to make me look good; I want to be able to use your talent even more. I want you to actually write some letters from scratch. Let's do a couple of practice runs. Write three hypothetical letters, and we will sit down and review them. Write one letter to Martha, congratulating her on her promotion; one to Don, notifying him his quarterly report is late; and one to Dawn, asking her the status of her latest project."

In reviewing the practice letters with Peggy, Maureen enthusiastically emphasized the good parts and mildly critiqued some areas needing improvement. She requested two more practice exercises and then began to give Peggy actual writing assignments. Maureen reviewed Peggy's work for about sixty days and then began encouraging her to send the letters without review. Peggy gained confidence. Maureen seized every opportunity to tell her how good her work was and how much time it was saving her. Within the year, Maureen began to rely on Peggy for more creativity, including outlines for actual client presentations.

The second reason for employees' lack of confidence to do a job is that they do not believe the standards can be met. They may believe the standards are inflated or unrealistic and that the job cannot really be done in accordance with the existing policies and procedures.

When employees are not meeting the standards and expectations, frequently their first line of defense is to attack the standards. Will your standards hold up under the attack? Are the standards being met by everyone? Why are some employees able to meet them and others not? If the answers to these questions are not crystal clear, the standards may need to be reconsidered.

♦ **Poor performing employees will challenge the legitimacy of your standards.**

Turnaround Strategy

The most effective way of dealing with challenges to standards, policies, and procedures is to meet them head-on during initial training. If employees have been properly trained, the legitimacy of the standards never comes into question. If you are just telling employees what to do without actually showing them what to do (and proving it *can* be done), the standards may be open to challenge. If the standards, policies, and procedures are not legitimized during training, it is *never* to late to do so. If it has not already been done, do it now! "This is what we expect you to do, and I will prove to you it can be successfully accomplished by following our policies, procedures, and guidelines. Here's how. . ."

■ Performance Impediments (Real or Imagined)

Performance impediments are conditions that directly hinder successful job performance over which the employee has little or no influence. Performance impediments come in various forms, including

- Lack of resources
- Barriers
- Circumstances beyond the employee's control

Lack of Resources

Resources include functioning, well-maintained equipment, the tools and supplies necessary to do the job, and support or help from others on a timely basis. Does the employee have the resources necessary to perform satisfactorily?

Turnaround strategy   Acquiring resources is not an employee's responsibility; it is the total responsibility of *management*. Managers actively solicit the organization's resource allocators to compete for available resources and ensure their people have everything necessary to do their jobs. If you are unsuccessful in acquiring the necessary resources for your people, the resulting poor performance cannot fairly be deemed their responsibility. If one employee is performing well and another is not, is there a question of uneven resource distribution? If so, you either correct the resource problem, or you accept the lower level of performance.

▶ If they don't have the resources, they cannot be held responsible.

Barriers

Are there barriers—real or imagined—hindering an employee from achieving an acceptable performance level?

> Let's assume you have four tree-trimming service teams working out of a central location. Each service team is expected to meet a standard of trimming X number of trees per day. Team one works in reasonably close proximity to the central location, driving an average of fifteen minutes before beginning work. Team two works farther out, driving approximately half an hour; team three typically drives forty-five minutes; and team four drives one hour.

Driving time is obviously a barrier to performance for teams three and four. If all teams are held to the same performance standards, those teams are at a distinct disadvantage. Team four loses two hours per day just driving back and forth to their work site. A barrier obviously exists if they are held to the same performance standards as team one which spends a total of only thirty minutes driving each day. The unequal travel time makes it much more difficult, or perhaps impossible, for teams three and four to achieve the same standard. If you really want to increase bad attitudes, start giving bonuses to teams for production above the standard. Teams three and four will probably never receive a bonus, and you wonder why they are so negative!

If some employees are reaching your standards and others are not, you need to ask whether there are barriers hindering the poor performers.

Turnaround strategy　Barrier removal is not the responsibility of the employee—it is a management issue. Management must identify the barriers, assess their impact, and develop appropriate strategies for going over, around, under, or through them.

◗ Existing barriers must be removed, or expectations must be lowered.

Circumstances beyond the Employee's Control

Probably the most common and flagrant examples of circumstances beyond an employee's control are the additional tasks and time demands impulsively assigned by a supervisor or manager.

> Susan is John's boss. Because Susan is "swamped" with work and experiencing more crises and deadlines than usual, she asks John if he can help her out and "do some additional tasks this morning." (Run to the printer, verify some figures, call suppliers to verify shipments, or perhaps do some of her personal errands.) Susan thanks John by saying how much she appreciates his willingness to help out and tells him, "Oh, by the way, we have a departmental meeting at 1:00, and I promise it will only last one hour." John's entire morning is consumed doing the additional work Susan has assigned him, and in the afternoon, the one-hour departmental meeting that started at 1:00 lasts until 4:15.
>
> At the end of the day when John has not successfully completed all of his tasks, Susan judges him harshly. She says, "John, I'm really disappointed. Everyone else in the department was able to get his work accomplished today, but for some reason, you did not."

Is this really John's fault? Many employees find it impossible to say no to their boss, and the boss may not care what impact the additional tasks will have on the overall achievement of employees' responsibilities. They are unrealistically expected to just get it all done! This is obviously a management problem, and one that employees do not control!

When employees experience circumstances beyond their control, frustration escalates, levels of stress increase, and job performance decreases. Lack of time is just one example of circumstances beyond employees' control. Others may be

- Consistent computer downtime
- Excessive customer complaints/demands
- Other employees' tardiness/absenteeism
- Seasonal peak demands

Turnaround strategy Performance impediments are alleviated only through management analysis, reaction, and correction. The employee's role is to raise management's awareness of the existence of the impediments. Unfortunately, many times when employees attempt to raise our awareness, we accuse them of whining and complaining, and we demonstrate a "shoot the messenger" reaction.

Each and every one of us could readily write down a litany of all of the legitimate impediments hindering us from doing our jobs—guess what, so can your employees!—and all too frequently we may be at the root of many of their impediments.

■ Attitudes of Resistance or Refusal to Do the Job

In the final analysis of poor performance, if employees

- Have the knowledge to do the job,
- Have the training to do the job,
- Understand the goals, mission, vision, and objectives of the organization,
- Understand the standards,
- Have met the standards in the past,
- Believe they can do the job effectively,
- Acknowledge the validity of the standards,
- Have the necessary resources to do the job well,
- Have removed barriers or adjusted expectations appropriately,
- Have had issues beyond their control reduced or eliminated,

then you must assume they are *choosing* not to perform the job satisfactorily. You attribute this choice and option to their attitudes.

Turnaround Strategy

The strategy for dealing with poor performance based on choice or attitude is very specific, and the outcome quickly becomes very clear. You need to establish crystal clear, short-term goals and increase your controls.

Goals   Goals must be short term and very specific. You cannot tell someone to get better, to improve, or to be nicer; there must be a very specific goal to be achieved.

- "Our production standard is 100 units per day. You are currently producing 83. You have thirty days to increase to 90 units per day, and within the following thirty days, our standard of 100 units per day must be met and maintained."

- "Our sales standards are a minimum average of $10,000 per month, or $30,000 per quarter. You have been averaging $22,000 per quarter. By the end of the next quarter (ending March 30th), your sales must equal $30,000."

Unclear goals, vague standards, or generalized statements of desired improvement do not result in increased performance. Effective feedback techniques must be used to ensure that employees are fully aware of the goals they are required to meet and their expected ongoing performance. Their agreement is unnecessary—but their awareness is.

▶ General descriptive goals are meaningless.

Controls   Once performance improvement goals have been established, increase the controls. These controls can take several forms:

- Increasing monitoring of the employee.

- Increasing mandatory reporting frequency.

- Requiring regularly scheduled, face-to-face debriefing and review sessions throughout the day.

- Establishing a consistent end-of-day/end-of-week review where specific progress (or lack thereof) can be monitored. Constructive corrective criticism and recognition (if appropriate) can be offered, and continuing performance commitments reestablished.

If the employee responds and the goals begin to be met, gradually loosen the controls as the employee's performance begins to improve. Employees earn a decrease in controls by successfully meeting the goals and/or changing their behavior.

Consequences

If goals and controls are not successful, there must be a consequence. At the end of the specified period of time, if the poor performance has not been corrected, you have no choice but to begin the disciplinary process (see Chapter 11). This process must be implemented as soon as possible after the unmet corrective deadline has passed. If you do not institute the disciplinary process, a very clear message is sent to employees. You legitimize their continued poor performance and affirm the validity of their bad attitude. You also lose control of the situation.

> ▶ **Failure to take action makes their choice not to perform a "forever kind of thing!"**

■ ■ ■

Unfortunately, in many organizations the attitude-based choice of poor performance has been allowed to prevail for an extended period of time. You may have been placed in this management situation. This long-term entrenched poor performance is very difficult to correct. As previously discussed, legal issues of past practice and entitlement enter into this scenario. However, it is never too late to begin to enforce your standards.

> **!** **Standards must be enforced uniformly and consistently. You can not single out individual employees; everyone must be held to the same consistent standard.**

The poorly performing employee will either respond quickly to goals and controls or refuse to respond at all—there is rarely any middle ground. Either way the outcome becomes very clear, very quickly. The next step is certain: celebration or discipline.

Unaddressed attitude-based poor performance becomes a contagious infection within an organization. If allowed to continue, it will have a quickly spreading, severely negative impact on the entire organization. A power struggle develops between employees and management, one in which management must actively engage and prevail. Do not give in to attitude-based poor performance.

Rule Out Other Causes

Before you assume poor performance is attitude-based, you must be sure all other potential causes of poor performance have been eliminated. It is very easy to attribute employees' poor performance to their attitude. Why?

Because it absolves the manager of all responsibility. When we cite people's attitude as the cause of poor performance, we put total blame and responsibility on them. While this may actually be the case in some circumstances, blaming employees' attitudes has become a very fertile dumping ground for many managers in many organizations.

▶ Attitude should be the *last* place you look, not the first.

So before you absolve yourself from total responsibility and blame the entire poor performance on the employee's attitude, take a close second look. Don't be too quick to embrace the obvious. What are the underlying circumstances—perhaps hidden well below the surface—that could be contributing to this attitude? Use the following assessment criteria to evaluate the situation.

Twelve Critical Questions to Assess the Root Causes of Poor Performance

	Yes	No
1. Does the employee understand the expectations and standards of the organization? Ask the employee to articulate/explain the expectations/ standards to you. Do not just ask—the employee should be able to state them in a clear, concise manner.	_____	_____

* If the answer is no, you have a communication issue.

| 2. Can the employee summarize the training she has received? Can she articulate or recreate the steps, guidelines, and procedures on which she was trained? | _____ | _____ |
| 3. Is there documentation/proof that the employee was ever trained on the tasks/skills? | _____ | _____ |

* If the answer to 2 or 3 is no, you have a training issue.

| 4. Observe the employee. Can you witness his ability to do the job? Can his physical/mental ability be demonstrated? Can you corroborate its existence? | _____ | _____ |

* If the answer is no, you have an aptitude/ability issue.

	Yes	No

5. Does the employee express doubts about her ability to do the job or about the validity of the standards? _____ _____

   * If the answer is yes, you have a belief issue.

6. Can the employee substantiate, or prove to your satisfaction, that he is lacking the necessary resources to do the job? _____ _____

   * If the answer is yes, you have a resource issue.

7. Are there observable barriers prohibiting the employee from successfully completing her tasks? _____ _____

   * If the answer is yes, you have a barrier issue.

8. Does the employee perceive he is somehow disadvantaged in the successful completion of tasks? Is the playing field uneven? _____ _____

9. Is the employee's perception real (legitimate), in your judgment? _____ _____

   * If the answer to 8 and 9 is yes, you have a barrier removal issue.

   * If the answer to 8 is yes and 9 is no, you have a perception issue.

10. Can the employee substantiate, to your satisfaction, the existence of undue interference or demands beyond her control? _____ _____

   * If the answer is yes, you have a lack of control issue.

11. Does the employee express a belief that his poor performance is justified by the actions of others? _____ _____

12. Does the employee make comments that her performance will improve when changes in management policies or procedures occur? _____ _____

   * If the answer to 11 and/or 12 is yes, you have an attitude issue.

> Mary Ann is an office manager for your biggest competitor. She has been in your industry for a number of years, has a wealth

of knowledge and experience, and is very capable and competent. Through your negotiating efforts, you have been successful in recruiting Mary Ann to join your organization. You consider this to be a great coup.

You have offered Mary Ann the opportunity to move from her current position as department head to an executive level vice presidency. You are creating a new customer service department and Mary Ann will assume the title of Vice President of Customer Service. Up to this point, you have not had a specific customer service department, with everyone in the organization handling customer service issues on an individual basis. You have decided to create a separate customer service department as a positive step in your continued growth. While Mary Ann has not officially performed as a customer service manager, you believe she has the experience, knowledge, and understanding to do an excellent job. Mary Ann sees this as a great opportunity, and you believe you are very fortunate to attract someone of her caliber.

On Mary Ann's first day on the job, Frank, your CEO, introduces her to everyone, sings her praises, and encourages everyone to be as supportive and helpful as possible. He then shows Mary Ann her office, gives her the keys to her new company car, and says, "I'm behind you 100%. If there's anything you need, let me know. You know what has to be done—now go do it." One of the reasons that Frank was anxious for you to hire Mary Ann was that with her experience and background, he and other key people in the organization would not have to waste precious time and money training her. After all, she was bringing a wealth of experience and knowledge with her. (Notice there is no discussion of goals, explanation of mission, vision, logistics, policies, or procedures.) You have literally taken Mary Ann to the side of the pool and pushed her in by saying, "Just go do it."

Within a relatively short period of time, Mary Ann begins to question whether she truly was meant to be in customer service. While she was a great office manager, she never really appreciated how much interaction customer service has with difficult customers. Some customers are unreasonable and just downright mean and cranky! She is not sure if she has the aptitude, patience, or compassion to successfully do this job. Also, your CEO, Frank, has begun to feel some frustration with Mary Ann. She is not doing the things he believes are necessary to get the customer service department up and running. While he has not voiced his frustration to her, it is beginning to show in their interaction. Mary Ann realizes something is going on, and she is not quite sure what it is.

She is recommending that two people be hired immediately for her department, anticipating an additional person in the next ten to twelve months, and projecting she will have a staff of five within a three-year period. She is also recommending some changes in existing policies and procedures, believing many of the customer service problems the company is experiencing are, in fact, created by your outdated and, at times, oppressive policies and procedures. She feels the organization shoots itself in the foot and creates hassles for your customers, which take extra time and effort to correct. She believes policy changes are necessary. Frank does not respond well to Mary Ann's plan. He denies her staffing plans saying, "I did not hire you to build an empire. I want *you* to do the job. When we begin to demonstrate success, we may add one person at the end of the first year, perhaps building to three people in five years. An ultimate staffing of five people is extremely doubtful, at best." He also tells Mary Ann, "I don't care what policies and procedures were in place when you were employed by our competitor. We do things our way here, and we are not going to change." He also begins to share with Mary Ann his disappointment in her performance saying, "You just are not doing any of the things that are necessary to build an effective customer service department."

Would we be surprised if Mary Ann develops a bad attitude? And when Mary Ann develops this bad attitude, Frank may well respond by saying, "Mary Ann, you have a bad attitude. I am extremely disappointed. If this attitude does not change, it may be necessary for us to part company. You either change and get with the program, or you might want to see if our competitor will give you your old job back." Is this really Mary Ann's attitude problem?

Some observations:

- When Mary Ann joined the organization, the appropriate time was not taken for orientation, policies and procedures training, establishment of goals, discussing philosophies, or clearly communicating expectations. This is a significant example of the employee's lack of proper knowledge or information to do the job.

- Mary Ann's questioning of whether she really has the aptitude, patience, or compassion to successfully do this job would indicate a blending of her lack of ability to do the job and her lack of confidence to do the job successfully.

- Mary Ann's belief in needing additional people and in policy and procedure changes, which are not being supported, reflects the existence of performance impediments (barriers = existing policies and proce-dures; lack of resources = not enough people to successfully do the job). Whether Mary Ann's perceptions of policy and procedure prob-lems or staffing demands are realistic really does not really matter at this point; they are her beliefs, which means they are her reality. Frank has done nothing to address those beliefs or offer alternatives.

Before you rush to judgment and blame an employee's attitude, time must be taken to analyze other possible contributing factors. Trying to correct Mary Ann's attitude will not be successful. If the other issues are addressed successfully, Mary Ann's attitude will correct itself.

■ ■ ■

In our next chapter, we will identify some additional negative behav-iors that often accompany poor performance and offer more corrective strategies.

10 Turning Around Poor Performance: *Strategies, Tactics, and Techniques*

In this chapter we will look at six behaviors typically associated with poor performance.

- Insubordination
- Personal Problems
- Absenteeism and Tardiness
- The Employee Who Is "Skating"
- Disruptive Passive-Aggressive Behaviors
- Procrastination

These behaviors usually exist in tandem with drops in production, and you may be dealing with an employee demonstrating several of these behaviors at the same time. The key is to isolate the behaviors and address each one individually. In the real world, you cannot fix everything at once—you may have to prioritize, addressing the most disruptive behavior first.

■ Insubordination

Insubordination is an employee's blatant refusal to carry out specific assignments or to follow policies and procedures when informed or requested to do so. This includes displays of disrespect toward leadership at any level. Insubordination may occur in public (in department/team meetings) or in private (one-to-one conversations) between the manager and employee. Insubordination may be manifested as aggressive actions, passive refusals, verbal attacks, nonverbal demonstrations of contempt, or intimidating behavior of any kind.

Insubordination is common and predictable in situations where

- New managers are appointed

- Managers are younger in age or time of service than the people they are appointed to lead

- Female managers are appointed to a predominantly male work group

- Employees have feelings of extreme resentment (perhaps feeling they should have been appointed to the job)

- Significant changes are made in existing traditional policies, and employees perceive a loss in the change

- Employees disagree with actions taken during a crisis

- Problems unrelated to the workplace cause stress and pressures that are acted out on the job

- Employees perceive that corrective action or discipline is not being appropriately initiated with poor performers or disruptive employees

- Employees have a personal need to demonstrate their courage or bravado by publicly defying management

Insubordinate behaviors are willful challenges to authority. Bad attitude employees may be driven by disrespect and/or doubt that the manager can or will respond to their challenges. Insubordination can be a testing of boundaries or limits. If employees sense weakness or hesitation, they will initiate a challenge to test their perceptions. (How far can they go until the boss starts to push back?)

Turnaround Strategy

The appropriate response to insubordination blends elements of counseling and a verbal warning (see Chapter 11). There are two initial "musts" in confronting insubordination: it must be dealt with quickly, and it must be dealt with privately.

Respond quickly   Response to insubordinate employees' behavior must be quick, decisive, and as close to the insubordinate action as possible. To hesitate or ignore the action invites escalation of the negative behavior and an explosion of collateral insubordination in others. This lack of response may actually enhance the stature of the insubordinate employees in the eyes of their peers and may increase their influence over others. Leadership of the workforce may informally (covertly) shift to them if the manager is seen as weak or unwilling/unable to respond appropriately.

New managers frequently hesitate to address insubordination early, fearing longtime, productive employees will quit or go over their heads to the next level of management. This fear can be paralyzing or extremely destructive and may be a death sentence to their leadership. Insubordination not dealt with immediately only gets worse. Employees begin to see disruptive behavior as an effective tool to control the manager. In reality, any subsequent decisions or ongoing actions of the manager will be influenced by prior examples of how the insubordinate employee has reacted. The continuous potential for disruptive and disrespectful behavior becomes an ever-present threat to the manager. To avoid the insubordination and potential public embarrassment, the manager is careful not to provoke the employee—constantly tiptoeing through a mine field. These managers cease to lead and merely become caretakers.

When considering your response to insubordinate behavior, remember the following adage:

▶ **A terrible ending is better than unending terror.**

A manager who is fearful of employees' reactions is experiencing "unending terror." If employees are going to quit or go over the manager's head, so be it. Flush this behavior early. Do not strengthen the threat through the weakness of inaction.

Respond privately   Initially, insubordination should be dealt with in private. Public reprimand is inappropriate and may appear as lack of control on your part. It is unacceptable and undignified to reprimand insubordinate employees in public. When employees feel either public embarrassment or encouragement from their peers, it is difficult for them to back down. They must defend their position or "play to the crowd." Their reaction may have very little to do with challenging the content of management's actions and becomes a demonstration of how bold they are.

When the insubordination takes place publicly or in a meeting, it is appropriate to say to the employee in the presence of others, "I would like to see you privately," or "I would like to temporarily adjourn the meeting. Let's reconvene in ___ minutes." Then summon the employee to a private discussion. It becomes obvious to all that you are going to address the insubordinate employee and that the behavior the others witnessed is unacceptable and will not go unchallenged. Dealing with insubordination in private spares the employee and the group the discomfort of a heated, public exchange. It also takes away the audience.

Bring insubordinate employees to your office or any area clearly identified with your management "turf." Do *nothing* to lessen their discomfort (signs and trappings of influence, power, and authority work in your favor).

▶ **The calmer you react the stronger you appear.**

■   ■   ■

Let's look at an example of typical insubordinate behavior and a seven-step technique for dealing with it successfully.

> ▶ Mario, the supervisor in the shipping department, receives a call from his boss, the vice president of operations, requesting him to temporarily assign two of his employees to the inventory control department. They are under a deadline to complete a special inventory, and they need some additional help for the next two days. Mario agrees to assign two people, and asks Nate and Millie to report to inventory control. Millie agrees, finishes her current task, and heads to the inventory site. Nate refuses to go, saying it isn't his job to count; it is his job to ship, and he was not going to participate in the inventory. Mario asks Nate if there are any extenuating reasons why he is refusing this assignment other than not wanting to do it. Nate responds, "No, it's just not my job." Mario then tells him his participation is not optional and that his job is to serve the company in any capacity requested. Mario insists that he report to the inventory site. Nate responds by clocking out, going home, and not reporting to work for two days (he calls in sick). When Nate returns to work, Mario requests to see him immediately and says, "Nate, I assigned you a task and you refused to carry it out. Rather than completing the assignment, you clocked out and left work."

The seven-step technique   Following is a successful technique for dealing with insubordinate behavior:

1. Describe the behavior and seek explanation. Describe the actions with as much fact, detail, and as little emotion as possible. Stay in control—do not rant and rave. Do not show any outward sign that this behavior has gotten to you. If you do, bad attitude employees will recognize the impact their behavior has on you and will continue to use it to upset and control you whenever they choose. Listen to their response. (Their response really doesn't matter—your response will not change; however, allow them to voice their opinions.)

2. Acknowledge the issues and deplore the behavior. State clearly your understanding that differences in beliefs, opinions, or feelings exist. Affirm employees' rights to their perceptions. (You are not agreeing with their perceptions; you are acknowledging their right to have them.) *Do not tell them they are wrong.* Focus on their unacceptable *behavior.* Clearly state your refusal to tolerate a repeat of their actions: "While I understand your feeling that inventory control is not your job, we all have the responsibility to assist in other areas as the need

arises. Your refusal to comply and insubordinate act of clocking out are unacceptable and will not be tolerated."

3. Establish the acceptable format for communication. "I will give your opinion every possible consideration, and I am willing to make any reasonable corrections; however, when I make a decision, I expect compliance whether you agree with the action or not. We will treat each other with respect and do our jobs as mature adults. Refusing to work is not acceptable. Under no circumstance will disrespectful behavior be tolerated."

4. State the consequences of this and any similar future incidents. "You will *not* be paid for the time you clocked out early, and that time will be considered an unexcused absence with the appropriate documentation entered into your file. The alleged sick days will be charged against your sick leave, *if* you can support them with the proper medical documentation. If not, they will also be considered unpaid, unexcused absences and will be documented as such. This is to be considered a verbal warning, and future incidents will be subject to our disciplinary policy."

5. Clearly state your "reluctant willingness" to use your authority, if necessary. "I will not hesitate to take whatever action is necessary to make sure this circumstance is never repeated. While I do not hold grudges and am willing to put this behind us, make no misjudgments about my future willingness to deal with this behavior."

6. Summarize. Ask employees to summarize for you, in their words (verbal or written), their understanding of the conversation and the future consequences, if the behavior is repeated. "To be sure I've made myself clear, please summarize our discussion and the consequences of future insubordination."

7. Document. Create a document, factually summarizing

    - The incident

    - Your response

    - The employee's response to the discussion

    - Potential consequences of continued insubordination

This document is entered into your ongoing documentation file (with the employee receiving a copy).

The key to dealing with insubordination is to stay focused on the employee's behavior. Behavior is something you can influence and control; you cannot influence, change, or control their attitudinal thought process.

■ Personal Problems

From time to time, everyone will experience challenges and problems outside the workplace that affect their job performance. As a manager, you certainly cannot sit in judgment of the individual impact of someone else's personal problems. Some employees are devastated by their personal problems, while others work through similar challenges, putting the problems behind them and getting on with their lives. Employees' personal problems become a management issue when

- They interfere with the consistent achievement of standards, objectives, and expectations
- Employees perceive they are justified for lowering their standards, objectives, and expectations
- They become a burden to others or have a negative impact on the overall performance of peers

Most organizations have clear and concise company policy declarations concerning the appropriate response to predictable personal problems. Such policies address

- The number of sick days per year
- Bereavement leave for the death of close family members (as well as definition of who qualifies as a close family member)
- Additional elective days off
- Guidelines concerning doctor visits, dental appointments, parent/ teacher meetings, etc.

The clearer the policy declaration, the less managerial judgment comes into play. The less discretionary judgment, the more fairness to all concerned. Consistent policy application and enforcement reduce the potential for employee abuse. In the absence of such a predetermined policy, inconsistency, unfairness, and resentment prevail.

Personal problems causing employees to suffer a disruption in productivity fall into three general categories: emergencies, short-term challenges, and chronic circumstances.

Emergencies

Emergencies vary. They can range from a family crisis due to illness, to injury, crime, or a cornucopia of other potential misfortunes. Emergencies tend to be acute circumstances requiring immediate attention. They must be addressed quickly, or they may escalate to short-term challenges, or continue long-term and become chronic. Your response to emergencies is very clear:

- Immediately give employees the appropriate time off to address their crisis.

- Insist that employees communicate their circumstances to you within three to four hours of leaving work. (You are concerned, and you want to know what is happening. When employees do not keep you informed by staying in touch, it is frequently an early warning sign of low candor.)

- Request documentation.

While the request of documentation may seem harsh or imply suspicion, it is an effective tool in avoiding abuse. It voids or at least reduces the number of false emergencies. It is important to require appropriate documentation from every employee experiencing an emergency; you must be consistent with the entire workforce. There must be no implied favoritism. True emergencies will generally create a paper trail—receipt from a doctor or hospital, copy of a police report, etc. If no documentation is available, so be it; however, a notation of the incident should be part of your ongoing documentation.

Short-Term Challenges

These problems interfere with performance for a predictable period of time. They often relate to issues such as transportation problems, temporary child care issues, relocation, or changes in domestic status.

Turnaround strategy   The correct response to short-term challenges is to

- Clearly identify the problem and its specific duration.

- Negotiate an agreement as to when and how the short-term challenge will be eliminated.

- Request documentation of the problem. (This must be done consistently with every employee, with the understanding that not all short-term crises can actually be supported by documentation.)

- Clearly identify how the employee will make up the lost time or productivity.

- Enforce the agreement and enter into the disciplinary process if the problem is not corrected.

Chronic or Long-Term Problems

These problems can range from drug and alcohol abuse, illness, injury, or ongoing marital problems to employees who are willing to seize *any* opportunity to excuse themselves from coming to work and being productive.

Turnaround strategies   Your responsive action must bear in mind one basic rule of organizational life: employees are responsible for dealing with their personal problems and meeting the legitimate standards, objectives, and expectations of the job they have agreed to do. It is *not* the company's responsibility to adjust its standards, objectives, and expectations downward in response to employees' personal problems.

Following is a four-step strategy for dealing with long-term personal problems:

1. Listen and maintain confidentiality. "Help me understand the challenge you are facing." Listen to the employee's description and perceptions of the problem. Providing a nonjudgmental listening post may be the best thing you can do. Many employees are willing to talk, but some are reluctant. Some will ask to talk with you to keep you informed, others to establish the basis for seeking your permission to perform less (wanting to have the standards and expectations lowered in light of their problems). Some employees will begin to share their problems only after being prodded by their manager; others will refuse to discuss them at all. Inevitably, the manager becomes aware of the problem either through rumor and gossip or by observing a change in the employee's patterns of behavior and performance. Listening to employees builds trust and respect and may add a personal dimension to a perhaps depersonalized workplace.

As we discussed earlier, few things destroy bonds of trust more than violations of confidentiality. Under *no* circumstances should you share information or knowledge of an employee's personal problems without the employee's permission. Is it any wonder that managers who have a track record of breaching confidentiality have employees who are reluctant to discuss their personal issues and problems? There is no statute of limitations on confidentiality. When employees leave the organization and confidential information is divulged or leaked, it sends very negative messages to the remaining employees.

> **❗ Beware of employees seeking pledges of confidentiality *before* they share information. "I've got something to tell you, *but* you must promise me that you won't tell anyone else and you won't say where you heard it." Watch out! They may be drawing you into a tangled web. They may be transferring responsibility to you and absolving themselves of accountability.**

You should respond to this situation as follows: "If this is something personal, I will promise you confidentiality. If this is something that affects me, other employees, other departments, or the organization, I *cannot* guarantee that I will not divulge the information. Use your judgment before you tell me."

2. Demonstrate empathetic, not enabling sympathetic, behaviors. Demonstrate your empathy and understanding of employees' problems. "I understand this is very difficult for you."

> **Do *not* sympathize. Frequently managers try to build a bridge of understanding by relating a similar story from their life's experiences.**
> 1. **If they need to talk, shut up and let them. They do *not* want to hear your stories.**
> 2. **Creating too close a connection can boomerang.**

> Jonathan came to work one day in obvious distress. He asked to see Liz, his manager, privately to discuss a personal problem. He revealed he was experiencing a serious marital problem; his wife had actually left him the day before. He had not slept all night, and he was in a high state of anxiety. Due to his condition and inability to focus on his job, he was requesting the day off. He wanted to let her know this was going to be a difficult time. While he would do the best he could, he knew his personal problems were going to interfere with his performance. He hoped she would understand.
>
> Liz, in her desire to be helpful, assured Jonathan that she did understand. She had, in fact, experienced a divorce herself several years ago and realized the pain and disruption that accompanies marital problems. She also went on to say, "Jonathan, I have first-hand experience with what you are going through. It took me over a year to get my head back on straight and regain my composure and productivity."

Such demonstrations of sympathy can be very destructive. This bridge of understanding served as an official stamp of approval for Jonathan to allow his job performance to deteriorate for an extended period of time (at least a year, if his divorce was as bad as his boss's—and no doubt, he perceived his would be worse!). Frequently, Jonathan would appeal to Liz saying, "You know how difficult this is for me . . . Just like when you went through it . . . I can't make it in today (or I have to go home early)." Liz bore significant responsibility for his resulting performance decline.

Many managers like Liz actually become coconspirators in the deterioration of an employee's performance when personal problems are involved. It is not uncommon to see a pattern of a divorce with a job change occurring a short time later. While this may be the result of someone trying to "reinvent the new me," it can also be an indication of personal problems being permitted into the workplace, resulting from managers who, while well-intentioned, are allowing their sympathetic response to contribute to the consistent deterioration of performance. You can be so understanding that the employees begin to take their job requirements too lightly. This may result in the employees leaving the organization, perhaps on their own or as the result of a formal disciplinary action due to their "understood" performance slippage.

> ◆ **You do employees no favors when you sympathetically "buy in" to their problems.**

When employees have personal problems, help them to identify the options that may be available to them, but do not become involved in either the problem or its correction. As we discussed in earlier chapters, while you may supply them with the phone number of someone who can help, do *not* place the call and make the appointment for them. If you take the responsibility of trying to fix it, you deepen their dependence. You will also bear the responsibility when the "fix" doesn't work. Chances are extremely high it won't work and the employee will conveniently have you to blame. Employees must take personal responsibility for addressing their own issues. Encourage accountability and responsibility; do not enable weakness or helplessness.

Some managers actually adopt a strategy of protectionism for employees experiencing personal problems by covering up for them, distorting production figures, or enhancing verbal reports about their contributions. While the positive intention may be to keep other managerial personnel "off the employee's back," this obviously makes the manager a willing partner (or accomplice) in the employee's ongoing deterioration. As active coconspirators, these managers should be held directly accountable for the ultimate negative results.

3. Reinforce standards, objectives, and expectations.

> ◆ **Be a source of corrective strength, not a weak link in perpetuating the problem.**

After acknowledging employees' problems, reemphasize their ongoing responsibility to meet the requirements of their job. Liz's response to Jonathan could have been, "I understand how difficult this is for you, and here is what we expect from you . . . Other parts of your life may be going badly, but I will help you to continue to do your job well. Work will be your success."

While to some this may sound boorish or insensitive, in reality you do employees a positive service by requiring them to maintain their performance even in the face of ongoing problems. Insisting they do allows them to experience some measure of success in their lives. While things outside of work may be in chaos, the workplace may become their only harbor of stability. Continued performance gives them some portion of their life where things are going right and gives them something to take pride in while navigating in a sea of personal turmoil.

Chronic, ongoing personal problems are *not* a legitimate reason for managers or the organization to reduce existing standards, objectives, and expectations. Personal problems do not alter the responsibility of employees to meet the requirements of their job.

4. Monitor employees to ensure performance and maintain accountability. Carefully monitor employees' performance, and when they are successful in maintaining their performance and not allowing their problems to interfere, take the time to recognize and celebrate their efforts. Do not allow their success to go unnoticed or unrewarded. Celebrations can take a number of forms, including

- Personal time spent with them
- A formal written letter of recognition
- A heartfelt, personal verbal acknowledgment
- A small gift certificate for a meal, sporting event, theater, CD
- Anything that would convey your pride in their efforts to overcome their problems

If employees do not perform to the level of acceptable standards and expectations, the disciplinary policy should be implemented. Please note: the disciplinary process is *not* implemented *in response* to personal problems; it is implemented *because of* poor performance. Any and all disciplinary actions must be performance-based. Employees' personal problems are their own issue—their performance is your issue. While they may accuse you (or the company) of being judgmental or uncaring about their personal problems, continually reinforce their responsibility to perform even in light of personal problems.

◆ **Employee performance is *not* negotiable.**

■   ■   ■

While concessions may be made to help employees through some of their personal problems, they must be made only after careful, extensive consideration. Any such concessions must be offered to *all* employees in similar circumstances. Consistency is the key. Are you willing to do it for everyone in similar circumstances? If not, do not do it for just one person!

■ Absenteeism and Tardiness

This is a problem best dealt with before it starts. The first line of defense is a clear, concise company policy. Emphasizing the policy at the time of employment underscores the company's position and reduces the frequency and severity of the problems for the long term.

> ♦ **Employees take seriously that which you seriously emphasize.**

The policy should be read and signed by all new employees as part of their initial hiring procedure. Two copies of the policy should be provided: one signed copy to be entered into the personnel file (indicating awareness and acceptance of the policy) and one for their personal records.

Turnaround Strategy

At the earliest sign of an emerging pattern of tardiness or absenteeism, you need to begin documentation of the problem and conduct a formal review of the policy with the employee.

- The written policy is revisited.

- A copy of the previously initialed policy is produced, substantiating awareness and understanding of the policy.

- The circumstances for the tardiness/absenteeism should be investigated. "Help me understand why this pattern of tardiness/absenteeism is developing" invites employees to explain their circumstances as opposed to defending their behavior.

- Any legitimate reasons for the behavior may be treated as previously discussed in the personal problems section.

- Restate the existing policy, and emphasize the unacceptability of this emerging pattern of tardiness/absenteeism. The responsibility to begin work on time each day has not changed. Employees are expected to maintain their employment agreement.

- Identify this discussion as a verbal warning, and state the consequences of continued incidents.

- Have the employee re-initial and date the existing document.

- Monitor ongoing results.

If the behavior improves   Do not take the behavior change for granted; recognize positive results. Let employees know you are paying attention. You saw the bad—make sure they know you also saw the good!

▶ **Recognition is important—what gets recognized gets repeated.**

If the behavior continues   The only option is to implement the disciplinary process. Complete, accurate documentation is vital, and demonstrating your willingness to enforce the organization's policy to the fullest extent is critical. Allowing the behavior to continue gives your stamp of approval to the employee and to *all* current and future employees as well. Your inaction digs a deep hole from which it will be difficult to climb out.

Consistency is the key to correcting tardiness/absenteeism.

- You cannot turn a blind eye to infractions.

- You cannot practice selective enforcement.

- You cannot allow the "boss's buddies" to set their own hours while holding others to rigid compliance with the rules.

When employees realize that tardiness/absenteeism is taken seriously, they test the policy less and less.

■ The Employee Who Is "Skating"

"Skating" refers to employees who are just getting by. They may be meeting the minimum performance standards (sometimes just barely), but they are capable of producing much more. Their minimum level of production is a choice.

Some examples of skating employees include

- Former high-achieving employees who are resting on their laurels

- Employees with long terms of employment who feel they have paid their dues

- Employees who may enjoy some special protection (perhaps the CEO's kid!)

- Employees pending retirement whose goal is to count the days until their retirement is official

These circumstances are especially challenging because these employees are actually meeting the minimum acceptable standards, objectives, and expectations. They are fully confident of their invulnerability to the disciplinary process and have a significant level of control over the situation. Managers are at a disadvantage here, and for those who are performance-driven, this may be one of their biggest nightmares!

Turnaround Strategies

Helpful strategies for "pending retirees," "laurel resters," and "past dues paid" employees include

Appeal to their pride, primacy, or legacy　Helping employees develop a clear awareness of their visibility and the impact their performance has on others can be very rewarding. Their years of service alone makes them very influential. Appeal to how they want to be seen or remembered by others.

- "Do you want to be remembered as someone who marched out with his head held high or who slithered out the back door with his head down in shame?"

- "Your background and experience are really looked up to in the organization. I would hate to have other employees think of you as someone who was not pulling her weight."

- "You have so much influence on the whole department/team, I really need your help with increasing everyone's productivity."

Increase their leadership role　Is there a way of making them responsible for helping or mentoring other employees? Very few veterans do not want to share their wealth of knowledge. Position them to contribute to the success, growth, and development of others.

▶ **If employees feel they are being put out to pasture, they act that way!**

Offer new challenges　In reality, skating employees may be experiencing high levels of boredom due to repetition. They may have been doing the same thing for so long, it is no longer a challenge to them. Familiarity breeds contempt. They may actually be functioning on autopilot. Give them something new and different to challenge them. This is not necessarily an entirely new job; it may be a new project responsibility. The new assignment can be in addition to their current duties. Also consider lessening the burden of repetition. Is it possible to analyze and reassign some of their ongoing, repetitious tasks? Providing relief from the drudgery may be just what the doctor ordered!

Increase their visibility   These employees may feel they deserve somewhat special status due to their extended years of service. While a promotion is not in order, perhaps an informally elevated status is. Can you position them to be seen as senior to their peers? In meetings have them

- Present new products/systems
- Conduct fundamental training reviews
- Participate in or conduct role-playing situations
- Represent you at some meetings or functions
- Offer their advice on pending decisions

They earn this increased visibility by increased performance.

Offer monetary incentives   For employees pending retirement, monetary incentives can be very successful. In many cases retirement income is influenced by the earnings during employees' final years of service. Is there a way to structure a performance-based increase that will help them to earn more in retirement? The dollars involved do not have to be large. Tying a salary increase or exit bonus to their personal performance, and perhaps the performance of the entire department, invites them to move from skater to mentor or motivator.

The Protected Employee

Some skating employees do so because they have special protection and believe their manager may be powerless to influence them. They may have ongoing relationships with higher-ups in the organization or special friendships with powerful people. They may be relatives of people at the highest level in the organization (the CEO's kid, for example).

These circumstances are not uncommon, and managers are often intimidated by this special protection. In reality, these circumstances have no bearing on your responsibility to manage. While they may be intimidating, they also put your management actions under a microscope, and your failings or hesitations become visible very quickly. If protected employees somehow reverse an action you have taken, they usurp your authority. If you fail to take an appropriate action, you willingly surrender your authority and allow yourself to be intimidated. All employees are expected to perform and meet the standards, objectives, and expectations of the organization. These employees are no different.

However, there are some specific tactics for dealing with protected employees.

- Documentation will be extremely important. If it comes down to your word against theirs, it is probable they will win. However, when it comes down to your facts versus their word, your facts will carry the day.

- Never take *any* unilateral actions without consulting your upward chain of command and organizational "specialists" (human resources, legal, etc.).

- Always keep the source of protection informed of the situation. Before you take action of any kind, apprise the protectors beforehand so they are not caught off guard. Give them copies of documentation, being careful to avoid any personalization or remarks of your assessment of the employee. Tell the protectors what problems you are experiencing, what you are doing to respond, and what you hope to accomplish. In the calm atmosphere of a pre-event business discussion, protectors are more likely to be supportive of your position. Also, when favored employees come to them complaining or pleading their case, you have provided the protectors with appropriate warning and information to be prepared to defend the action. Since you informed them *prior* to your action, they are, in fact, defending a decision they were part of. Do *not* go to the protector and request permission to address the problem. It is your responsibility; do not give it away. *Do* go to them and extend the courtesy of information and notification.

> **!** If protectors are caught off guard, they may have an emotional knee-jerk reaction, and the outcome may not be in your favor. Once committed, they may not be able to back up, and you may bear the brunt of their face-saving efforts. All this can be avoided by preaction consultation.

Specially protected employees are a fact of life. While your options may be limited, they do exist. Use them or forever lose them!

■ Disruptive Passive-Aggressive Behaviors

Passive-aggressive behaviors come in many variations and levels of intensity, including

- Sabotage (commonly acts of omission, not commission)
- Talking behind people's backs
- Spreading negative rumors or gossip

- Agreeing with the manager to his face and disagreeing to everyone else behind his back

- Making agreements, and when *intentionally* not kept, pleading a misunderstanding

- Undermining a manager's position by spreading untruths to upper levels of the organization

Turnaround Strategy

The most effective way of dealing with passive-aggressive behaviors is through direct confrontation: first in private, then publicly (only if necessary). This conversation should be very short and *general*. Do *not* fall into the trap of providing specific details. The more specific your description, the more specific their denial. Also, a show of controlled anger can be very helpful to your cause.

1. Ask to see passive-aggressive employees privately (no witnesses).

2. State very clearly your awareness of their behavior and that you want it stopped immediately. "I know what is going on, and I want it stopped. Now!" (Do *not* go into specific detail. They want you to be specific so they can selectively contend or pick apart your statements.) Do not budge.

   How will they respond? They will deny, deny, deny. You will witness their "wounded buffalo righteous indignation." Nonverbal gestures of disbelief, incredulity, or contempt will precede their statements of offense at your audacity. (No doubt you will receive the "hair ball in the throat" demonstration—mouth agape, wounded look, and short coughing or choking sounds—you will know it when you see it.) How could you accuse them of such a thing? They will *never* acknowledge the legitimacy of your statements. Twenty years later they will still be proclaiming their innocence!

   Passive-aggressive employees will attempt to push you hard to become more specific.

   - "What do you mean?"
   - "Who said something about me?"
   - "Give me an example."

   Your response: "We both know what is going on, and it is in your best interest to stop it!" (End of conversation.) If you do attempt to explain yourself and become specific in your accusation, they will bog you down in the minutia of denial.

◆ The less said, the better.

Even in the face of the denials, the behavior will probably cease. Passive-aggressive behaviors usually die quickly once exposed. They flourish due to perceived anonymity. By confronting passive-agressive employees you strip them of their anonymity. Once their cover is blown, they rarely continue to risk the behaviors.

If the behavior continues   If the passive-aggressive behaviors continue, monitor and document any and all incidents. While hard to prove, passive-aggressive behaviors are a legitimate basis for taking action.

Public confrontation may be necessary, if these behaviors are not corrected. This is always distasteful and usually results in an intense negative reaction from the employee involved, but you may have no other option. Public confrontation sends a strong message to passive-aggressive employees and the entire group that you are aware of the continuing behavior. Others will begin to distance themselves from the problem employee. The entire group realizes you are aware of the root of the poison tree. If nothing else, public confrontation reduces the influence the passive-aggressive person may have on others.

> ▶ John's company had just announced its intent to acquire one of its smaller competitors. The target of the takeover had six regional offices, and as head of administrative services, he was asked to develop a plan for blending the six new offices with their existing eight. The intent was to consolidate as much as possible and eliminate any duplication of services.
>
> To develop the plan, John formed a short-term cross-functional team to consider all possible options. Included on the team was Cheryl, a manager in their Denver facility. As the discussions progressed, John began to feel that Cheryl was not supportive of any ideas that directly affected her or her facility. Changing everything else was fine, but any changes affecting her were resisted. She would not provide data on a timely basis, and John had reason to believe she was politicking with other members to influence their thoughts. He suspected she was making some deals. As plans to close her facility and expand the Dallas office progressed (requiring her to relocate), her efforts intensified.
>
> John talked with her privately about her behavior, and she became very sullen and uncooperative. He continued to see signs of her recruiting other team members to support her positions. Faced with no other choice, John decided to confront her publicly.

"I am aware of some of the things that are happening. Some of us are making decisions based on personal issues as opposed to what is best for the company and everyone else involved. I know that when our meetings are over, there are attempts to sway people's thinking away from what we have agreed upon. The things we supported in the meeting, all of a sudden, will never work, and opinions are changed dramatically from one meeting to the next. Cheryl, you and I have had several conversations concerning this type of behavior. I want to state as clearly and seriously as I can that I do not think it is fair for you to plead your personal issues instead of staying focused on our goal of creating the most efficient plan possible. It is not acceptable to alter our recommendations based upon one person's personal agenda. Let's not have any more of it."

This public confrontation is the last resort. It is one of the few times a manager should violate the rule of private criticism. Public confrontation is distasteful, but it is the appropriate tool in extreme circumstances. The immediate results are additional intense denial on the part of the offending employees, but chances are they will either cease the behavior or quit. If they quit, throw them a great going-away party!! (Cheryl resigned abruptly from the team and left the company within four months.)

■ Procrastination

Dealing with employees who procrastinate is a common management challenge. Procrastination is very frustrating and has a negative impact on productivity, efficiency, and the morale of others. Understanding its primary causes may be helpful.

Causes

Procrastination occurs for three primary reasons (there are others; these are the three biggest): fear of failure, resistance, and boredom.

Fear of failure   Employees may be afraid of not knowing how to do the task or may be concerned they will not do the job perfectly. They may feel this task will finally expose their self-perceived incompetence. Perhaps intimidated by the task, they may not even know how to begin. They are probably afraid to acknowledge any need for help, fearing it will be seen as weakness or incompetence. This fear results in paralysis and they do nothing.

Others procrastinate not in actually starting the task, but in completing it and turning in the results. They will complete it, but they do not consider it finished because they perceive that it is never quite good enough, never quite done. It is never completed to their satisfaction. They are constantly looking for a little extra time to get it done right and to their personal expectations. The problem is there is *never* enough time for them to complete the task just the way they want it!

Resistance to the task   They may just not want to do it—period! They don't agree with it or believe it is unimportant. They don't believe that it is worth postponing their current tasks to get it accomplished.

Boredom   When employees are bored with what they are doing, they frequently procrastinate to avoid the repetition. This type of procrastination is usually experienced with routine or ongoing tasks. Much of the procrastination we experience around repetitive reporting requirements (daily, weekly, monthly) is, in fact, rooted in boredom.

Turnaround Strategies

Each case is addressed differently.

Fear of failure

1. Remove the fear from the task. Communicate to employees that you are not expecting perfection with their first attempt. Tell them you are looking for a rough draft or a first pass. Ask them to take the task as far as they can and then you will help if necessary to finish. Clearly communicate you do not expect them to be perfect.

   ◆ **Taking away the need to be perfect reduces the fear.**

2. Guide them through the initial steps of the task. If they fear knowing how or where to begin, outline the beginning actions for them ahead of time. "Tell me three things you will do to get this project/task started." If they cannot come up with three things on their own, help them out. "Here is what you might consider doing first. . . ."

3. Help them understand where they can go for help: to you, to experienced employees who are willing to assist, to written material or documentation, or to sources outside of the organization that may be helpful.

Resistance to the task

1. Clearly establish the importance of the task you are assigning. Help them to understand why you are asking them to do it, why it is important to be accomplished, and why it must be done on a timely basis.

If employees do not understand the priority of the task, they will tend to submerge it with all of the other tasks they are going to do as soon as they get the time. (These are the tasks that never get done because they never have the time.)

2. Establish the downside to not completing the task effectively and on time. This may be a personal downside to them, to the organization, or perhaps to the next person in the chain of the process. It is important for them to understand who and what else may be dependent upon them performing in a timely manner.

Boredom

1. As we discussed earlier, rotation of tasks is an effective technique for dealing with issues of repetition-based boredom. Is it possible to alleviate some of the boredom by rotating the tasks to someone else? This is not intended to dump all of the boring tasks on one person but to rotate some of the repetitive tasks among a group.

2. Help to structure employees' tasks so they can accomplish them in a series of multiple short sessions. Let them know they are not expected to accomplish them all at once. Four fifteen-minute periods are less boring than one hour-long session!

3. Truly assess the value of the boring tasks. Are they important or urgent? Is it busy work with relatively low payoff in productivity? How much of it could actually be eliminated?

> Renee has fifteen phone calls to make to confirm vendor shipments. She perceives this to be an extremely boring task as well as a hassle (she is put on hold, switched from person to person, etc.). She does not attach a lot of importance or urgency to these calls. Instead of asking her to make all fifteen phone calls in one sitting, it might be better to encourage her to make five calls three different times throughout the day.

Additional tactics for dealing with procrastination

1. Avoid paying off procrastination behaviors. You may unwillingly be creating a positive outcome for the procrastinating employee. If you criticize an employee for procrastinating on a task and then take the task away and assign it to someone else (or do it yourself), the employee may see this as a very effective way of getting out of doing it. Wouldn't you be perfectly willing to absorb a little bit of criticism if it

means the loss of responsibility? Taking the task away is seen as a reward. Procrastination works! This behavior should not result in the successful avoidance of the work.

2. Use positive recognition to counter procrastination. Heap positive recognition on procrastinating employees when they start the task, when they stay on task, and when they finish the task.

    What gets recognized gets repeated. If you want to change procrastination behaviors, rewards will help that process. Recognition will bring positive behavior change where criticism has failed.

3. Establish consequences. Procrastination must have consequences. If something is not done on time, there must be a downside for offending employees. Effective consequences include requiring employees to stay late until the task is completed satisfactorily. If they do not have it done on time, they are expected to have it completed before they leave for the day. If the task is not completed on time, let *them* fix the problem (not you).

◆ **Procrastination should always have consequences.**

In summary, performance-based negative behaviors cannot always be successfully overcome. In the next chapter we will discuss what to do if you are not successful in turning the behaviors around: the next steps of counseling, confrontation, and documentation.

The Disciplinary Process:
Counseling, Confrontation, and Documentation

In this chapter, we will address the use of the disciplinary process for dealing with bad attitudes and poor performance. We have given you all of the component parts, and now we will tie it all together from the first discussion about an emerging problem through the eventual dismissal of the employee, if necessary.

▶ The key to successful outcomes is early intervention.

The reasons for early counseling and confrontation include

- Silence = acceptance and approval.
- Behavior uncorrected is behavior repeated.
- The earlier you respond, the less you have to fix.
- Reacting to negative behaviors early eliminates the creation of ingrained bad habits.

Many managers wait for the annual performance appraisal to address problems of poor performance or disruptive behaviors. This delay, while perhaps well intentioned, usually compounds the problem. Delay allows the problem and poor productivity to become entrenched (months go by without reaction or correction). Delay diminishes the chances of achieving a quick turnaround. Delay causes the performance appraisal to be negatively loaded. You pile on a year's worth of problems (compounded by management inaction), and any positive input is diminished. There has never been a significant organizational problem when in the aftermath someone didn't say, "If only we had reacted sooner, this *never* would have happened."

Why do managers practice avoidance behaviors? Why do they hesitate to begin the counseling and confrontation process early? Why do they put off intervention in the hopes the problem will somehow correct itself? The reasons are quite simple.

- Counseling and confrontation are not instinctive behaviors. (Managers tend toward avoidance rather than interaction—it's easier!)

- Counseling and confrontation skills are not taught in most organizations.

- Many managers doubt their confidence and ability to counsel a problem employee.

- Many managers may fear the employee's reaction—this fear leads to procrastination.

- Many managers feel they do not enjoy the full support of higher-ups in the organization. They fear that any action they initiate will be criticized or reversed.

- Counseling and confrontation skills aren't utilized frequently enough to be kept sharp. (Under the "use them or lose them" theory, these skills may atrophy due to infrequent use.)

What is the difference between counseling and confronting an employee? *Counseling* is a preplanned, informal discussion initiated by managers to raise employees' awareness concerning the emergence of problems with their performance or behaviors. The counseling session offers specific examples of the problem and provides clear, realistic action steps for problem resolution. It also involves employees in formulating change. *Confrontation* is an unplanned response to an urgent incident occurring in the manager's presence or the result of a meaningful complaint or acute workplace crisis.

> ♦ **Counseling responds to emerging patterns. Confrontation is incident-induced.**

■ Counseling

Counseling is appropriate when problems with performance or behavior can no longer be ignored, tolerated, or condoned. These emerging patterns are not just isolated events; their correction is necessary.

Counseling Strategy

The guidelines for counseling sessions are very similar to the interactive communication steps discussed at length in Chapters 5 and 6.

- Depersonalize the discussion—*what*, not *who*

- Use a neutral, nonthreatening location (perhaps off-site)
- Communicate assertively, not aggressively

The eight-step counseling model   This model follows the interactive communication guidelines.

1. State your observations. "Here's what I perceive is happening."
2. Listen to the response. "Tell me your thoughts."
3. Interactively summarize all responses. "Let's summarize our perceptions."
4. State the specific corrective action. "Here's what needs to be done differently."
5. Seek feedback. "I want to be sure we have communicated effectively. Let's summarize the changes we have agreed to."
6. Mutual agreement for implementation. "How will the change be accomplished?"
7. Identify monitoring measurement and follow-up. "How will we know we are being successful?"
8. Summarize the agreements and end positively. "When you do . . . and I do . . . , I'm sure we will be successful."

Note that in this eight-step model, three steps focus on summarization: step 3 summarizes the perceptions, step 5 summarizes the correction of the problem, and step 8 summarizes the agreement to change and monitor.

Counseling Session Results

In the simplest of terms, there can be only two possible results of an employee counseling session: the employee either corrects or continues the behavior.

The performance/behavior improves   When employees correct their poor performance or disruptive behavior, heap as much positive reinforcement on them as possible. One of the worst mistakes you can make is to allow positive responses to go unnoticed.

◆ What gets recognized gets repeated.

If employees successfully achieve correction and you ignore it, you teach them it really was not important—it really did not matter, and they won't take you seriously next time.

▶ **Celebrate the correction.**

The performance/behavior continues   The manager is faced with a dilemma. The options are to counsel again, raise the stakes by beginning the disciplinary process, or ignore the outcome and hope it goes away (we won't even go there!).

Initiate a repeat counseling session addressing the failure to keep the agreement. Your opening statement is, "Tell me what it means when we have an agreement to do things differently and that agreement isn't kept? What conclusions should I draw?" Entering into this dialogue with the employee may reveal legitimate circumstances or substantial reasons why the performance/behavior has not been corrected.

As we discussed in Chapter 9, performance correction may be beyond employees' control.

- Have they been properly trained?

- Are they choosing to not make the change?

- Are there other issues beyond their control?

- Are there previously undetected barriers to performance?

- Do they have the physical/mental aptitude/ability to do the job?

- Are they lacking in resources to successfully achieve acceptable performance?

Complete the eight-step counseling model again with the addition of a consequence—further lack of response must carry a downside: the implementation of the disciplinary process.

■ Confrontation

While counseling sessions are preplanned events, confrontations are *immediate actions* containing a component of urgency. Confrontations take place when

- Managers witness an action that violates company policy, procedure, or safety regulations.

- Serious accusations are made by a customer or someone else in the organization against an employee, demanding immediate attention and investigation.

- Employees take a unilateral action exceeding the scope of their authority.

- Ongoing violations of existing policies or procedures are discovered, and managerial action must be taken.

These are just a few examples of circumstances requiring an immediate confrontational response from the manager. Lack of response implies weakness, demonstrating reluctance to deal with the issue (or managerial intimidation). It implies tacit approval and may, in fact, be considered negligent if unsafe conditions are permitted to continue.

Confrontation Strategies

When confrontations are dealt with effectively, there can be positive changes in performance or behavior with little or no disruption in the relationship between manager and employee. Dealt with ineffectively, confrontation results in no positive ongoing change and increases negative emotion and conflict.

Confrontations are frequently ineffective because they focus on blame instead of correction. The typical ineffective confrontation is a two-step process consisting only of criticism and correction.

Ineffective confrontation model   This model or pattern, as shown in the following figure, is focused on blame, telling employees they were wrong, and establishing what they should have done, but it provides no explanation or teaching opportunity. The criticism and correction model results are no learning, no growth, no development, and little or no future initiative or risk taking.

In the future, when faced with a decision to take an action, employees will probably choose inaction. Not having confidence in their own decision making and wanting to avoid the boss's wrath or criticism, they choose to do nothing.

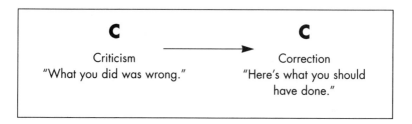

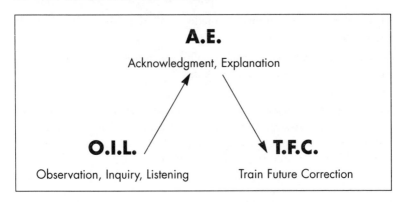

Effective confrontation model   The successful three-step confrontation model, as shown above, includes

1. Observation, Inquiry, Listening. Determine what happened and why it was done.

    - "I'm not quite sure what happened. Can you fill me in?"

    - "Help me understand what action was taken and the thought process behind it."

    - "It appears to me this action violated our policies and procedures. Can you help me understand what happened?"

2. Acknowledgment and Explanation. Acknowledge employees' effort. Explain the critique.

    - "I appreciate your taking action."

    - "That wasn't necessarily the best action to take. Here's why. . ."

3. Train Future Correction. How will you do it differently next time?

    - "This is the action I would like you to take next time. Let's review."

Use of this process results in recognition of the employee's attempts and efforts, provides a learning experience, and prepares the employee to think through the problems differently in the future. Used appropriately, this three-step process effectively teaches and promotes growth, development, and future success. It stands in contrast to the criticism/correction model that blames and invites a negative reaction.

It is a cold, hard fact of managerial life that much of the negative, emotional, and defensive reaction we experience from our employees is actually created by the manager's inappropriate style of confrontation. When attacked and criticized, employees defend themselves. Successful managers are in the teaching business, not the attacking business.

▶ **Blaming people gets you nowhere. Fixing future behavior gets you everywhere.**

As we move to a discussion of the disciplinary process, it is important to address the two key components of documentation and measurement.

■ Documentation

An important component of any management process is accurate corroboration and recordkeeping. Documentation is an important responsibility for every manager. Documentation is misunderstood by many and dreaded by most, and is generally considered a pain. Questions of documentation are the first ones asked by the human resources department or your boss when you recommend taking any action with problem employees. "Do you have proper documentation?" is usually answered with, "No, but I'll get some."

Documentation is not complex or difficult. It is merely an accurate, factual representation of events and discussions concerning a specific employee. Documentation should be void of emotion and be supported by whatever verification or proof is available. Proper documentation must always address

- The standard, objective, or expectation in question
- The specifics of the infraction or violation
- Verbal discussions (if appropriate)
- The employee's response

Guidelines for Documentation

Documentation must be habit   Train yourself to document daily. Probably the best time to document is the last few minutes before you leave the workplace. As you prepare to exit, ask yourself, "What happened today that needs to be documented?" Proper documentation is not difficult; however, it does require commitment and effort.

Document early   Begin the documentation process at the *first* signs of disruptive behavior or poor performance. Waiting too long to document is the proverbial "closing the barn door after the horse has left." Do not wait until you have a full-blown problem to begin to document.

> ♦ **One of the best friends you will ever have is a documentation file you never have to use!**

Document every employee   Do *not* document only the employees from whom you anticipate problems. Consistently document significant events with every employee. You may be creating negative legal repercussions by having documentation files only on certain employees. Be consistent in your documentation. Do not permit your documentation files to create the illusion of favoritism or your being out to get certain people.

Balance the documentation file   Do *not* document only negative events. A documentation file detailing only problems could be proof of a pattern of bias. If you document only the negative events, you could be proving that you really are out to get the employee. When an employee does something positive, that should be documented and entered into the file as well. You never weaken your position by acknowledging an employee's positive achievements. You clearly prove your objectivity. If a disciplinary action is necessary with an employee, you can clearly establish "Here's what he or she does well. Here's what he or she does not do well (the problems we are experiencing). Unfortunately, in this case, what is not done well overrides the good. We found it necessary to take this appropriate disciplinary action." This reflects a position of strength.

Documentation checklist

- Document performance and behavior only—never document attitudes.
- Factoring in your emotional response causes documentation problems.
- Double-check the validity and accuracy of your documentation. The employee *will* challenge your facts. Will they hold up under review?
- If the facts are in doubt, do *not* document.
- Documentation must be consistent.
- Documentation must be fair.
- Document correction as well as further infraction.

■ Measurement

> ♦ **The importance of measurement in correcting performance problems cannot be overstated.**

Bad attitude employees frequently claim their job cannot be measured. While some jobs may be difficult to measure, most lend themselves to some form of measurement, which may include a blend of subjective/objective observations (the less subjectivity the better). Bad attitude employees prefer subjective measurement; they rate themselves subjectively high and accuse you of being unfair and picking on them if you don't agree. Objective measurement reduces or eliminates the influence of opinion and self-serving subjective conclusions; objective measurement is crucial with the bad attitude poor performer.

Measurement tools, such as graphs, histograms, Paredo charts, S.P.C.s (statistical process control charts), and so on, should be used to track the performance of bad attitude employees. Proving it on paper speaks volumes, and it is difficult for them to wiggle away with the facts staring them in the face! These tools provide the opportunity to visually display your thinking. Proper use of these tools allows you to put your thought process on paper. They remove opinion, guesswork, and subjectivity. Performance can be measured against goals, objectives, standards, or past results. When the measurement is not favorable, the need for correction is obvious. The need for correction cannot be based solely on subjective perception, and visually displayed thinking is necessary. Your goal is objectivity, not subjectivity.

If employees persist in proclaiming their performance cannot be accurately measured, consider this response: "If what you do cannot truly be measured, I have no basis upon which to employ you, pay you, or determine any increase in your compensation. How can I assess your value if I can't measure what you do?" Faced with this reality, they may rush to create a method of measurement. Predictably, this initial proposal will be heavily weighted in their favor, and it may serve only as a starting point for negotiation. It is a beginning, and don't judge employees harshly if they attempt to slant the measurement in their favor. Your job is to implement as much objective and accurate measurement as possible. Results speak for themselves.

Key observation: By their nature, disruptive behaviors do not lend themselves to quantified measurement. Their documentation may be anecdotal; however, the effects of these behaviors may be measurable in the

- Number of lost customers
- Number of customer/client/patient complaints
- Number of disrupted meetings
- Actual rates of turnover

◆ **Poor performance that is *not* measured will *not* be corrected.**

Lack of objective measurement reduces performance questions to opinion. Your opinion is they are not doing the job satisfactorily. Their opinion is they are doing just fine, thank you. When such differences of opinion exist, correction is impossible. Perception of *unmeasured* poor performance is *subjective* (and open to challenge and interpretation). Perception of *measured* poor performance is *objective* (the proof stands on its own). Which type of poor performance do you think is easier to correct?

Now we will consider the disciplinary process.

■ The Disciplinary Process

An essential component in reacting positively to poor performance is the proper use of the disciplinary process. Used properly, the disciplinary process is a valuable tool. Used improperly (or not at all), you waste a valuable leadership tool and may actually contribute to or compound continued poor performance and negative behaviors.

The disciplinary process *is*

- An effective, formal process to help identify, correct, or bring consequences to poor performance and disruptive behavior.

- A process for complying with legal and ethical requirements in the event an employee must be severed from the organization.

- The latter stages of a continuum, the concluding formal steps in a sequence of managerial options of problem correction.

The disciplinary process *is not*

- A mechanism to punish.

- A tool to bludgeon employees into submission.

- The option of first choice to deal with employee problems.

There are key points to remember:

- Do *not* use the disciplinary process casually, impulsively, or in a reactionary manner.

- Do *not* start the disciplinary process without a complete commitment to follow through.

- Do *not* begin the disciplinary process unless you are ultimately willing to lose the employee.

- *Do* use the disciplinary process consistently with all employees.

- *Do* realize the failure to use the disciplinary process properly *will* result in the spread of poor performance, disruptive behaviors, and bad attitudes. (There is no such thing as localized disciplinary failure.)

Guidelines for the Disciplinary Process

Use the disciplinary process consistently   The disciplinary process must be implemented in an objective, well-planned manner. It must be used consistently with all employees who fall into negative performance or behavior patterns. If two employees are consistently tardy, you cannot discipline one and not the other. Such unfairness legitimately increases resentment and bad attitudes. It also creates a legal liability for the organization (and perhaps the manager personally). If you begin the disciplinary process and fail to follow it through to conclusion, you teach employees to disregard the process, as well as the words of their manager; their responsibility to perform at an acceptable level; and the standards, objectives, and expectations of the organization.

Use the disciplinary process with caution   Once the process has begun, it can take on a life of its own. It may well result in the resignation or dismissal of the employee. ("Termination" is the appropriate word; however, it conjures up visions of Arnold Schwarzenegger, a submachine gun in each hand, literally eliminating his foe. We choose the less graphic description of dismissing the employee.) Some organizations misuse the disciplinary process by trying to punish or get the attention of a good employee who is temporarily experiencing low levels of performance. The result has been the loss of an employee they had no intention of losing. Once the disciplinary process is instituted, three things can happen:

1. Employees correct their performance, and everyone lives happily ever after.

2. Employees do not correct their performance, and you must take the disciplinary process to its ultimate conclusion of dismissal.

3. Employees choose to resign whether they correct their performance or not.

As you see, of the three possibilities, two of them result in the employee leaving the company. While this outcome may at times be cause for celebration, it may also have negative results. It is true no one is irreplaceable; however, there are people who are less replaceable than others. Additional factors come into play such as peak season, key customer relations, and levels of employee influence. Do not take the use of the disciplinary process lightly. You may lose someone when you can least afford to do so.

Hesitation has significant downside consequences   Failing or hesitating to implement the disciplinary process when it is necessary sends a strong, negative message to all employees. It proclaims performance deterioration is acceptable, and continued poor performance will not be disciplined. This contagion spreads rapidly throughout the organization. High-achieving employees *resent* it when poor performers go uncorrected. It makes them feel foolish and taken advantage of. "Why should I work my tail off when nobody cares what these other people do?" Frequently managers choose not to discipline an individual employee; instead they punish the entire group, team, or department.

> Jeff frequently violates flextime agreements, not actually working a full day (coming in later than agreed or leaving early). Instead of addressing his behavior individually, Laurie, his manager, rescinds the flextime policy for all! Now, no one can take advantage of flextime. Everyone reverts to the previous rigid starting and ending requirements, and overall morale goes in the sewer!

This group-focused reaction is, at best, unfair and elicits a huge negative reaction from the top performers as well as from those who never violated the flextime rules. Failing to discipline problem employees or punishing the many for the sins of the few (or the *one*) is a management weakness and a great way to accelerate overall performance decline and bad attitudes.

When you allow some employees to continue their substandard performance while demanding high levels of performance from others, you create the inherent unfairness that is the cornerstone of resentment. (The top performers' resentment would be perfectly justified and the direct result of management weakness or incompetence.)

▶ **Tolerated poor performance is approved poor performance and becomes continued poor performance.**

An effective disciplinary process is part of a continuum in the sequence of counseling, warnings (not *threats*), consequences, and suspensions. Before we outline an effective, legally defensible disciplinary process, it is appropriate to add a warning.

Follow your existing organizational disciplinary process guidelines. If you implement changes, they must be the result of a diligent thought process

and approved with the involvement and agreement of all levels of the organization (especially top-level executive management, legal counsel, and human resources professionals). Do *not* make unilateral, impulsive changes to your existing policy. Use the disciplinary process *consistently*. Any existing collective bargaining or other contractual agreements must be honored. Laws vary from state to state, and any changes in your disciplinary process must be in accordance with laws and regulations governing your state.

Disciplinary process checklist   Following are twelve critical questions to address before you begin the disciplinary process.

1. Is the problem serious enough to implement the disciplinary process?

2. Is this an objective, fact-based action or a subjective, emotion-based action?

3. Have you investigated all unusual or mitigating circumstances?

4. Does your documentation clearly support your perception of poor performance or disruptive behaviors?

5. Does your documentation establish a legally defensible position?

6. Have you properly addressed the removal of barriers or the allocation of resources affecting this employee's performance?

7. Are you treating this employee any differently than anyone else in the company's present or past employment?

8. Could this employee have any right to claims of unfair treatment or circumstance?

9. Have all proper procedures and guidelines been followed as established by the human resources department?

10. Have you addressed all reasonable options for helping the employee improve their performance/behavior problems?

11. Have all influential parties been consulted and their support obtained prior to beginning the disciplinary process (your manager, human resources department, legal counsel, others)?

12. Have all employment and collective bargaining agreements, as well as any contractual procedures, been carefully reviewed and considered prior to beginning the disciplinary process?

! **If you cannot confidently answer all twelve of these questions to your satisfaction, do not begin implementation of the disciplinary process.**

Should your managerial actions be subject to review by higher-ups, human resources, the legal department, or challenged in the courts or through a grievance procedure, these twelve questions will loom large.

Steps in the Disciplinary Process

There are five steps in the disciplinary process:

- Counseling sessions
- Verbal warnings
- Written warnings
- Suspension
- Separation

Counseling sessions As discussed, effective counseling sessions raise employees' awareness of their poor performance or disruptive behaviors and provide specific positive recommendations for solution.

Verbal warnings A verbal warning is a formal communication notifying an employee of the actual beginning of the disciplinary process. The verbal warning must be clearly announced to the employee. It is not acceptable to have a casual conversation concerning performance and later claim this served as the verbal warning. Some organizations use a dual verbal warning policy—the first unwitnessed; the second with a witness present.

The role of witnesses in the disciplinary process is frequently misunderstood. Witnesses are merely present to corroborate factually the events of the meeting—they are not there to validate poor performance issues or serve as an advocate or adversary of either management or employees. They are present to be able to state clearly and accurately what took place in their presence. Witnesses are neutral. The witness must always be someone in a position *above* the employee involved. It is not acceptable to use an employee's peers as witnesses. This subjects the employee to potential (and unnecessary) public embarrassment. (*If* employees request their own witness and select one of their peers, that is acceptable as *their* choice.)

The use of witnesses at the verbal warning may be optional, at the discretion of the manager involved. Obviously, if witnesses are required by policy, contractual agreement, or law, compliance is not optional. The presence of a witness conveys a message of extreme seriousness. When is it appropriate to send this message? Play this "seriousness card" when it is to your best advantage. If your gut hunch is telling you the employee will respond positively to the verbal warning and correct the situation, the use of a witness may be premature overkill. The employee may not respond well to what is perceived as an attempt to intimidate. However, if your gut hunch tells you that you are going to war with this employee, the presence of a witness is appropriate and advantageous. When in doubt, use a witness. (This is the only phase of the disciplinary process where a witness may be optional. All other phases *require* a corroborative witness.)

Following is an eleven-step model for verbal warnings:

1. Formal acknowledgment that this meeting constitutes a verbal warning. "This discussion is a verbal warning and formally begins the disciplinary process. It is my hope that further disciplinary steps will not be necessary."

2. Restatement of the standards, objectives, and expectations of the organization. "This is what is expected of you. . ." (Substantiated by whatever legitimate documentation is available, that is, policy manuals, signed agreements).

3. Clear identification and documentation of the poor performance or disruptive behavior. "The performance has not been acceptable and here is why . . ." or "The disruptive behavior continues in spite of our previous discussion. I offer these examples . . ."

4. State the specific correction necessary. General statements are *not* acceptable. The correction must be specific and measurable. "Here is what is necessary to improve the performance behavior and avoid future disciplinary measure . . ."

5. Statement of how ongoing performance will be measured. (The employee must have reasonable access to the measurement.) "Your performance will be measured by . . ."

6. Statement of ongoing monitoring tools and methods of feedback on performance. "Your performance will be measured by . . . It will be readily available for your review. We will meet weekly to discuss the progress. You will be expected to bring this information with you each time we meet."

7. Specific timeline for performance and behavior correction. "Your performance must meet our minimum standards of ___ within ___ days."

   What is an appropriate timeline? The length of the timeline is determined by the process involved as well as past policy. Employees must be given enough time to actually correct their performance. If it will take a month to turn the performance around, you cannot give them only two weeks to do so. If you give employees six months to correct their performance, you are sending the message that their poor performance is really *not* a critical issue. In reality, if you can wait six months for employees to correct their problems, *you do not have a problem!* Only fix things that really matter. Thirty-day timelines are usually appropriate. However, any and all influencing factors must be considered.

8. Statement of managerial support to help the employee make the correction. "My goal is to correct the problem quickly and avoid any further disciplinary action. Here is what I/we will do to assist you."

9. Identify additional resources available. "Copies of our training manuals will be available." "You may attend another training class or seminar." "Our trainer will spend ___ days with you in the next ___ weeks to provide additional training."

10. Consequences of continued poor performance. (The consequences of continued poor performance may be a final verbal warning or escalation to a written warning.) "If we are not successful in correcting this problem a second verbal warning will be issued, or we will escalate the process to the next step of a formal written warning. It is my hope that will not be necessary."

    Do not threaten to fire the employee. Such threats are based on emotions, punishment, and retribution. Employees are well aware of their rights, and governmental and organizational policies and procedures. They know such threats are hollow and meant only to intimidate. When the threat to fire is not carried out, the manager looks weak and loses face.

    If necessary, the following statement may be appropriate: "Ultimately, if this problem is not corrected, it could result in your being asked to leave the organization. There are many steps in the process before that could happen, and I want to do everything possible to avoid such an outcome."

11. Restatement/summary of the verbal warning. It is extremely important to test the effectiveness of the verbal warning communication. Have employees summarize and repeat back in detail their understanding of the warning. It is important to determine what information actually got through. It is the manager's job to determine the employees' level of comprehension. If they do not completely understand their responsibility for correction or the consequences of not doing so, the chances of successful change are nonexistent. It is likely that a restatement or clarification of some of the issues will be necessary. In a verbal warning situation, emotions can run high. Vestiges of resentment may interfere with listening and comprehension. Selective listening patterns are extremely common. Taking the appropriate time to clarify and restate the critical aspects of the verbal warning provides greater potential for future success. A variation of this restatement

technique is to ask employees to put their understanding in writing or in an informal outline. Have them summarize their interpretation as well as the tone of the meeting. While this may not always be possible, when it is, it will give you a clear understanding of their depth of comprehension. It also eliminates any subsequent claims of misunderstanding or lack of clear instruction.

▶ Overcome denial by effective restatement.

Within twenty-four hours of the verbal warning, a written summary of the meeting should be created by you and given to the employee. A copy should be placed in your documentation file. This does *not* constitute a formal written warning. It serves as a formal recap of the verbal warning and is a part of your ongoing documentation.

Failure to correct the poor performance after verbal warnings results in escalating the process to the next level.

Written warnings   The written warning is an escalation step in the disciplinary process. It indicates a continued lack of success in addressing the problem, along with an increase in the seriousness of the situation. This is also the first official notification to the human resources department and upper-level management (perhaps legal as well) of the existence of a significant performance or behavior problem.

The written warning is primarily the verbal warning put in writing, with a copy being placed as permanent record in the employee's personnel file. It follows the same format as the verbal warning with the following additions:

- The written warning begins with a summarization of the previous counseling sessions and verbal warnings (frequency, dates, times).

- The consequence of the written warning is obviously different. It must be clearly identified (either a second written warning or form of suspension in compliance with your existing policy).

- A witness is mandatory for a written warning. *This is not an option!*

At the completion of the written warning session, the employee is asked to sign the document and is given a copy. The employee may refuse to sign the document or may take the copy and tear it into small pieces in a demonstration of defiance, disagreement, or contempt. Do not be distracted by any provocative negative behavior. It is intended in part to incite you and possibly to draw you into a negative emotional reaction. The employee's signature is not necessary. That is one primary reason a witness is necessary. The witness, truthfully and accurately, corroborates that the employee was asked to sign, refused to do so, and was given a complete copy of the document. This statement is attested to in writing, on the face of the written warning document, and is sent to the human resources department. It becomes a permanent entry in the employee's personnel record. What the employee does with the document is not your business, just be sure you can prove the employee received a copy.

If a second written warning is appropriate, follow this same format, including the first written warning information in the opening summary, and address the next step consequence. If the written warning does not result in appropriate performance or behavior change, the process escalates to suspension.

Suspension   Suspension is intended to impress upon employees the seriousness of their circumstance, provide a period of reflection concerning their future employment, and invite them to clarify their commitment to improve their performance/behavior. There are three types of suspensions: paid administrative leave, unpaid temporary suspension, and a combination of paid leave and unpaid suspension.

1. Paid administrative leave. Employees may be suspended with pay for a short period of time (usually one day maximum). Paid administrative leave for an extended period of time is counterproductive. It can be perceived to be an additional paid vacation and is hardly seen as a negative consequence. A paid suspension considers the following three issues:

    ▪ Paying employees does not escalate the negative emotional factors involved in the ongoing problem. There is no short-term loss of income to contribute further to resentment or to foster feelings of victimization.

    ▪ Employees' families are not punished. The organization is not perceived to be dealing with problem employees by unfairly punishing the family by depriving them of income.

    ▪ When employees are being paid, you can require performance. You can require them to take the appropriate time to consider their situation, to consider their options, and to submit their intentions or plan in writing.

    If the goal is to correct the performance/behavior and continue employment, employees can be required to develop a specific action plan detailing what will be done and how it will be done. If the employee is not being paid, he cannot be required to develop or submit a plan (on his own unpaid time).

▶ **Pay = performance**
  No pay = no performance and no control

The leave period is intended to encourage employees to decide whether they truly want to continue in the employ of the organization, or if it is in their best interest to seek employment elsewhere. You can expect employees to return from this period of administrative leave with an increased willingness to correct the problem or an agreement to move on.

2. Unpaid temporary suspension. This is recommended for a period of three to five days. The intention is to allow employees to experience "negative microeconomics" or a short trial period of unemployment.

- They experience not having a job for three to five days.
- Their income is disrupted up to 60% of one week's earnings, 25% of one month's earnings.
- They forfeit the use of company property and equipment (company car, laptops).
- They are not permitted on company property during their suspension.
- They cannot conduct any business on behalf of the organization in any form for the duration of the suspension.

During this time of "microeconomic unemployment," employees will determine whether they wish to correct the problem performance/behavior or separate from the organization. When employees are suspended without pay, they cannot be required to develop an action plan; however, they can be expected to provide an employment decision upon their return.

3. Combination suspension. A two-step blending of both types of suspension can be very useful. If the written warning is not successful in bringing about the necessary improvement, a paid administrative leave day can be implemented. If this fails, escalate to the three to five days of unpaid temporary suspension. There are key considerations in this recommendation.

- Paid administrative leave is nonpunitive, and the use of this option emphasizes the intention of the organization and manager to correct, not punish.
- Potential legal exposure is further lessened by extending the notice time of the disciplinary process. While the time of the disciplinary process is extended, it is also escalated incrementally with each step intended to convey increased urgency and ensure progress toward a final outcome (correction or separation). Extending the process alone, without appropriate escalation, only bogs down in repeated

warnings which become repetitive and unproductive with little or no consequence.

- The cold hard reality is that unpaid temporary suspension usually does *not* result in long-term, positive correction once the process reaches this stage. Separation becomes a foregone conclusion. With correction as the ultimate goal, anything that can be done to lengthen the process without lessening the urgency is beneficial. Adding the step of paid leave may allow time to be your ally. You owe employees every opportunity to save their job. The unpaid temporary suspension with its low percentage payoff is delayed as long as possible without diminishing the process.

- Unpaid temporary leave can be seen as a welcome form of retribution for management. It may be perceived that management enjoys punishing employees. Your goal is to correct, not punish, and adding the step of paid administrative leave *may* lessen the negative perception. Management may be seen as less eager to punish and to invoke the final step reluctantly.

When an employee returns from any form of suspension, there are two possible outcomes: the employee resigns or the employee pledges to correct performance and behavior.

It is always a prudent strategy to assume that employees will resign upon their return. Prepare all of the necessary documents to effect their resignation in advance. If they do not resign, the documents can always be voided. As with all steps after the verbal warning, a witness must always be present when the employee returns from suspension.

If the employee resigns upon return from the suspension,

- Process the resignation immediately (already prepared)
- Issue the final check (if legally required to do so at that time)
- Wish him well

While the employee may offer notice, you are under no obligation to accept it. In reality, one of the worst things you can do is to allow the previously suspended employee to work out a resignation notice. Sabotage, workman's compensation claims, theft, destruction of records, or a continued general undermining of management are all inevitable results. An employee set on extracting retribution can do a lot of creative damage. There is no law requiring an organization to accept a notice. Even if you have a contractual agreement committing you to pay employees for a period of time, you are better off paying them to stay away.

If the employee pledges to improve performance, welcome him or her very positively. Compile a written document that clearly summarizes all of the steps in the disciplinary process to date and that clearly states that the next incident or infraction will result in dismissal. Ask the employee to sign this document and give him or her a copy. (Rarely does an employee refuse to be cooperative or to sign the document at this stage. The employee realizes the seriousness of the situation and usually demonstrates positive cooperation and compliance.)

When the employee signs this document and returns to work, one of two things will happen.

- The employee successfully corrects his or her behavior or performance, and everyone lives happily ever after. And this success story will add to your legend as a highly skilled manager, capable of eliciting turnaround performance. If this happens, celebrate, and include the employee.

- The employee fails to live up to the agreement, and the unacceptable behavior or poor performance continues. If this happens, the employee must be dismissed. Failure to do so destroys credibility, the organization, and the entire disciplinary process. If the employee is not dismissed, it proves not only to this employee, but to all others as well, that you are not willing to enforce company standards and expectations, these policies are not to be taken seriously, and you are weak and unwilling to take action.

Separation (termination)   If the employee leaves the organization as a result of the disciplinary process due to resignation or dismissal, the following guidelines should be followed:

- A witness is mandatory during *all* potential separation events.

- *Never* strip the employee's dignity. (No matter how disrespectful or abusive, never respond in kind.)

- Maintain confidentiality forever. (Just because the employee is gone does not absolve you of your responsibility.)

- Avoid postseverance character assassination at all costs.

- Do not permit the employee to return to company property. (There are significant security considerations for you, your coworkers, and other management personnel.)

- Express your regret over the outcome. Do not apologize.

When an employee is dismissed, consider offering outplacement assistance in seeking a new job. Training and assistance with interviewing, networking, or resume writing may be very helpful and seen by others as a humane gesture by the organization. It is in your best interest to help the dismissed employee find employment.

All requests for employment references from potential future employers for your separated problem employees should be referred to the human resources department or upper management. You could be considered legally liable for any detrimental statements.

The Care and Feeding of Survivors

The remaining peers, teammates, or workmates of the severed employee must be attended to in the aftermath. Many organizations treat resignations or dismissals with a wall of silence. It appears at times to be an attempt to rewrite history. The empty desk or chair is treated like it was never occupied in the first place. This may reflect management's discomfort with the separation process, or it can be a lack of knowledge or confidence in dealing with the event professionally. Ignoring or trivializing the event does not change the reality. The remaining employees have questions, perceptions, and perhaps fears that must be addressed.

It is important to meet with the remaining intimate work group (those most affected by the separation) and address the issue in a straightforward manner.

- Acknowledge that the severed employee is no longer with you. (They already know it; however, they need to hear it officially from you.) Treat your employees as adults. Provide the dignified communication they deserve.

- Acknowledge that a behavior/performance problem existed. The best phrase to use is "As you know, we were having ongoing problems." Do *not* divulge proprietary or personal information or the particulars of the incident. Merely acknowledge that ongoing problems have existed. They know that ongoing problems have existed. They have been hearing only one side of the story (the side that is not favorable or supportive of you).

- Acknowledge that proper policies and procedures were followed. This last statement is extremely important and assures them this process was done by the book and they have nothing to fear from a subjective witch hunt. Reassure them they will not be next on the hit list. Your assurance of the appropriate procedures being followed is in stark contrast to what they have been hearing from the recently severed problem employee.

Taking these steps reinforces to the employees that

- You are willing to exercise your managerial rights and use the disciplinary process and policies when necessary.

- The standards, objectives, and expectations of the company are valid and are to be taken seriously.

- You do not want them to fear any personal vulnerability.

The predictable responses of the survivors will be that approximately 10% of them are angry. They perceive you were unfair and mistreated their friend. Approximately 10% of them are happy. They disliked the departed employee and perceive you were negligent in not dismissing him or her sooner. Approximately 80% of them accept the facts and are ready to get on with their lives.

Effective use of the disciplinary process is a very useful tool in turning around or eliminating poor performance and disruptive behaviors. Understanding the process is not easy—it is very complex and compounded by legal, moral, and policy issues that challenge any manager and every organization. Used properly, the disciplinary process is an asset. Used improperly, it is a nightmare, and when we fail to use it at all, it is chaos.

12 Motivating Bad Attitude Employees

Motivating bad attitude employees is difficult. In Chapter 4 we discussed the motivational shift in today's workplace. In the past, employees were motivated to avoid loss and reacted by working harder to the threat of something being taken away from them. Today employees are motivated more by achievement or growth—much of the fear is gone. What makes employees work harder or be more productive has been altered dramatically. Tactics that were successful in the past have become counterproductive.

Your challenge is to recognize that many of the current trends in motivation do not necessarily apply to your bad attitude employees. Being motivated to achieve or gain something may be unrealistic for them— their lack of confidence inhibits their ability to grow, achieve, acquire, and succeed. Attempting to motivate bad attitude employees by fear is ineffective; it results in no positive change in workplace behavior. It merely reinforces what they already believe to be true, and it may actually harden their resolve to fight back. When motivation is based on taking something away, it reinforces their perceived persecution and victimization. It becomes a catharsis that blossoms into a siege mentality—protect yourself and trust no one. These people *expect* attempts to be made to take things away; when it is threatened or actually happens, their response is, "I told you so. I knew this would happen." It causes them to fight back passive-aggressively, underground, covertly.

Motivation based on taking something away exacerbates bad attitudes and accelerates the performance freefall. The entrenched negative mindset of bad attitude employees makes them unresponsive to many of the current successful motivational strategies.

In this chapter, we are going to discuss

- The role of the manager in motivation
- Creation of a motivational culture
- Strategies for success
- The unmotivating reducers of job satisfaction

But first, to further understand the motivational challenge, it is important to consider A. H. Maslow's hierarchy of human needs and how they influence bad attitude employees' motivation. Maslow developed a theory that established three categories of human needs and how these influence motivation. His work has been highly regarded by psychology and management theorists.

■ Bad Attitude Employees and Maslow's Hierarchy of Needs

Physiological and Safety Needs

For most employees these needs are met by having a steady, secure job that enables them to provide the basic requisites of life (for themselves and their family): staying warm and dry and avoiding hunger. In the past, this job security was controlled exclusively by the organization. "The organization giveth, and the organization taketh away." The potential threat of removing this security drove employees to conform and perform.

Today, the guarantee of security has shifted from the organization to the individual. Security no longer means having a guaranteed job; it is the possession of personal skills to guarantee employability. Individual employees determine their own security by their willingness to learn, develop, change, and perform. Security is equal to the contribution made to enhance the organization; the greater the contribution and inventory of skills, the greater the security. Employees with the right set of skills ensure their ability to always have a job—to always be employable—and not necessarily by the same organization.

Bad attitude employees have not made this journey to self-determined security. Today's personal security puts accountability and responsibility squarely on their shoulders. They are much more comfortable in deflecting that accountability and responsibility, and they continue to look unrealistically to the organization for the guarantee. As the erosion of the organization's ability to guarantee security accelerates, bad attitude employees see the threat to their security as an unavoidable reality over which they have no control (the inevitable impending doom). Bad attitude employees' physiological and safety needs are more at risk, not enhanced, in this current economic cycle. They have actually experienced an erosion of their basic needs.

Affiliation and Belonging Needs

The need to belong and fit into the organization is strong for all employees, including those with bad attitudes. However, bad attitude employees do not believe they can achieve acceptance through any positive contribution. Their fitting in or acceptance will be achieved by negative contributions. They may shun acceptance from their productive mainstream peers. ("I'll never get it, so I don't want it.") Rather, they pursue acceptance from employees displaying similar negative attitudes: those demonstrating poor performance and disruptive behaviors.

Excluding, shunning, or ostracizing bad attitude employees from belonging to the group does not motivate them to correct their behavior and earn acceptance. Many managers think that exclusion of bad attitude employees will motivate them to achieve inclusion. This couldn't be further from the truth; it merely reinforces their perceived negative reality. While they may desire inclusion, they are *not* motivated to work toward achieving it. Denying them positive fulfillment of affiliation and belonging needs drives them deeper into the negative camp. You will pay a price for their exclusion.

Self-Esteem and Self-Actualization Needs

The importance of self-actualization and overall job satisfaction has risen significantly. But achieving these goals in the redefined workplace can be much more difficult. Those experiencing the most difficulty tend to migrate toward bad attitudes. Positive self-perception and the satisfaction of doing important, worthwhile work and making meaningful workplace contributions are severely challenged in bad attitude employees. For many managers, having a positive impact on issues of self-esteem and self-actualization offers the most fertile opportunity for increasing bad attitude employees' motivation. This takes commitment, patience, and a high tolerance for frustration on your part.

■ The Role of the Manager in Motivation

First of all, take yourself off the hook.

▶ **It is not your job to motivate bad attitude employees.**

It is not your job to motivate anyone. The bottom line is that every individual is responsible for his or her own motivation. It is up to each employee to establish his or her own reasons for coming to work and motivations for reaching whatever level of success is desired. As a manager, it is your responsibility to create a productive environment conducive to people achieving their individual goals. It is a fallacy that a good manager has to be a good motivator. It is unrealistic to expect managers to keep employees constantly motivated.

> ▶ Years ago I had the pleasure of managing a young man named Charles. He was a very high performer, but by today's definition he would be considered a "high maintenance" employee. He demanded a lot of attention, and early in his career he would frequently challenge me by saying, "I'm not very motivated; I'm feeling down. You're my boss; do something to motivate me." My response was, "I was not put on this earth to motivate you. I have all I can do to be responsible for keeping myself motivated. But I am willing to help—let me know what you want to achieve, and I'll help you get there!"

We often equate managerial motivation with the ability to keep employees pumped up. Frequently managers who perceive themselves to be good motivators believe they are good talkers and are skilled at effective emotional appeals. Unfortunately employees often give their managers lip service or the appearance of increased responsiveness, when, in fact, they may be dismissing their boss as shallow and emotionally immature.

People who are considered to be good motivators (athletic coaches, the clergy, politicians, professional speakers) usually are able to instill a short-term burst of increased emotion and commitment. This lasts for a limited time and tends to cascade quickly. Sustaining commitment and performance long-term is an individual accomplishment. People must reach down deep within themselves to find their drive or motivation. It cannot be given to them by an outside source.

What good does it do you to raise your employees' emotions for a short time? While there are situations when an emotional appeal to "win one for the Gipper" may be successful, these instances should be few and far between. When legitimate and heartfelt, these appeals are effective; when contrived, they appear meaningless and humorous. Workplace motivation should not be short-term or based on emotion.

Setting Goals

Your managerial efforts are better invested in creating an overall motivational environment and discovering the personal motivators of individual employees. Once their motivational triggers are identified, partner with them to help them achieve their goals. Employees are motivated to achieve what is important to *them*. They are not going to increase their performance to achieve either your goals or the goals set for them by the company. They will work hard enough to keep their job. Exceptional and turn-around performance is driven by achieving *their* goals. These triggers vary with each individual, and the best path to discovery is inquiry—ask them. While there are some significant motivational issues that most employees have in common, all have specific issues that motivate them as individuals. Discovering these unique individual motivators is an essential key in helping any employee to achieve.

Bad attitude employees are doubly challenging because they may be reluctant to disclose their motivational triggers and goals. In fact, they may not really know what these are themselves. Goals can be a major issue for bad attitude employees. If confidence and esteem are low, it is not an uncommon pattern for goals not to be set or even attempted. If employees do not believe they can achieve goals, why expose themselves to the prede-termined failure of setting them in the first place? Many bad attitude employees totally dismiss the goal-setting process. This may be a reflection of their perceived inadequacy. However, if pushed or mandated to establish goals, they frequently respond by submitting extremely high, unreachable objectives. Why would bad attitude employees set such unattainable goals? Because they get to be right! Their rejection of the goal-setting process cre-ates this scenario: you make them set goals, they set them too high, they fail, they win. They were right and you were wrong! In the goal-setting process with bad attitude employees, you may have to negotiate goals downward to realistic, achievable levels. High achievers try to sandbag you with lowball goals. They set them low and blow them out of the water. Bad attitude poor performers set goals high and fail. In life, we all get to be right!

Setting extremely high, unachievable goals may be mistakenly consid-ered a successful method to obtain at least some measure of performance increase. Managers may think, "Well, if I/they only achieve half of the objective, that will at least be some increase." In reality, this is rarely the out-come. When managers set unrealistic goals, motivation to achieve them may be high initially. However, when it becomes clear the objectives will not be met, activity and effort are replaced by frustration. Why even try? This reality usually sets in very early in the process and results not only in partial completion of the goals, but also reduces performance and lowers morale and motivation. It is not uncommon for performance to drop below the level achieved before the unrealistic goal was set. Unattainable goals do not yield even partial improvement. Even if they did, why would you invite people to fail? Partially achieved goals and objectives are forms of failure. Establish realistic goals and allow employees to celebrate success and be motivated to achieve even more.

As a manager, you should establish two levels of incremental goals—organizational responsibility and personal achievement. Bad attitude employees may feel overwhelmed by all of their organizational responsibilities. They believe the demand is just too great, and they simply can't accomplish it all. Help them to break their responsibilities and long-term goals into short-term, manageable increments. This will put their responsibilities into a manageable perspective. The big "undoable" becomes a series of small "doables."

▶ **Help your employees put their foot-long challenges into inch-long segments.**

This may provide a feeling of increased control and help reduce the intimidating, overwhelming burden.

Help your employees discover their personal goals. Discuss their thoughts of accomplishment. What do they want to achieve? What is their next step? If you can discover and align their goals with the overall goals of the organization, an increase in motivation will be unavoidable! There are times when bad attitude employees' goals are actually at cross-purposes with yours and the organization's. (You want an increase in production; they are just hanging on until retirement.) In many cases, bad attitude employees do not have a clue as to their goals. If possible, patiently help them to identify realistic, positive, personal goals. Patience is a virtue here, and bad attitude employees probably need the guidance.

■ Create a Motivational Culture

The manager's role is extremely challenging. While your influence to motivate positively is limited, your opportunity to unmotivate negatively is ever-present. Your challenge may be less to motivate your employees than to make sure you don't screw it up. Focus on creating a motivational culture that invites employees to achieve, take initiative, and share in the spotlight. Avoid creating a culture that removes or hinders the elements of motivation.

The basic tenets of a motivational culture include

- Establishing high levels of trust
- Maintaining dignity and respect
- Establishing retribution-free communication
- Sharing recognition and rewards

Establish High Levels of Trust

Employees tend to be more motivated in high-trust environments. There is confidence that the intent of management is legitimate and that all are focused on the greater good. Communication is more open, and there is a greater willingness to sacrifice. In low-trust environments, the need to protect oneself has a higher priority than performance, and skepticism abounds. Employees are motivated to do nonproductive things!

Trust cannot be demanded; it is earned over a period of time based on ongoing observation and experience. You do not built trust based upon what you are *going* to do. Trust is something given by others based upon the legitimacy of what you have *already* done. Trust is elusive and subjective. It can be extended or withdrawn capriciously, and once trust is violated, it is rarely, if ever, reestablished. Trust and motivation are intertwined—fear destroys trust and motivation; actions speak much louder than words.

The components of trust are numerous and elusive, but three of the most consistent are: honesty, keeping agreements, and fairness.

Honesty   Honesty means not intentionally distorting the truth, not intentionally withholding pertinent information, and truthfully admitting when you don't know. It is telling the truth, as you know it to be, and delivering the message in a tactful manner without hurting the people on the receiving end of the information. You are perceived to be honest when people can take what you say at face value and not have to question. "I know what they said, but what did they really mean?"

▶ **Reading between the lines is searching for dishonesty.**

Keeping agreements   Keeping your word is an integral building block in the creation of trust. If you say you are going to do something, do it. This means returning phone calls, following up on paperwork, and getting back to someone on questions or comments. Frequently in today's workplace we make agreements that we do not intend to keep or that have such a low level of commitment that they are forgotten as quickly as they are created. Napoleon is reported to have said, "The best way to keep your word is never to give it." In reality, we are better off saying no or not giving commitment than promising something and not following through. Just as you do not trust people who do not keep their agreements, your employees do the same. Agreements that you perceive have a low priority may have much greater worth to the employee. If your employees do not believe that your word is your bond, they will undoubtedly have a low level of trust in your leadership. No one is motivated to perform for an organization or manager they perceive cannot be believed.

Motivation by its very nature involves taking risk and pursuing initiative. In low-trust environments there is very little risk taken or initiative shown. These become secondary to C.Y.A. (cover your anatomy) activities. Often low risk-taking and lack of initiative are mistakenly diagnosed as low motivation. Employees are judged harshly, when, in fact, it is management's lack of trustworthiness causing the problem.

> Erin worked in customer service. Her job was to address customer problems of quality and service. Her department head repeatedly implored her: "Use your judgment; do what you think is right to make the customer happy." Erin was always hesitant to do anything out of the norm because of her boss's track record of criticizing her for past decisions he perceived as too costly. Erin frequently said, "He tells me to use my judgment, but as soon as I do something unusual to satisfy a customer, he jumps all over me."
>
> This resulted in Erin's constantly seeking her boss's approval for actions well within her authority to take. She wanted his prior approval to avoid exposure. Customer complaints that should have been solved quickly and easily were prolonged, frequently causing customers great frustration and probably resulting in lost future business. She also required extensive documentation of complaints from customers frequently demanding reshipment of small parts or a written report from a field representative to verify the customer's minor allegations.

Erin's reluctance to take risk and initiative was not due to low motivation or lack of ability—it was a normal response to being hung out to dry once too often.

Fairness   Fairness is a subjective term. What is considered fair by one person is considered unfair by another. In considering the role of fairness in motivation and establishing trust, the key component is consistency. Employees value consistent fairness. A manager's response to predictable circumstances or ongoing incidents should not vary with mood or experience of the moment. If employees feel compelled to determine whether their manager is in a good mood before asking a question or making a request, it shows a lack of confidence in the manager's consistency and fairness. Favorable responses undoubtedly depend on the boss's mood. If the manager has just experienced a bad incident or is under pressure from those above in the organizational chain, the chances are employees may fear they will receive a less than favorable response. Trust is created when responses are predictable and consistent regardless of the mood or the pressure of the day. Embedded in this trust is the fact that all employees are treated equally. Managers should not have two sets of policies: one for the in-crowd and one for the out-crowd. Everyone is extended the same consideration. Motivation runs high when uniform fairness is the rule, not the exception.

Maintain Dignity and Respect

In a motivational culture, everyone must be treated with dignity and respect regardless of his or position within the organization. This is demonstrated by

- Consistent extension of common courtesy
- Avoiding public embarrassments
- Zero tolerance for harassing behaviors
- Zero tolerance for abusive behaviors
- Zero tolerance for the vilification of past employees
- Refusing to talk about others behind their backs

When employees perceive that they are not being treated with appropriate dignity and respect, resentment escalates. Many respond in kind, treating others in the same undignified and disrespectful manner (overtly with peers, covertly with management). Dignified and respectful behavior also includes refraining from putdowns, negative judgments, or editorial comments.

Acceptable Statements

- "I disagree with this proposed change."
- "Something doesn't sound quite right."
- "There may be other issues to consider."

Unacceptable Statements

- "That is the stupidest, dumbest idea I have ever heard!"
- "How could anyone expect me to believe something so absurd?"
- "Don't just look at this in a selfish, greedy, uncaring way, with no regard for anything or anyone else."

◗ **Indignity and disrespect increase the virulence of the bad attitude infection.**

Establish Retribution-free Communication

Open and honest communication is one of the cornerstones of a motivating environment. Creating an environment of retribution-free communication means that everyone in the organization can raise issues, voice disagreement, or ask for explanations without fear of punishment or backlash. In highly authoritarian management environments, asking questions or voicing skepticism is considered at best to be politically incorrect and at worst career damaging. It is an unhealthy environment when employees fear raising issues.

▶ Kathy's organization shifted from a typical hierarchical alignment to a team orientation. The change was intended to increase overall motivation and morale and to get employees (team members) more involved and committed to their jobs. The traditional boss was to have less influence, and more team decisions and collective problem solving were to become the norm.

Kathy attended the regularly scheduled weekly team meeting. The meeting was attended by all five team members including the team leader (a fellow employee now acting as team leader in a rotated sequence). The team coach (former manager) was not in attendance. The team was encouraged to raise issues for discussion, resolve conflicts, and make decisions with as little influence from the coach as possible. During the meeting Kathy openly voiced her displeasure with a recent organizational decision to reduce some coverage in the employees' health benefit program. During the discussion, the team agreed the recent benefit reductions did not make them happy, but they understood the company's position. Everyone, including Kathy, agreed to support the change and hoped the situation would be temporary and short-term. At the close of this discussion the team went on to other business.

As Kathy was on her way home, she was beeped and ordered to return to work. She was summoned into a meeting with the team leader and coach and criticized for the questions she raised at the meeting. She was told that under no circumstances was she ever to make comments critical of any organizational policy, and if she continued to be a negative influence on the team, changes might have to be made.

Obviously, trust was obliterated between Kathy and her team leader. She also learned the painful lesson that the proclamation of employee empowerment and encouragement to actively engage in decision making and process development was cosmetic at best. Open communication meant only positive discussion and not voicing a contentious position. She learned that any deviation from the company line resulted in reprimand and threat. Needless to say, her participation in future team meetings was minimal. Motivation and initiative plummeted. As other team members experienced similar situations, the effectiveness of the team declined. Leadership reverted to an authoritarian style, and employees were criticized for lack of motivation and interest in their jobs.

It is an unhealthy alliance, whether in the personal or organizational arena, when the issues of one party are not given equal weight with the issues of the other. When employees' concerns, questions, or skepticism are suppressed, motivation becomes a battle casualty.

All communication must be done in a respectful, dignified manner. No one is permitted to assail the character of others, question their intelligence, or impugn their motive; however, when presented in an appropriate way, all communication is welcome. If a discussion is off limits due to security or proprietary information, this can be clearly stated without criticism or implied threat to the employee. Badgering or repeatedly raising closed issues is also *not* acceptable behavior for employees. It is appropriate for managers to acknowledge the employees' unhappiness and move on. "We have discussed this in the past. Nothing has changed, and I don't think that it will. We have to acknowledge our disagreement (displeasure) and move on."

The more open the communication, the fewer signs of low motivation and low morale. You will experience significantly less crabbing, whining, or raising of negative issues. Limits will be tested, but once people realize that all communication is welcome, they will be less compelled to probe the limits.

▶ **Freedom in communication = increased motivation.**

Share Recognition and Rewards

Unfortunately, in many organizations recognition is hoarded by management. Rewards are not shared or distributed equally among the people actually responsible for the achievement. An employee may have an idea, and a manager may seize it and sell it upwards as his own. When recognition for success is forthcoming, the manager will spotlight himself rather than the department or team members who actually made it happen. Fewer things are more discouraging than seeing someone take credit for an idea or accomplishment that came from someone else. The door to motivation and accomplishment slams shut, and frequently employees pursue a vendetta to get even.

Traditionally, high recognition and reward have been the domain of executives and sales departments. In a highly motivating environment, all employees participate appropriately and are recognized and rewarded to levels commensurate with their contribution. Those actually making things happen should share in the rewards.

> ▶ A manufacturing company was being honored by one of its key suppliers as customer of the year. The vendor was honoring the company for its significant increase in purchases, promptness in paying, and cooperation in solving customer service problems. The CEO of the company being honored was asked to attend the vendor's annual awards banquet and be honored in front of the vendor's entire workforce and their families. While the CEO was flattered with the honor and invitation, she felt the people responsible for the honor should be the ones receiving the recognition. The eight employees in the department actually using the vendor's product were invited to accompany the CEO to receive the credit they deserved. *They* were invited to travel at company expense. *They* were invited to share in the spotlight. After all, *they* were the ones responsible.

> ❗ **Avoid recognition and rewards that are exclusive. When we honor only one person as employee of the year, we may alienate the entire workforce. We motivate one and unmotivate everyone else. When we honor one person for generating the most creative idea of the year, we discount all other employees who may have participated in an idea-generating program. Recognition and reward should be as inclusive as possible.**

▶ **Inclusion = motivation.**

Ask yourself: How can we honor more rather than fewer? A threshold of performance can be established, and everyone who meets the qualifying requirements is honored en masse. This invites more people into a shared recognition and rewards program instead of isolating a chosen few. The motivational impact is distributed to the many, not limited to the few.

In exclusive reward and recognition environments, it is not uncommon for one person or an elite group of employees to be honored repeatedly. This repetition may be the focus of humor, including suggestions that the award be named after the repeat recipient. When the inevitable happens and another employee emerges to take the top spot, the crestfallen may experience significant public embarrassment. This loss of face could result in the employee leaving the organization rather than assuming a position of less than number one. This can be devastating to the organization. Proper use of recognition and reward is one of the most productive motivational opportunities in your tool kit. Improperly used, it can become a significant deterrent.

■ Strategies for Success

Now that you know your role in motivating your employees and have created a motivational environment, here are some additional strategies for success. These strategies focus on helping the employee become more motivated and making the work more motivating.

Increase Skills Inventory

With job security being defined by the individual employee's capability and production, helping employees to learn new skills and sharpen their existing skills increases their value to the organization, to themselves, and perhaps to their next employer.

Bad attitude employees often view training as a frustrating, not enlightening, experience. For training to be an effective motivational opportunity, it must be presented by competent instructors, it must be reinforced by management, and it must not be punished.

Training must be presented by competent instructors   Not everyone is an effective trainer. Training is a skill that must be learned, practiced, and developed. Proper selection of trainers is extremely important. Do not expect your bad attitude employees to experience increased motivation at the hands of an unskilled trainer.

The ability to perform does not guarantee the ability to teach. In many organizations, the top performer automatically becomes the trainer, and the training becomes an unmotivating exercise in "you stand there and watch me work." Top performers, the gifted ones, may find it extremely difficult to identify with those who do not possess their level of skill and ability. Training should not go to the top performer by default.

As a manager, do you review your company's training efforts? Is the training in your organization provided by effective, competent people who have been trained to successfully transfer knowledge and develop skills in others? If the training is provided by a department that is perceived by employees to have no experience in the real world, such training is very easy for employees to reject. Bad attitude employees interpret this to be another example of management not understanding them or knowing what their difficult world is really like. Bad attitude employees do not identify with someone who hasn't been there and done it. Lack of experience is easily scoffed at or dismissed. It gives bad attitude employees an excuse—it gives them someone to blame.

Training must be reinforced   Reinforcement is an important part of the learning process. So often employees receive training, and when they return to their department, the training is ignored or ridiculed. "I don't care what they told you in training class. Here's how I want you to do it in my department." This is frequently the management attitude greeting employees returning from training. Training must be reinforced by leadership at the departmental or team level, or it quickly becomes extinct, and future training efforts are dismissed as unimportant. It is very easy for bad attitude employees to become frustrated and develop feelings of victimization, with lack of motivation as the only possible outcome. "They tell me one thing. You tell me another. What am I supposed to do?" It gives them something to blame—it absolves them of responsibility.

Training must not be punished   For many employees, training is inherently negative. The time spent in training and learning new skills has to be "made up" when they return to their department. If employees attend a three-day training class, they return to three days' work backlog along with their ongoing current task assignments. They must work overtime, forfeit days off, or work harder to accomplish the tasks of today, tomorrow, and those left over from the days of training. Bad attitude employees perceive this to be inherently unfair, another exploitation, and proof that training should be avoided. Realistic adjustments in workload, along with short-term lowering of expectations and productivity, are appropriate in training situations.

Training must include all of the basic fundamentals   Bad attitude employees are frequently critical of management decisions and resentful of many of the organization's oppressive policies and procedures. This criticism and perception are based on a very narrow me-focused view. Have you ever considered broadening this view by providing fundamental basic business training? If you expect employees to understand the actual costs of running the organization, you should teach them what those costs are. It is easy to assume employees possess very basic business skills that perhaps you take for granted, when in fact, they have never been exposed to the information. Providing a better understanding of the forces driving their environment can be very enlightening. The "ah ha!" is extremely motivating. This also helps employees to effectively apply their intellect and reasoning to the challenges they face.

Training as an incentive   You may not truthfully be able to guarantee an employee's job, promotability, or pay increase if the employee increases his or her performance or eliminates disruptive behaviors, but you can offer training as an incentive. "If you achieve these specific goals, I will see that you receive the training necessary to help you learn . . . I want to help you increase your inventory of skills." (If they do, you do.)

Training is a double-edged sword. Done effectively, it is a tremendous opportunity to provide permanent peak motivation for employees. Done ineffectively, it significantly discourages. The loss is twofold: loss of motivation and loss of opportunity to do something about it.

Communicate Information

Information is very motivating. Everyone wants to be in the in-crowd, but the bad attitude employee rarely is. When every employee receives information equally on a timely basis, parity is created. Equality is motivational. As discussed earlier, when bad attitude employees' flow of information comes only from the grapevine, that information is going to be negative. The employees have no positive, factual information to balance against the rumor and gossip.

Give Employees Influence and Input

This has been referenced many times throughout our book. We cannot overstate the motivational value of

- Allowing employees to determine how something is going to be done
- Listening to employees and valuing their intellect and input
- Giving employees as much influence and control as possible over their intimate work environment

Acknowledge Individuality

We all want to be seen as individuals. Bad attitude employees perceive they are merely a number. They believe they are not valued as individuals. "I am an interchangeable part that could be swapped out or replaced at any time." Giving bad attitude employees positive individual attention is very motivating. This can be individual time spent with them concerning non-work-related topics. It is showing personal interest in them or their families or sharing nonworkplace common interests. Let them know their value to you and the organization.

♦ **Depersonalization is a motivation killer.**

> ▶ José managed a group of service technicians. His most chal-
> lenging problem employee, Zack, was a boxing fan. José had a
> passing interest in the sport of boxing, and from time to time, he and
> Zack would have discussions on recent events or current boxing news.
> José decided to increase his individual attention and time spent with
> Zack and chose to use boxing to build a personal bridge. He began
> to pay closer attention to news of the boxing world, subscribed to a
> boxing magazine, and began to have more frequent, in-depth, and
> meaningful discussions with Zack. He passed the boxing magazine
> along to Zack when he was finished reading it, with notes in the mar-
> gins and highlights. They attended closed-circuit boxing events togeth-
> er. As this connection began to blossom, Zack's performance began
> to improve, and his bad attitude began to subside. Zack felt he was
> acknowledged by his manager as an individual and appreciated
> José's efforts. His willingness to perform increased, and his desire to
> be disruptive decreased when he began to feel he was being appre-
> ciated for something more than a strong back and productive hands.

So often with bad attitude employees like Zack, the only contact we have with them is in group settings or one-to-one contact when things are not going well. Assess the ratio of positive to negative contact you have with your bad attitude employee. Rarely, if ever, do we have a non-work related discussion, and rarely, if ever, are our discussions around some-thing individually important or meaningful to the employee. Instead of the employees always listening to your stories, take the time to listen to theirs.

Flextime, telecommuting, and assistance with childcare issues also offer motivational opportunities to respond to employees' personal, fluc-tuating needs in the workplace of today.

Connect Employees to the Results of Their Work

If employees do not fully comprehend the importance of producing quali-ty results, they are rarely motivated to perform to the best of their ability. If work is not perceived as being meaningful, employees have no reason to be motivated to do it well. If an employee processes forms and merely takes them from the in-basket and dumps them in the out-basket when finished, it may be difficult to identify with the ultimate outcome. It is difficult to be motivated to do something well when you do not see the big picture. Helping employees to be connected to the result may mean an on-site visit to a customer, a dialogue with internal customers, or a visit to a remote department or team to see what actually happens to the work once it has been completed and forwarded.

> In the hospitality industry, probably the most important employees from the hotel guest's point of view are the housekeeping and maintenance personnel. Hotel guests live in the outcomes created by these employees. During a hotel stay, we rarely meet the manager. We experience the front desk personnel momentarily during check in and check out, but we are totally surrounded by the housekeeping and maintenance departments' results. The greatest front desk clerk in the world cannot make up for a poorly cleaned or maintained room. Yet these departments are often disregarded at the hotel. Low pay, no recognition, budget cuts, etc., send a message of unimportance and low value. Consistently reinforcing the importance of these employees will increase motivation. Failing to do so only instills performance lethargy.

Acknowledge Transferrable Skills

Do your employees possess skills used outside of the workplace that can somehow be incorporated into their job or used creatively by the organization? If they are active in their community, they could head up the United Way campaign or another charitable activity. If they are active in Little League or recreation programs, they could coordinate intramural teams and activities. Horticulture or gardening skills could be used to maintain a specially designated memorial garden. Many bad attitude employees who do not experience fulfillment from their jobs, supplement this need with extensive activities during their off hours. It is not uncommon for the off-hour activities to become more important to them than their jobs. They may take time off from work to accommodate demands from these extracurricular activities. We should not be surprised when they actively pursue activities from which they derive the greatest personal gain. Can these skills and activities somehow be incorporated and recognized in the workplace?

Have Fun

Employees want to enjoy their jobs. They do not want work to be all drudgery; they want to have some fun and enjoyment. And typically, bad attitude employees are not having much fun. They may not be instinctively fun people.

There are a number of things you can do to help. The wave of interest in volunteerism and organizational commitment to community service can be a great way of injecting fun and fulfillment at the same time. Many companies are giving people time off from their workday to volunteer, as well as encouraging groups of people to become involved in their off-hours. Some organizations provide funding for service activities (pay for materials when employees provide their labor for fix up projects, for example). Obviously, this cannot be mandated, but providing an opportunity for employees to be of service and have some fun can be very motivating.

Organizational celebrations are necessary and fun. If the department or team is doing well, spring for pizza and have a lunchbreak conversation that has nothing to do with the workplace. One manager made an agreement with his department of eight people that every time they hit their monthly goal, he would come in on Saturday morning and wash each one of their vehicles by himself. Interestingly, the bad attitude employees found this to be *very* motivating. They would do almost anything to punish their boss. The boss's perspective was "If they do something good to get me to do something they perceive I don't want to do, this is not all bad!" Your people may be motivated to perform to punish you!

■　■　■

Let's look at the most significant do's and don'ts to consider in the motivation of your bad attitude employees.

The Top Ten Ways to Motivate Your Bad Attitude Employees

1. Give personal positive attention
2. Listen attentively
3. Identify options or acknowledge the unfixables
4. Provide ongoing specific feedback on performance
5. Praise positive change or performance increase
6. Give away "how" decisions whenever possible
7. Develop their skills
8. Have some fun
9. Reward and recognize all contributors to success
10. Negotiate their goals

The Top Ten Motivation Killers

1. Not being listened to
2. Lack of vision (goals)

3. Responsibility without authority/influence
4. Lack of feedback
5. Poor information flow
6. Uncorrected poor performance in others
7. Inadequate resources (including time)
8. Repetitious work
9. Disorganization
10. Lack of closure

13 Bad Attitude Employees and Change

Discomfort in the face of change is a very common human reaction. We are all uncomfortable with change to some degree. Change disturbs our complacency, calls us to new territory, and introduces elements of the unknown. We take comfort in the safety of knowing where we are; the intimidating, fearful, and perhaps inhospitable nature of where we are going is always a compelling uncertainty.

♦ **Organizational life = the certainty of change and the uncertainty of outcome.**

When organizational change is first announced, it is common for the positive, high achievers to be the most uncomfortable. While they will eventually accept and do well with the new developments, they may have an extremely negative reaction to impending change. These are the employees who may have the most to lose in a changing environment. Things are going well for them now. "It ain't broke—why fix it?" This initial negative response is usually short-lived. When awareness of the inevitability of change sets in, these positive, productive people are able to embrace the change and proceed successfully. While they would rather not have to change, they are confident in their ability to achieve success. They see themselves as having significant control and influence over their future.

Douglas K. Smith, co-author of *The Wisdom of Teams,* has written an excellent book, *Taking Charge of Change: 10 Principles for Managing People and Performance* (Addison Wesley, 1996). He describes three phases of an individual's willingness to change. Employees are either ready, reluctant, or resistant to change. Smith says, "The majority of people, in my experience between 60 and 80 percent of any sizeable organization, are neither resistant nor ready; they are anxious and reluctant about what lies ahead." This reluctance, as Smith describes it, is quite normal; and using the strategies described in this chapter, we believe you can change reluctance to readiness in most cases.

Bad attitude employees are resistant from the very beginning of the change process. If not effectively neutralized, this resistance can harden into extremely negative disruptive behavior, including intentional sabotage (acts of omission as well as commission).

Bad attitude employees' resistance to change is permanent and often escalating. Some resist change so extensively, they are consumed by it. These long-term change resisters frequently end up as part of the body count in downsizing. Their lack of confidence, coupled with their perceptions of victimization with little or no control over their future, makes change a very scary and unsettling journey. If bad attitude employees see their past success as the result of luck or just being at the right place at the right time, the future is very uncertain. This uncertainty is based on their perceived insignificance and lack of control or influence.

- "This could be the time I'm not 'lucky' enough to be successful."
- "This could be the time my incompetence is finally exposed."
- "This could be the time when the inevitable impending doom becomes reality."

To better understand bad attitude employees' resistance to change and to assist them in being successful in a change environment, we must consider the nature of change, the types of change, and the inevitable issues of change.

■ The Nature of Change

Change is inevitable and ongoing. It is an evolutionary process of constantly redefining reality. As the constant challenges we face change, responses too must adjust if we are to remain competitive and achieve success. To deny change is to pretend that things always remain the same; the only variable is acceleration. While the pace of change may quicken or recede, the guarantee that we *will* change is inescapable.

For many, change may be seen as a specific stable process of moving from point A to point B. Change is something you do and then it is over, not to be repeated; it is not perceived to be an ongoing process. It is similar to the young mother awakening her son for his second day of kindergarten. When she says, "It's time to get up for school," he replies, "Oh no, I don't have to go to school. I went already." While some may wish that life was a series of very stable progressions, the consistent, unending, revolutionary change in today's workplace is anything but stable. Change cannot be avoided. We have no choice but to embrace change or rapidly become obsolete and insignificant.

Change is inescapable. If people leave one organization because the rate and disruption of change are unacceptable, they would actually *become* the change in their new organization. They would create in themselves that which they resisted in their previous job. They would be expecting the change resisters in their new organization to "get with the program. Change is inevitable—it is our future." They would judge harshly those in their new environment who displayed the same behaviors they practiced in their past environment. As their new environment consistently redefined itself, they may eventually find it necessary to move again. As some pursue this odyssey, they become wandering nomads in the job market. Avoiding change is like trying to stop the forces of nature. It is impossible; it cannot be done.

The Types of Change in Today's Workplace

In reality, there are only two types of change: change that is inflicted (commanded—over which we have no control) and change that is elected (chosen—that which we welcome). Either we are made to change or we choose change of our own free will. Given our penchant for resisting change and clinging to the present, inflicted change is by far the more prevalent change we experience. We tend to elect change only when the downside of remaining the same becomes increasingly more painful or the upside of gaining something new becomes increasingly more attractive. When the resistance to the change becomes uncomfortable, the change becomes worthwhile.

Organizational change is inflicted upon the vast majority of employees in the organization.

♦ Change is elected by few, inflicted upon many.

The decision to change is made by a few top leaders of the organization. Few, if any, others have influence over the decision. This, in and of itself, is neither negative nor detrimental; it is reality. The overwhelming majority of workplace changes are inflicted on the overwhelming majority of people.

The Inevitable Issues of Change

In any change circumstance, there are always two compelling, inevitable issues: what we are giving up and what we perceive we are gaining. In any change there are loss and gain; there are separation and attainment. The extent to which we focus on either of these issues determines the extent of our resistance or acceptance to change. If we perceive what we are giving up is too valuable to us or the pain of separation is too great or the price too high, we resist change. If we believe what we are giving up is actually harmful to us or the expense is minimal, compared to the good to be achieved, we embrace or pursue change. Avoiding pain can be a very motivating reason to accept change.

■ Organizational Change

Different levels of the organization experience change in various ways.

Level	Type of Change	Focused Issue
Ownership Executive Senior management	Elected	Gain. Where we are going. The good to be accomplished.
Middle management Senior technical positions	Inflicted	Loss. What we are giving up balanced with acknowledging some potential gain.
Employees/Staff (nonmanagement/ leadership personnel)	Inflicted	Loss. The pain of what is being taken away. (Some see little potential for gain—most see the downside of loss.)

Change is actually chosen, selected, or elected by very few. Change then cascades down to others as an infliction. The vast majority of the organization has no choice, input, or influence in the decision.

At the very top level, people in the organization are excited about where they are going and what is to be gained; they perceive change as positive. They acknowledge potential loss and that it will be uncomfortable for some, but the benefits far exceed the price to be paid. In their excitement, they sell change down through the organization with enthusiasm and celebration. They may attempt to introduce and implement change by pep rally. They may strike up the band and expect everyone to get on board for the journey to the future. In reality, most people in the organization do not wish to make the trip.

People who are unenthusiastic about impending change are seen as negative or resistant to change. Those in upper levels of organizations are frequently frustrated by the lack of commitment and enthusiasm of others. They do not understand why everyone does not share their excitement about the change. They may attempt to command enthusiasm and acceptance through authoritarian dictates. "You *will* support the change, and you *will* be excited about it; you will *not* resist or withhold your support."

◆ **Acceptance of change cannot be commanded—but it can be created.**

■ Bad Attitude Employees and Change

Change—bad attitude employees don't want to go there. The perception of inflicted change is seen as further proof of their victimization, disenfranchisement, and lack of control. It adds to the continuous string of bad events. Negative emotion is a component of any inflicted change, and bad attitude employees thrive on it.

Bad attitude employees become entrenched in their perception of loss in the face of inflicted change. As much as they proclaim to dislike today, they dislike even more being forced to give it up and move into tomorrow.

◆ **The bad of today is overridden by the unknown of tomorrow.**

The resistance of bad attitude employees is rooted in their defense of what they are giving up. They react to what is forcibly taken away and defend against criticism, loss, and potential unfairness.

Defense Against Criticism

Bad attitude employees frequently interpret the introduction of change to be a criticism of their past. Being compelled to change must mean what we have done in the past was unacceptable, wrong, or unproductive. They may actually see change as a form of blame. They are being blamed (or criticized); they have no responsibility; others must be held responsible for any bad outcomes. They may acknowledge the need for others to change, but not themselves. Defending against this blame is very important to bad attitude employees. Blame is a tool they consistently use to devalue others. Blame perceived to be aimed at them is seen as a further devaluation of themselves. Blame is to be avoided and resisted at all costs.

It is important not to position change as a criticism of the past. Change is a very positive statement about shifting the economic challenges. Our effective past behaviors, processes, and procedures will not provide success in the face of our changing challenges. Change is about today and tomorrow, not about yesterday.

Defense Against Loss

This issue reflects the fear of bad attitude employees. Their fear of potential loss is huge, including the loss of

- Job
- Face
- Stability
- Quality
- Prevailing advantage
- Economic status

- Influence
- Access

- Identity
- Relationships

- Responsibility
- Things

Bad attitude employees fear the loss of the known and the uncertainty of the unknown. They fear increased future requirements. They fear any new commitments, demands, or accountability that may be inflicted upon them. They demonstrate an overwhelming fear of their inability to be successful. They may fear they are not capable of learning new skills or adjusting to the challenges of the future.

Defense Against Potential Unfairness

This issue reflects the resentment of bad attitude employees. They may see themselves becoming even more victimized by favoritism or internal politics. They question whether

- They will be required to increase their effort with no increase in compensation.
- There will be an inequitable distribution of the workload.
- Others will receive more compensation than they do for the same level of effort or responsibility.
- Their responsibility and accountability will increase, while those of others will be decreased.

In short

▶ **They fear the inevitability of being taken advantage of.**

■ Turnaround Strategies

Douglas K. Smith states, "As a change leader, you need to consider informal and nonhierarchical as well as formal hierarchical ways to influence people's performance agendas." He offers three alternatives:

- Hierarchy or *telling*. By virtue of a power position, people can be told or commanded to achieve performance goals and objectives.
- Exchange or *trading*. Establishing a tradeoff, "If you do, I'll do" scenario. Things the employee wants can be traded or exchanged for successfully accomplishing change objectives.
- Mutuality or *teaming*. Working in concert with employees to achieve mutually agreed upon (and mutually beneficial) goals and strategies.

Telling is usually not successful with bad attitude employees. It pushes their resistance underground. Trading can be successful if employees perceive value in what they acquire. Teaming has limited success only to the extent employees see the mutually established goals to be valid. Chances are your acceptance renders the goals automatically unacceptable to the disruptive employee.

To implement change successfully with bad attitude employees, you need a full complement of strategies in your turnaround tool kit. The strategies that follow give you a broad range of options.

The Four-Step Process

A successful strategy with bad attitude employees is a four-step "partial blend" of Smith's three alternatives.

1. Explain and interpret.

   Explain in as much detail as possible, supported by as much fact and data available, the specific reasons why you are making the change. Do not assume employees understand the reasoning behind the change, regardless of how plain or obvious it appears to you. Do not expect employees to agree with the change. Their agreement is totally under their control, not yours. Do not hold yourself responsible for their acceptance or rejection. Your goal is not to get them to *approve* the change; your responsibility is to help them *understand* the thought process and reasoning behind the change.

   It is also important to communicate the ongoing nature of change—that it is a mere step in the journey, and that what you are asking them to do now will not last forever. The embracing and accomplishment of one change is the essence of the blossoming of another. Identify for bad attitude employees the fluid, ongoing, connected flow of change. "When you do this, I will be asking you to continue the momentum and embrace the additional ongoing change that is necessary and inevitable."

   You should also emphasize the value of the gain. Employees' perception of the gain of the change will reflect the importance you place on it for them. If you present the gain as unimportant or inconsequential, that is how they will receive it. The value they place on the gain will probably be about 50% of the value you present. If you present the gain as very high, they will perceive it to have some value. If you present the gain as very low, they will see it as subterranean.

2. Listen to their perceptions of loss, fear, or resentment.

   Bad attitude employees will not move forward and embrace change until their issues of what they are giving up have been addressed.

Throwing a pep rally before we have listened and processed their issues serves only to be antagonistic. Encourage employees to articulate their issues. Listen, validate, and acknowledge the reality of these issues; then prepare employees to move forward. Their issues will never be reasons for aborting the change, but they may well be the basis for some interim adjustment. Failure to listen effectively escalates resentment and resistance.

3. Make bridging agreements.

Bridging agreements are intended to ease employees into the realities of change. Consider short-term adjustments, accommodations, or agreements to lessen the initial negative impact of the change. Reacting positively to some of their issues allows them to win and lessens their perception of victimization and vulnerability. This may mean implementing change incrementally as opposed to abruptly. It may mean providing ongoing feedback sessions where you meet to listen to employees' interpretations and experiences. This provides opportunities to celebrate the positive aspects of the changes and react quickly to correct any negative perceptions.

4. Establish accountability and consequence.

Communicate in a clear and concise manner the upside to be gained by the positive accomplishment of the change as well as the downside to be absorbed in the failure to achieve. There is rarely successful change without consequence. The consequence may be a positive one to be embraced or a negative one to be avoided.

> ▶ **For bad attitude employees, there will be no change unless there is a consequence.**

Your expectations of the employee in the change process must be made very clear. Any blurring can easily lead to distortion or misunderstanding. Unclear accountability always gives bad attitude employees a loophole for excuse or blaming. The communication must be very clear. "Here is the change we are making. Here is exactly what you will be held accountable for. . . ." Inherent in accountability is the measurement tool. Employees must be aware of how their performance/accountability is going to be measured.

- They should know what they are being held accountable for.
- They should know how the success or failure is going to be measured.
- If they are given the proper tools (training, equipment), then the barriers to achieving the change are removed or circumvented.

The only result then can be successful implementation or failure due to chosen resistance. (Choosing not to perform was addressed in Chapter 9.)

The ultimate outcome may be dismissal of bad attitude employees. The success of necessary change cannot be held hostage to their refusal or inability to overcome their resistance.

■ ■ ■

Here are some more strategies for your turnaround tool kit—twelve critical components for successfully overcoming resistance and driving change.

Announce the Change Early and Often

Provide as much notice as possible to let people know that change is coming, what it looks like, and when it is going to happen. Bad attitude employees, especially, need as much advance notice as possible. Meaningful, planned change should not be a surprise. Give them interim reminders so that when the change actually happens, it is a natural progression, not an abrupt disruption.

The day-to-day journey through change does not always go smoothly. The pain and discomfort of loss and the unfamiliarity of any new process or task, coupled with the ongoing stress and pressures of remaining competitive and constantly improving, combine to take a toll on everyone. If there is not a future payoff, the journey hardly seems worth it. For the athlete, the payoff is victory; for the student, the payoff is graduation. For your employees, the payoff or gain must be meaningful, or they will perceive no compelling reason to embrace "your change."

Employees will not embrace change and increase productivity so that *you* can be promoted or for the company to become more profitable, earning *others* greater profitability in a future sale. In an economic cycle where employees are motivated less by protecting against loss and more by personal attainment, success will be achieved when they see their own ends being met. What is the payoff? Is it monetary, personal development, enhanced security, or increased influence? If the payoff does not translate to the employees' level, forget it! Use your creativity to make sure it does.

▶ **Pain and discomfort must be balanced by positive gain.**

Assess and Announce the Depth and Magnitude of the Change

Announcing and implementing change incrementally is deadly to an organization. It has been described as amputating a limb one inch at a time.

Announce and implement the entire change at one time. Breaking it up does not lessen the impact. It merely stirs resentment and antagonism and prolongs the agony. Incremental announcement and implementation also create the perception that management has no clue as to what they are doing and that every day brings a change merely for the sake of change. The greater the pain induced by the change, the more important it is to deal with the pain once.

Celebrate Past Achievements

Celebration is an important aspect of change. Any change initiative should start with a celebration of past achievements and competency. Change can be perceived as criticism, if it is interpreted as a repudiation of the past. Establish the validity of the past, and honor people for their achievements. "As we look at where we are going and the changes we must make to remain competitive, let's take the time to summarize all of the things we have already accomplished. While there is always room for improvement, we need to recognize that we're really good at what we do."

Articulate Your Confidence Specifically

Explain to your employees the basis for your confidence in their ability to implement the change successfully. Tie your confidence to past performance as much as possible. "We have demonstrated our ability to change in the past, and I'm sure we'll be able to duplicate that experience." Helping them to identify past success is an excellent way to empower their confidence in future achievement.

♦ **Success isn't new—they have already done it!**

Open Up the "How"

As much as possible, involve employees in how the change is going to be achieved successfully. "Here's what we are going to do. Here's why we are going to do it. Here's when it's going to happen. How do you think we can best bring this about?"

The more they impact the *how*, the less they are victimized or exploited by the change. Partnerships in change are forged by involving people in the decision-making process. Employees are the ones who will actually make the change happen. They have great knowledge and expertise concerning how to make the change happen most effectively. Take advantage of their intellect.

Train the Change

If you are asking employees to do things differently and/or take on additional responsibilities, they must be trained to do so. *Assume nothing.* Do not expect bad attitude employees to ask for training help. They perceive such requests as admitting weakness. While they will not acknowledge the need for training up front, they will hold the issue in reserve. It will be very convenient later on to blame their lack of success on your failure to train them properly.

If you want them to ford the river, they must be taught water safety and how to defend themselves from piranha and poisonous snakes. Just be sure they know how to swim!

▶ **Change is predestined to failure when not supported by appropriate training.**

Balance Ongoing Discussion with Effective Action

While we have stressed the importance of communication, it is necessary to point out that stalling by requesting more information, more discussion, or clarification can be a tactic used by bad attitude employees to delay the implementation of change. As further discussions are necessary, they must be accompanied by implementation action. "We will continue to talk while we are beginning to implement the change. We will not continue to talk without taking appropriate action." Communication enhances change. It does not provide justification for delay. (The more we preannounce, the less ongoing discussion is necessary.)

Monitor Incremental Activity and Results

Do not take pledges of readiness and willingness to implement change at face value; it may be only lip service. Bad attitude employees may attempt to con you by being supportive to your face yet actively resisting behind your back. The results speak for themselves.

▶ **Trust everyone—and cut the cards.**

Do you have a clear understanding of how you will accurately and objectively determine the true performance of the people you are holding accountable for implementing change?

Monitor and Celebrate the New Achievements

Again we stress the importance of celebration. Seek opportunities to recognize and reward

- Successful beginnings
- Interim success
- Goal satisfaction
- Demonstrated flexibility
- Achievements above and beyond

Do not wait until the end of the change process to celebrate. At the *first sign* of openness to change and the *first attempt* to implement the

change, celebrate openly and very visibly. What is recognized and reinforced gets repeated. "I know we are new at this, but I am really impressed
with the fact that you/we did . . . this morning. We have already begun to
make this change happen."

Confront Resistance

Do not allow resistant behavior to go unnoticed or unchallenged.
Unchallenged resistance is approved and affirmed resistance. The key is to
invite discussion and not box employees into defending their actions (or
inaction). "Tell me what it means when . . ." is an excellent technique to use
in confronting their resistance. "Patrick, help me understand what it
means when we have an agreement to . . . (using the new process) and I
observe that agreement not being kept. Help me understand that."

Change resistance quickly becomes contagious, spreading rapidly
throughout the group, team, or organization. Decisive change leaders
react immediately to prevent the spread of infection.

Implement Consequences

When there is a positive payoff for positive results, implement it. When
there is a negative consequence due to resistance or failure, it is important
to communicate the consequence very early in the process and hold people responsible for their actions. Negative consequences are very real—do
not hide them or protect employees from them. When negative consequences occur, allow their impact to be felt. The workplace is an adult
environment; adults are accountable for their actions. If discipline or dismissal is appropriate, the employee is the sole determinant of the outcome.

Display the "Courage to Live the Change"

This is a term Douglas K. Smith uses to address the importance of your
"doing as you say." Your employees will assess your willingness and commitment to any change by your actions, not your words.

▶ **It is not what you say you will do, but what you really do that determines the validity of your change leadership.**

Any sign of hypocritical "not walking the talk" on your part will be
seized by bad attitude employees as justification for their resistance.

In reality, if your commitment and willingness to implement change
are not solidified, you must address those issues deep within yourself
before you turn to your employees. Asking them to do what you do not
totally support will have a negative result!

■   ■   ■

In conclusion, to embrace, resist, or reject change is an individual issue all employees (and managers) must decide for themselves. We are all personally responsible for how we choose to react to the everchanging work environment. Bad attitude employees will struggle with their demons of change. Their resistance or refusal to march into tomorrow may be their undoing.

As a manager, your role is to

- Present change as an ongoing, healthy, positive reality

- Help bridge the past, present, and future through listening, analyzing, responding, and adjusting to the unpredictable occurrences inherent in change

- Monitor outcomes to ensure the ultimate goals and objectives of the organization are achieved

In the final analysis, it is the responsibility of all employees to meet the organization's standards, expectations, and objectives, regardless of their attitude toward performance.

◆ Bibliography

Arnold, John D. *When Sparks Fly: Resolving Conflicts in Your Organization*. New York: McGraw-Hill, 1992.

Brady, Erik. "Nike, There Is a Silver Lining." *USA Today*, August 2, 1996, page 14.

Brinkman, Dr. Rick, and Kirschner, Dr. Rick. *Dealing with People You Can't Stand*. New York: McGraw-Hill, 1994.

Canfield, Jack. *Self-Esteem and Peak Performance*. Boulder, CO: Career Track Publications, Audio, 1987.

Caroselli, Dr. Marlene. *The Language of Leadership*. Amherst, MA: Human Resource Development Press, Inc., 1990.

Covey, Stephen R. *The 7 Habits of Highly Effective People*. New York: Simon & Schuster, 1989.

Dinkmeyer, Don, Ph.D., and Eckstein, Daniel, Ph.D. *Leadership by Encouragement*. Delray Beach, FL: St. Lucie Press, 1996.

Fournies, Ferdinand F. *Why Employees Don't Do What They're Supposed to Do*. New York: McGraw-Hill, 1988.

Fuller, George. *The Workplace Survival Guide: Tools, Tips and Techniques for Succeeding on the Job*. Englewood Cliffs, NJ: Prentice-Hall, 1996.

Griessman, B. Eugene. *Time Tactics of Very Successful People*. New York: McGraw-Hill, 1994.

Hacker, Carol A. *The High Cost of Low Morale and What to Do about It*. Boca Raton, FL: St. Lucie Press, 1997.

Handy, Charles. *The Age of Unreason*. Boston, MA: Harvard Business School Press, 1989.

Jellison, Jerald M. *Overcoming Resistance: A Practical Guide to Producing Change in the Workplace*. New York: Simon & Schuster, 1993.

Katzenbach, Jon R., and Smith, Douglas K. *The Wisdom of Teams: Creating the High Performance Organization*. New York: Harper Business, 1993.

Kinder, Mickey. *Motivating People in Today's Workplace*. Boulder, CO: Career Track Publications, Audio, 1989.

Mackay, Harvey. *Dig Your Well Before You're Thirsty*. New York: Doubleday, 1990.

Ott, J. Steven. *Classic Readings in Organizational Behavior*. Belmont, CA: Brooks/Cole, 1989.

Peter, Tom. *The Pursuit of WOW!* New York: Random House, 1994.

Pevtzow, Lisa. "Dissatisfied Workers Hurt Productivity." *Princeton Business Journal*, April 30, 1996.

Pritchett, Price. *Firing Up Commitment during Organizational Change: A Handbook for Managers.* Dallas, TX: Pritchett & Associates, Inc., 1996.

Pritchett, Price. *Mind Shift: The Employee Handbook for Understanding the Changing World of Work.* Dallas, TX: Pritchett & Associates, Inc., 1996.

Rhode, Helga, Psy.D. *Dealing with Conflict & Confrontation.* Boulder, CO: Career Track Publications, Audio, 1993.

Robinson, Margot. *Egos and Eggshells: Managing for Success.* New York: Stanton Harper Books, 1993.

Ryan, Kathleen D., and Oestreich, Daniel K. *Driving Fear Out of the Workplace.* San Francisco, CA: Jossey-Bass, 1991.

Sashkin, Marshall, and Kiser, Kenneth J. *Putting Total Quality Management to Work.* San Francisco, CA: Berrett-Koehler, 1993.

Secretan, Lance H.K. *Reclaiming Higher Ground.* New York: McGraw-Hill, 1997.

Seligman, Martin E.P., Ph.D. *Learned Optimism: How to Change Your Mind and Your Life.* New York: Pocket Books, A division of Simon & Schuster, 1990.

Shandler, Donald, Ph.D. *Reengineering the Training Function.* Delray Beach, FL: St. Lucie Press, 1996.

Smith, Douglas K. *Taking Charge of Change: 10 Principles for Managing People and Performance.* Reading, MA: Addison-Wesley, 1996.

Smith, Gregory P. *The New Leader: Bringing Creativity and Innovation to the Workplace.* Delray Beach, FL: St. Lucie Press, 1997.

Solomon, Muriel. *Working with Difficult People.* Englewood Cliffs, NJ: Prentice-Hall, 1990.

Weeks, Dudley, Ph.D. *The Eight Essential Steps to Conflict Resolution.* Los Angeles: Jeremy P. Tarcher, Inc., 1992.

◗ Index